TRUSTS LAW

Joyce Liew Mouawad

Series editors: Amy Sixsmith and David Sixsmith

REVISE SQE

First published in 2021 by Fink Publishing Ltd

Apart from any fair dealing for the purposes of research, private study, or criticism or review, as permitted under the Copyright, Designs and Patents Act, 1988, this publication may not be reproduced, stored or transmitted in any form, or by any means, without the prior permission in writing of the publisher, or in the case of reprographic reproduction, in accordance with the terms of licences issued by the Copyright Licensing Agency. Enquiries concerning reproduction outside those terms should be sent to the publisher.

Crown Copyright material is published with the permission of the controller of The Stationery Office.

©2021 Joyce Liew Mouawad

British Library Cataloguing in Publication Data
A catalogue record for this book is available from the British Library
ISBN: 9781914213038

This book is also available in various ebook formats.
Ebook ISBN: 9781914213106

The right of Joyce Liew Mouawad to be identified as the author of this Work has been asserted by her in accordance with sections 77 and 78 of the Copyright, Designs and Patents Act 1988.

Multiple-choice questions advisor: Mark Thomas
Cover and text design by BMLD (bmld.uk)
Production by River Editorial
Typeset by Westchester Publishing Services
Commissioning by R Taylor Publishing Services
Development Editing by Peter Hooper
Indexing by Terence Halliday

Fink Publishing Ltd
E-mail: hello@revise4law.co.uk
www.revise4law.co.uk

Contents

About the author	iv
Series editors	iv
Introduction to Revise SQE	v
SQE1 table of legal authorities	xiv
Table of cases	xv
Table of statutes	xvi

1	The three certainties	1
2	Formalities for the creation of trusts	24
3	Constitution of trusts	43
4	Exceptions to the maxim that equity will not assist a volunteer	61
5	Beneficial entitlement	80
6	Purpose trusts	97
7	Resulting trusts	114
8	Family home trusts	130
9	Liability of strangers and the fiduciary relationship	148
10	Trustees	168
11	Trustees' liability	189
12	Equitable tracing and equitable remedies	207
	Index	227

About the author

Joyce Liew Mouawad is a non-practising barrister, lecturer in law and module leader, specialising in equity and trusts and land law. She has taught for 25 years at undergraduate and postgraduate level, including in-house CPD courses and University of London LLB External revision courses both in the UK and abroad. She has published academic textbooks in the fields of equity and trusts, land law and wills and administration of estates, and has considerable experience in writing revision-style books for law candidates.

Series editors

Amy Sixsmith is a Senior Lecturer in Law and Programme Leader for LLB at the University of Sunderland, and a Senior Fellow of the Higher Education Academy.

David Sixsmith is a Senior Lecturer in Law and Programme Leader for LPC at the University of Sunderland, and a Senior Fellow of the Higher Education Academy.

Introduction to Revise SQE

Welcome to *Revise SQE*, a new series of revision guides designed to help you in your preparation for, and achievement in, the Solicitors Qualifying Examination 1 (SQE1) assessment. SQE1 is designed to assess what the Solicitors Regulation Authority (SRA) refer to as 'functioning legal knowledge' (FLK); this is the legal knowledge and competencies required of a newly qualified solicitor in England and Wales. The SRA has chosen single best answer multiple-choice questions (MCQs) to test this knowledge, and *Revise SQE* is here to help.

PREPARING YOURSELF FOR SQE

The SQE is the new route to qualification for aspiring solicitors introduced in September 2021 as one of the final stages towards qualification as a solicitor. The SQE consists of two parts:

SQE1
- Functioning legal knowledge (FLK)
- two x 180 MCQs
- closed book; assessed by two sittings, over 10 hours in total.

SQE2
- Practical legal skills
- 16 written and oral assessments
- assesses six practical legal skills, over 14 hours in total.

In addition to the above, any candidate will have to undertake two years' qualifying work experience. More information on the SQE assessments can be found on the SRA website; this revision guide series will focus on FLK and preparation for SQE1.

It is important to note that the SQE can be perceived to be a 'harder' set of assessments than the Legal Practice Course (LPC). The reason for this, explained by the SRA, is that the LPC is designed to prepare candidates for 'day one' of their training contract; the SQE, on the other hand, is designed to prepare candidates for 'day one' of being a newly qualified solicitor. Indeed, the SRA has chosen the SQE1 assessment to be 'closed book' (ie without permitting use of any materials) on the basis that a newly qualified solicitor would know all of the information tested, without having to refer to books or other sources.

With that in mind, and a different style of assessments in place, it is understandable that many readers may feel nervous or wary of the SQE. This is especially so given that this style of assessment is likely to be different from what readers will have experienced before. In this *Introduction* and revision guide series, we hope to alleviate some of those concerns with guidance on preparing for the SQE assessment, tips on how to approach single best answer MCQs and expertly written guides to aid in your revision.

What does SQE1 entail?

SQE1 consists of two assessments, containing 180 single best answer MCQs each (360 MCQs in total). The table below breaks down what is featured in each of these assessments.

Assessment	Contents of assessment ('functioning legal knowledge')
FLK assessment 1	• Business law and practice • Dispute resolution • Contract • Tort • The legal system (the legal system of England and Wales and sources of law, constitutional and administrative law and European Union law and legal services)
FLK assessment 2	• Property practice • Wills and the administration of estates • Solicitors accounts • Land law • Trusts • Criminal law and practice

Please be aware that in addition to the above, ethics and professional conduct will be examined pervasively across the two assessments (ie it could crop up anywhere).

Each substantive topic is allocated a percentage of the assessment paper (eg 'legal services' will form 12-16% of the FLK1 assessment) and is broken down further into 'core principles'. Candidates are advised to read the SQE1 Assessment Specification in full (available on the SRA website). We have also provided a *Revise SQE checklist* to help you in your preparation and revision for SQE1 (see below).

HOW DO I PREPARE FOR SQE1?

Given the vastly different nature of SQE1 compared to anything you may have done previously, it can be quite daunting to consider how you could possibly prepare for 360 single best answer MCQs, spanning 11 different substantive topics (especially given that it is 'closed book'). The *Revise SQE FAQ* below, however, will set you off on the right path to success.

Revise SQE FAQ

Question	Answer
1. Where do I start?	We would advise that you begin by reviewing the assessment specification for SQE1. You need to identify what subject matter can be assessed under each substantive topic. For each topic, you should honestly ask yourself whether you would be prepared to answer an MCQ on that topic in SQE1.
	We have helped you in this process by providing a *Revise SQE checklist* on our website (revise4law.co.uk) that allows you to read the subject matter of each topic and identify where you consider your knowledge to be at any given time. We have also helpfully cross-referenced each topic to a chapter and page of our *Revise SQE* revision guides.
2. Do I need to know legal authorities, such as case law?	In the majority of circumstances, candidates are not required to know or use legal authorities. This includes statutory provisions, case law or procedural rules. Of course, candidates will need to be aware of legal principles deriving from common law and statute.
	There may be occasions, however, where the assessment specification does identify a legal authority (such as *Rylands v Fletcher* in tort law). In this case, candidates will be required to know the name of that case, the principles of that case and how to apply that case to the facts of an MCQ. These circumstances are clearly highlighted in the assessment specification and candidates are advised to ensure they engage with those legal authorities in full.

Revise SQE FAQ (continued)

Question	Answer
3. Do I need to know the history behind a certain area of law?	While understanding the history and development of a certain area of law is beneficial, there is no requirement for you to know or prepare for any questions relating to the development of the law (eg in criminal law, candidates will not need to be aware of the development from objective to subjective recklessness). SQE1 will be testing a candidate's knowledge of the law as stated at the date of the assessment.
4. Do I need to be aware of academic opinion or proposed reforms to the law?	Candidates preparing for SQE1 do not need to focus on critical evaluation of the law, or proposed reforms to the law either.
5. How do I prepare for single best answer MCQs?	See our separate *Revise SQE* guide on preparing for single best answer MCQs below.

Where does *Revise SQE* come into it?

The *Revise SQE* series of revision guides is designed to aid your revision and consolidate your understanding; the series is not designed to replace your substantive learning of the SQE1 topics. We hope that this series will provide clarity as to assessment focus, useful tips for sitting SQE1 and act as a general revision aid.

There are also materials on our website to help you prepare and revise for the SQE1, such as a *Revise SQE checklist*. This *checklist* is designed to help you identify which substantive topics you feel confident about heading into the exam – see below for an example.

Revise SQE checklist

Trusts Law

SQE content	Corresponding chapter	*Revise SQE checklist*		
Requirements of an express trust: The three certainties • Certainty of intention	Chapter 1, Pages 4–9	I don't know this subject and I am not ready for SQE1. ☐	I partially know this subject, but I am not ready for SQE1. ☐	I know this subject and I am ready for SQE1. ☐

Trusts Law (continued)

SQE content	Corresponding chapter	*Revise SQE checklist*		
Requirements of an express trust: The three certainties • Certainty of subject matter	Chapter 1, Pages 10-13	I don't know this subject and I am not ready for SQE1 ☐	I partially know this subject, but I am not ready for SQE1 ☐	I know this subject and I am ready for SQE1. ☐
Requirements of an express trust: The three certainties • Certainty of objects	Chapter 1, Pages 13-18	I don't know this subject and I am not ready for SQE1 ☐	I partially know this subject, but I am not ready for SQE1 ☐	I know this subject and I am ready for SQE1. ☐

PREPARING FOR SINGLE BEST ANSWER MCQS

As discussed above, SQE1 will be a challenging assessment for all candidates. This is partly due to the quantity of information a candidate must be aware of in two separate sittings. In addition, however, an extra complexity is added due to the nature of the assessment itself: MCQs.

The SRA has identified that MCQs are the most appropriate way to test a candidate's knowledge and understanding of fundamental legal principles. While this may be the case, it is likely that many candidates have little, if any, experience of MCQs as part of their previous study. Even if a candidate does have experience of MCQs, SQE1 will feature a special form of MCQs known as 'single best answer' questions.

What are single best answer MCQs and what do they look like?

Single best answer MCQs are a specialised form of question, used extensively in other fields such as in training medical professionals. The idea behind single best answer MCQs is that the multitude of options available to a candidate may each bear merit, sharing commonalities and correct statements of law or principle, but only one option is absolutely correct (in the sense that it is the 'best' answer). In this regard, single best answer MCQs are different from traditional MCQs. A traditional MCQ will feature answers that are implausible in the sense that the distractors are 'obviously wrong'. Indeed, distractors in a traditional MCQ are often very dissimilar, resulting in a candidate being able to spot answers that are clearly wrong with greater ease.

In a well-constructed single best answer MCQ, on the other hand, each option should look equally attractive given their similarities and subtle differences. The skill of the candidate will be identifying which, out of the options provided, is the single best answer. This requires a much greater level of engagement with the question than a traditional MCQ would require; candidates must take the time to read the questions carefully in the exam.

For SQE1, single best answer MCQs will be structured as follows:

A woman is charged with battery, having thrown a rock towards another person intending to scare them. The rock hits the person in the head, causing no injury. The woman claims that she never intended that the rock hit the person, but the prosecution allege that the woman was reckless as to whether the rock would hit the other person.	**The factual scenario.** First, the candidate will be provided with a factual scenario that sets the scene for the question to be asked.
Which of the following is the most accurate statement regarding the test for recklessness in relation to a battery?	**The question.** Next, the candidate will be provided with the question (known as the 'stem') that they must find the single best answer to.
A. There must have been a risk that force would be applied by the rock, and that the reasonable person would have foreseen that risk and unjustifiably taken it. B. There must have been a risk that force would be applied by the rock, and that the woman should have foreseen that risk and unjustifiably taken it. C. There must have been a risk that force would be applied by the rock, and that the woman must have foreseen that risk and unjustifiably taken it. D. There must have been a risk that force would be applied by the rock, and that both the woman and the reasonable person should have foreseen that risk and unjustifiably taken it. E. There must have been a risk that force would be applied by the rock, but there is no requirement that the risk be foreseen.	**The possible answers.** Finally, the candidate will be provided with **five** possible answers. There is only one single best answer that must be chosen. The other answers, known as 'distractors', are not the 'best' answer available.

Now that you know what the MCQs will look like on SQE1, let us talk about how you may go about tackling an MCQ.

How do I tackle single best answer MCQs?

No exact art exists in terms of answering single best answer MCQs; your success depends on your subject knowledge and understanding of how that subject knowledge can be applied. Despite this, there are tips and tricks that may be helpful for you to consider when confronted with a single best answer MCQ.

1. Read the question twice	2. Understand the question being asked	3. If you know the answer outright	4. If not, employ a process of elimination	5. Take an educated and reasoned guess	6. Skip and come back to it later

1. Read the entire question at least twice

This sounds obvious but is so often overlooked. You are advised to read the entire question once, taking in all relevant pieces of information, understanding what the question is asking you and being aware of the options available. Once you have done that, read the entire question again and this time pay careful attention to the wording that is used.

- **In the factual scenario:** Does it use any words that stand out? Do any words used have legal bearing? What are you told and what are you not told?
- **In the stem:** What are you being asked? Are there certain words to look out for (eg 'should', 'must', 'will', 'shall')?
- **In the answers:** What are the differences between each option? Are they substantial differences or subtle differences? Do any differences turn on a word or a phrase?

You should be prepared to give each question at least two viewings to mitigate any misunderstandings or oversights.

2. Understand the question being asked

It is important first that you understand what the question is asking of you. The SRA has identified that the FLK assessments may consist of single best answer MCQs that, for example,
- require the candidate to simply identify a correct legal principle or rule
- require the candidate to not only identify the correct legal principle or rule, but also apply that principle or rule to the factual scenario
- provide the candidate with the correct legal principle or rule, but require the candidate to identify how it should be properly applied and/or the outcome of that proper application.

By first identifying what the question is seeking you to do, you can then understand what the creators of that question are seeking to test and how to approach the answers available.

3. If you know the answer outright

You may feel as though a particular answer 'jumps out' at you, and that you are certain it is correct. It is very likely that the answer is correct. While you should be confident in your answers, do not allow your confidence (and perhaps overconfidence) to rush you into making a decision. Review all of your options one final time before you move on to the next question.

4. If you do not know the answer outright, employ a process of elimination

There may be situations in which the answer is not obvious from the outset. This may be due to the close similarities between different answers. Remember, it is the 'single best answer' that you are looking for. If you keep this in your mind, it will thereafter be easier to employ a process of elimination. Identify which answers you are sure are not correct (or not the 'best') and whittle down your options. Once you have only two options remaining, carefully scrutinise the wording used in both answers and look back to the question being asked. Identify what you consider to the be the best answer, in light of that question. Review your answer and move on to the next question.

5. Take an educated and reasoned guess

There may be circumstances, quite commonly, in which you do not know the answer to the question. In this circumstance, you should try as hard as possible to eliminate any distractors that you are positive are incorrect and then take an educated and reasoned guess based on the options available.

6. Skip and come back to it later

If time permits, you may think it appropriate to skip a question that you are unsure of and return to it before the end of the assessment. If you do so, we would advise
- that you make a note of what question you have skipped (for ease of navigation later on), and
- ensure you leave sufficient time for you to go back to that question before the end of the assessment.

The same advice is applicable to any question that you have answered but for which you remain unsure.

We hope that this brief guide will assist you in your preparation towards, and engagement with, single best answer MCQs.

GUIDED TOUR

Each chapter contains a number of features to help you revise, apply and test your knowledge.

Make sure you know Each chapter begins with an overview of the main topics covered and why you need to understand them for the purpose of the SQE1 assessments.

SQE assessment advice This identifies what you need to pay particular attention to in your revision as you work through the chapter.

What do you know already? These questions help you to assess which topics you feel confident with and which topics you may need to spend more time on (and where to find them in the chapter).

Key term Key terms are highlighted in bold where they first appear and defined in a separate box.

Exam warning This feature offers advice on where it is possible to go wrong in the assessments.

Revision tip Throughout the chapters are ideas to help you revise effectively and be best prepared for the assessment.

Summary This handy box brings together key information in an easy to revise and remember form.

Practice example These examples take a similar format to SQE-type questions and provide an opportunity to see how content might be applied to a scenario.

Procedural link Where relevant, this element shows how a concept might apply to another procedural topic in the series.

Key point checklist At the end of each chapter there is a bullet-point summary of its most important content.

Key terms and concepts These are listed at the end of each chapter to help ensure you know, or can revise, terms and concepts you will need to be familiar with for the assessments.

SQE-style questions Five SQE-style questions on the chapter topic give you an opportunity to test your knowledge.

Answers to questions Check how you did with answers to both the quick knowledge test from the start of the chapter and the SQE questions at the end of the chapter.

Key cases, rules, statutes and instruments These list the key sources candidates need to be familiar with for the SQE assessment.

SQE1 TABLE OF LEGAL AUTHORITIES

The SQE1 Assessment Specification states the following in respect of legal authorities and their relevance to SQE1:

> On occasion in legal practice a case name or statutory provision, for example, is the term normally used to describe a legal principle or an area of law, or a rule or procedural step (eg *Rylands v Fletcher*, CPR Part 36, Section 25 notice). In such circumstances, candidates are required to know and be able to use such case names, statutory provisions etc. In all other circumstances candidates are not required to recall specific case names, or cite statutory or regulatory authorities.

This *SQE1 table of legal authorities* identifies the legal authorities you are required to know for the purpose of the SQE1 Functioning Legal Knowledge assessments for *Trusts Law*.

Legal authority	Corresponding *Revise SQE* chapter/pages
The Law of Property Act 1925	
s 53	Chapter 2: Formalities for the creation of trusts, page 24
s 52	Chapter 3: Constitution of trusts, page 43
The rule in *Re Rose* [1952] Ch 499 The rule in *Strong v Bird* [1874] Lr 18 Eq 315	Chapter 4: Exceptions to the maxim, page 61
The rule in *Saunders v Vautier* (1841) 4 Beav 115	Chapter 5: Beneficial entitlement, page 80

TABLE OF CASES

Armitage v Nurse [1997] 3 WLR 1046 (KEY CASE)... 197, 206

Barlow Clowes International Ltd v Vaughan [1992] 4 All ER 22... 217
Barlow Clowes International v Eurotrust Intl [2006]1 All ER 333... 153
Bennett v Bennett [1879] 10 Ch D 474... 120
Boardman v Phipps [1967] 2 AC 46... 161-2
Boyce v Boyce [1849] 16 Sim 476... 10-11
Burns v Burns [1984] 1 All ER 244... 137-8

Cannon v Hartley [1949] Ch 213... 54
Clayton's Case [1816] 35 ER 767 (KEY CASE)... 217, 226
Comiskey v Bowring-Hanbury [1905] AC 84... 5
Cowan v Scargill [1985] Ch 270... 179
Curran v Collins [2015] EWCA Civ 404... 137

Eves v Eves [1975] 1 WLR 1338... 136-8

Federal Republic of Brazil v Durant International [2016] AC 297... 216
Foskett v McKeown [2000] 3 All ER 97... 212, 214

Gilmour v Coats [1949] AC 426... 106
Grey v IRC [1960] AC 1 (KEY CASE)... 32

Head v Gould [1898] 2 Ch 250... 193
Hodgson v Marks [1971] 2 All ER 682... 117
Hunter v Moss [1994] 1 WLR 452... 12-13

Jones v Lock [1865] 1 Ch App 25... 8, 48-9

Keech v Sandford [1726] 25 ER 223... 157
King v Chiltern Dog Rescue [2016] 2 WLR 1... 68

McPhail v Doulton [1970] 2 All ER 228... 14
Mascall v Mascall [1985] 49 P & Cr 119... 63-4
Midland Bank plc v Wyatt [1994] EGCS 113... 7
Midland Bank v Cooke [1995] 4 All ER 562... 138
Musset v Bingle [1876] WN 170... 101

National Anti-Vivisection Society v IRC [1948] AC 31... 106
Nestle v NatWest Bank [1994] 1 All ER 118... 192

Oppenheim v Tobacco Securities Trust [1951] AC 297... 106
Oughtred v IRC [1960] AC 206... 34

Palmer v Simmonds [1854] 2 Drew 221... 10
Pascoe v Turner [1979] 1 WLR 431... 140
Patel v Mirza [2016] UKSC 42 (KEY CASE)... 118-19, 129
Paul v Constance [1977] 1 WLR 527... 7, 26
Pullan v Koe [1913] 1 Ch 9... 53

R v District Auditor ex parte West Yorkshire Met County Council [1986] 26... 17
Re Adams & The Kensington Vestry [1884] 27 Ch D 394... 5
Re Astor's ST [1952] Ch 534 (KEY CASE)... 99
Re Barlow's WT [1979] 1 WLR 278... 17
Re Biss [1903] 2 Ch 40... 157-8
Re Clore's Settlement Trusts [1966] 1 WLR 955... 183
Re Denley's Trust Deed [1969] 1 Ch 373 (KEY CASE)... 103, 113
Re Endacott [1960] Ch 232 (KEY CASE)... 99-103, 108, 113
Re Golay's Trust [1965] 1 WLR 1969... 11
Re Haines [1952] 11 WLUK 23... 102
Re Hallett's Estate [1880] 13 Ch D 696 (KEY CASE)... 215, 226
Re Kayford [1975] 1 WLR 279... 9
Re Lillingston [1952] 2 All ER 184... 69
Re London Wine Co. (Shippers) Ltd [1986] PCC 21... 12
Re Osoba [1979] 2 All ER 393... 124
Re Plumptre's Marriage Settlement [1910] 1 Ch 609... 54
Re Ralli's WT [1964] Ch 288 (KEY CASE)... 66, 79
Re Rose [1952] Ch 499 (KEY CASE)... xiv, 61-5, 73-4, 77, 79
Re Smith [1928] Ch 915... 90
Re The Trusts of the Abbott Fund [1900] 2 Ch 326... 123
Re Thomson [1930] 1 Ch 203... 161
Richards v Delbridge [1874] LR 18 Eq 11... 51

Saunders v Vautier [1841] 4 Beav 115 (KEY CASE)... xiv, 80-1, 88-91, 94-6
Sen v Headley [1991] 2 All ER 636... 69-70
Stack v Dowden [2007] UKHL 17... 132
Strong v Bird [1874] Lr 18 Eq 315 (KEY CASE)... xiv, 61-3, 65-7, 74, 77-9

T Choithram International SA v Pagarani [2000] UKPC 46 (KEY CASE)... 64, 79
Thompson's Trustee in Bankruptcy v Heaton [1974] 1 All ER 1239... 162

Vandervell v IRC [1967] AC 291... 31-3

Wilkes v Allington [1931] 2 Ch 104... 68
Woodward v Woodward [1995] 3 All ER 980... 69

TABLE OF STATUTES

Bills of Exchange Act 1882, s 32... 50

Charities Act 2011 (CA) 104-5, 108, 112
   s 1... 104-5
   s 3... 104-5, 108
   s 9... 104

Civil Liability (Contribution) Act 1978 193
Criminal Justice Act 1993, s 52... 118

Equality Act 2010, s 199... 120

Inheritance and Trustees' Powers Act 2014 180-1

Law of Property Act 1925 (LPA) xiv, 24-37, 40, 42, 43, 50, 60, 117, 135-6, 151
   s 52... xiv, 50
   s 52(1)... 50, 60
   s 53... xiv, 24-5, 26-8
   s 53(1)... 24-5, 26-37, 40, 42, 43, 50, 135-6, 151
   s 53(1)(b)... 24-5, 26-8, 37, 40, 42, 43, 135-6
   s 53(1)(c)... 25, 28-37, 40, 42, 50
   s 53(2)... 37, 136, 151
   s 60(3)... 117
   s 136... 50
Law of Property (Miscellaneous Provisions) Act 1989 (LP(MP)A), s 1... 50
Limitation Act 1980... 196, 198-9, 201, 206
   s 21... 198-9, 201

Mental Capacity Act 2005 172

Perpetuities and Accumulations Act 1964 s 3... 86
Perpetuities and Accumulations Act 2009
   s 18... 100
Public Trustee Act 1906 174

Senior Courts Act 1981, s 50... 219
Stock Transfer Act 1963 50

Trade Union and Labour Relations (Consolidation) Act 1992, s 236... 220
Trustee Act 1925 171-5, 181, 183, 194, 197, 206
   s 31... 180
   s 32... 181, 183
   s 36(1)... 172-3, 175
   s 36(6)... 172
   s 39(1)... 175
   s 40(1)... 174
   s 41... 171, 173, 175
   s 61... 197, 206
   s 62... 194, 206
Trustee Act 2000 158, 159, 176-9, 187, 197
   Part V... 158
   s 1... 176-7, 187, 197
   s 3... 178

s 8... 178
s 31... 159
Trusts of Land and Appointment of Trustees Act 1996 (TOLATA 1996) 172-3, 175, 187
   s 19... 172-3
   s 20... 173

Wills Act 1837 (WA) 24, 26, 28
   s 9... 24

1

The three certainties

■ MAKE SURE YOU KNOW

This chapter will cover one aspect of the requirements of an express private trust: the three certainties. You must be able to identify each certainty and be familiar with the legal principles in order to effectively apply the law to client-based scenarios in your SQE assessment.

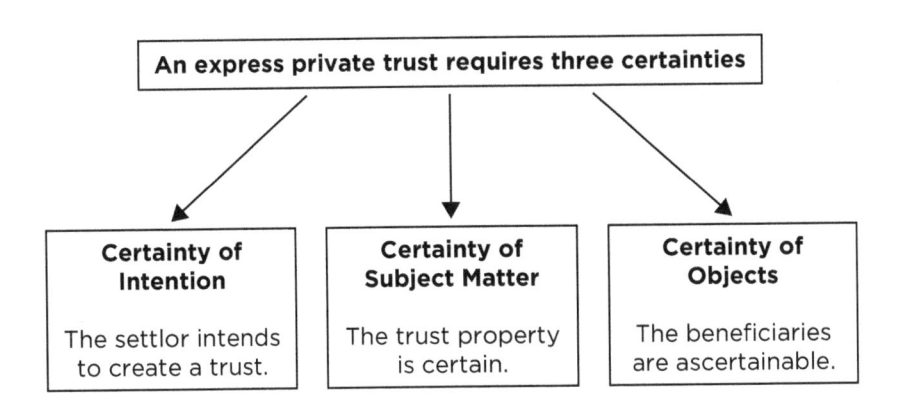

```
        An express private trust requires three certainties
        ┌──────────────────────┬──────────────────────┐
        ▼                      ▼                      ▼
 Certainty of          Certainty of           Certainty of
  Intention           Subject Matter             Objects

The settlor intends   The trust property      The beneficiaries
 to create a trust.      is certain.          are ascertainable.
```

■ SQE ASSESSMENT ADVICE

The topic of the three certainties is fairly straightforward and easily digestible. As you work through this chapter, remember to pay particular attention in your revision to:
- The requirement that all three certainties must be present for a valid trust and how to identify each certainty. The relevant factors in determining certainty of intention.
- The fact that certainty of subject matter includes certainty of property and certainty of beneficial interest.
- The different tests to determine certainty of objects for fixed trusts and for discretionary trusts.

2 The three certainties

In the SQE assessment, you may expect a question on whether a particular gift meets the three certainties. Another possible type of MCQ could be a given scenario on whether the testator's words and/or actions resulted in the creation of a trust.

Bear in mind that a valid trust must satisfy all three certainties as well as the formality requirements and must be completely constituted (see **Chapters 2** and **3**). Remember to read this topic in conjunction with formalities and constitution of trusts.

■ WHAT DO YOU KNOW ALREADY?

Have a go at these questions before reading this chapter. If you find some difficult or cannot remember the answers, make a note to look more closely at that during your revision.

1) True or false: An express trust can only be created in a written document.
   [Introduction to express private trusts, page 3]
2) True or false: The settlor must use the word 'trust' in order to demonstrate certainty of intention to create a trust.
   [Certainty of intention, page 4]
3) True or false: A person of means must watch what they say to others as any statement they make regarding their property will be regarded as an intention to hold the property on trust for another.
   [Certainty of intention, page 4]
4) Daisy is seeking your advice: she owns 1,000 shares in Google Inc. and would like to leave most of it to her sister Billie in her will. In which of the following is there certainty of subject matter?
   a) The majority of my shares in Google Inc. to my sister Billie.
   b) 800 of my shares in Google Inc. to my sister Billie.
   [Certainty of subject matter, page 10]
5) In which of the following examples is there conceptual certainty?
   a) I leave all the money in my account at Lloyd's Bank on trust for my best friends.
   b) I leave all the money in my account at Lloyd's Bank on trust for my Facebook friends.
   [Certainty of objects, page 13]

INTRODUCTION TO EXPRESS PRIVATE TRUSTS

Before we get to the substantive law on the three certainties, here is a quick reminder of the basics of trusts law:
- All non-charitable trusts are **private trusts**.
- An express trust is intentionally created by the **settlor**.
- The creation of a trust can be **inter vivos** or **testamentary**.
- When dealing with a will, the settlor is referred to as the **testator**.
- The settlor can act as trustee or they can appoint others to act as **trustees**.
- The trust must also have **beneficiaries**.

> **Key term: private trust**
>
> A private trust is any trust that is not charitable. The trust is said to be an express trust when the settlor intentionally created it.

> **Key term: settlor**
>
> The settlor is the person creating the trust.

> **Key term: inter vivos**
>
> During the lifetime of the settlor.

There are many ways a settlor can create a trust:
- In writing, either formally by executing a trust instrument or in a will; or by letter or a written note.
- By words or conduct.

It is a question of construction whether or not a trust has been created. The court will look at the words in the document (if written) or the words and conduct of the settlor (if not in writing) when deciding whether a valid trust has been created.

> **Key term: testamentary**
>
> A testamentary creation of trust is a trust created in a will.

> **Key term: testator**
>
> The testator is the person who created the will.

> **Key term: trustees**
>
> The trustees hold the legal title of the trust assets and are under a duty to administer the assets for the benefit of the beneficiaries.

4 The three certainties

> **Key term: beneficiaries**
>
> The beneficiaries are entitled to benefit from the trust and they hold the equitable title to the trust assets. The beneficiaries are said to have the beneficial interests.

For the SQE assessment, you should bear in mind that when ascertaining whether a valid trust has been created, you must consider all the relevant requirements. These requirements are explained in this chapter, as well as in **Chapter 2** and **Chapter 3**.

THE THREE CERTAINTIES

To create a valid trust, the settlor must ensure that all three certainties are present:
- Certainty of intention
- Certainty of subject matter
- Certainty of objects

Let's look at each in detail below.

CERTAINTY OF INTENTION

To create a valid trust, it must be clear that the settlor, by their *words* or conduct, had the *intention* to create this trust. That is why the certainty of intention is sometimes referred to as the certainty of words. There is no set form of words to use, so long as it is clear that the settlor intended to create a trust.

> **Revision tip**
>
> Remember the maxim (principle) 'equity looks to the substance rather than the form'. When ascertaining a person's intention, the court looks beyond that person's words to include their conduct and any factors the court considers to be relevant.

Take, for example, the following clause in John's will: 'My house to my partner Sam so that she can continue to look after our children'. This could be construed as:
- An absolute gift to Sam (if the court found that John had no intention of creating a trust), or
- A trust where Sam is the trustee holding the house for the children (if the court found that John had the intention to create a trust).

Certainty of intention 5

In the rest of this subtopic, we are going to explore common scenarios where the court must decide if there was certainty of intention.

The use of precatory words

As you can see from the example in John's will above, people do not always make their intent clear and use what the courts consider to be **precatory words**.

Key term: precatory words

These are words expressing confidence, wish, belief, desire, hope or recommendation, eg 'It is my wish', 'I sincerely hope', 'I have no doubt', etc.

The use of precatory words is unlikely to result in the creation of a trust. The case examples in **Table 1.1** give examples of this and will help you see how it can be applied in practice.

Revision tip

The case law mentioned in the table below is useful for aiding your understanding of the law and you may encounter a similar scenario in your SQE assessment. However, you will not be required to memorise the case names.

Table 1.1: Case examples of precatory words

Case example	Ruling
Re Adams & The Kensington Vestry [1884] 27 Ch D 394 'Unto and to the absolute use of my wife ... *in full confidence* that she will do what is right as to the disposal thereof between my children ...'	In this case, the words 'in full confidence' were precatory in nature and were considered not to be sufficiently imperative to show an intention to create a trust.
Comiskey v Bowring-Hanbury [1905] AC 84 'Absolutely *in full confidence* that she will make such use of it as I would have made myself and that at her death she will devise it to such one or more of my nieces as she may think fit *and in default to be divided among my nieces*'.	In this case, although precatory words were used, the testator also included a **gift over in default of appointment**. This imposed a mandatory obligation. The court was able to find an intention to create a trust here as the settlor made it clear in the whole context of the will that a trust was intended by including instructions for the nieces to acquire a benefit in any event.

> **Key term: gift over in default of appointment**
> Where a settlor has created a trust which gives the trustee a discretion on distribution of the trust property, the settlor may sometimes include an alternative gift in the event of a failure to distribute the property.

Take a look at **Practice example 1.1** below in relation to precatory words.

> **Practice example 1.1**
>
> Your client is a personal representative of her brother's estate. Her brother, a widower, died recently leaving two adult daughters. His will had the following clause, 'All my savings in my bank account for my only sister in full confidence that she will do right by my children'.
>
> Your client wishes to know if she is entitled to the money or whether she is to hold it on trust for her nieces. What is the court's likely approach?
>
> **The words used are precatory in nature and are unlikely to impose a mandatory obligation on your client. In the absence of any contrary intention in the will, the court will most likely find this to be an absolute gift to her.**

To summarise, the use of precatory words would generally not create a trust unless it is clear from the whole context of the document that the testator intended to create a trust.

What if the settlor included the word 'trust'? Do you think that demonstrates certainty of intention?

The use of the word 'trust'

Inclusion of the word 'trust' may not necessarily create a trust if there was no genuine intention on the part of the settlor to do so.

For example, if a father's will reads: 'I leave my whole estate to my only daughter; I *trust* she will make good use of it to continue to love and care for my beloved grandchildren'. Did the father intend to make his daughter a trustee holding for the benefit of the grandchildren? Or was the use of the word 'trust' merely precatory and this was an absolute gift to the daughter?

Based on what we know of the court's approach to the use of precatory words, this is likely to be construed as an absolute gift to the daughter despite the use of the word 'trust'.

> **Practice example 1.2**
>
> Mr and Mrs W are joint legal owners of a matrimonial home. Mr W executed a declaration of trust of the house in favour of his wife and children. He placed the trust deed in his safe. He later obtained a business loan from a bank using the house as security, the bank was unaware of the trust. When his business went into receivership, Mr W produced the trust deed. The creditors are claiming the house. Can the wife and children rely on the trust and thus prevent the creditors from claiming the house?
>
> These are the facts of *Midland Bank plc v Wyatt* [1994] EGCS 113, where the court found Mr W's declaration of trust to be a sham and therefore voidable. This case established that a declaration of trust does not automatically result in the creation of a valid trust. The court will look beyond the words used by the settlor to determine their true intention.

Next, we will consider whether the settlor's informal words and actions can create a trust.

Informal words and actions

A written document is unnecessary so long as the settlor shows sufficient intention to create a trust. Informal words are acceptable if the intention to create a trust is clear; there is no need to use the word 'trust'.

The case of *Paul v Constance* [1977] 1 WLR 527 is a good example of the informal words and actions of Mr Constance demonstrating his intention to create a trust. He had left his wife and moved in with Mrs Paul. He opened a bank account in his sole name (instead of joint names) to avoid embarrassment due to the fact that they were unmarried. Constance had frequently told Paul that the money in the account is 'as much yours as mine' and any joint bingo winnings were paid into that account. The court found that Constance intended to create a trust of the money in his bank account for Paul through a series of declarations and conversations on his part. However, the court acknowledged that this was a borderline case and awarded Paul half of the money in the account with the other half going to Constance's wife. Had this not been considered a borderline case, Paul would have been awarded all the money in the account.

> **Exam warning**
>
> In the SQE assessment, if you are required to ascertain whether a valid trust has been created, remember to consider not just the settlor's words and actions but also all the other relevant information included in the question.

Have a look at **Practice example 1.3** on the effect of a person's words or conduct:

> **Practice example 1.3**
>
> Mr Jones returned home after being away for business and was criticised for failing to bring a present for his infant son. He flourished a cheque for £900 payable to him and said, 'I give this to baby for himself', placing the cheque in his son's hands. He then took back the cheque and declared, 'I am going to put it away for him'. Jones died soon after and the cheque was found amongst his papers. What do you think of Jones' actions? Did his second declaration show certainty of intention to hold the money on trust for his son?
>
> These are the facts of *Jones v Lock* [1865] 1 Ch App 25, where it was argued that Jones' words, 'I am going to put it away for him' showed an intention to hold the money on trust for his son. However, the court held that there had been no valid declaration of trust, explaining that it would be 'of very dangerous example if loose conversations of this sort … should have the effect of declarations of trust'.

This practice example reinforced the principle of substance over form when considering a settlor's intention to create a trust. With that in mind, we will look next at how the settlor's conduct alone can demonstrate intention.

The settlor's conduct

So far, in all the examples above, the court had the settlor's words, whether written or oral, to consider when construing the settlor's true intention. What if the settlor never spoke of their intention? Or if there was no document recording their intention? Can conduct alone be used as evidence of an intention to create a trust? Consider **Practice example 1.4**.

Practice example 1.4

A mail order company where customers paid in advance opened a separate account into which all money received from customers whose goods had not been delivered were paid. The account was named 'Customer Trust Deposit Account'. Money was only taken from that account once the goods had been dispatched. The company went bankrupt and the liquidators sought a declaration as to the ownership of the money in that account.

Who do you think is entitled to claim the money in that account? The customers who had yet to receive their goods, or the liquidators?

These are the facts of *Re Kayford* [1975] 1 WLR 279, where the court held that the separate account was evidence of intention to create a trust. The money in the account belonged to the customers.

Use the summary in **Figure 1.1** to help you remember the salient points on certainty of intention.

Certainty of Intention

The settlor must intend to create a trust.

↓

Precatory words are generally insufficient. Question of construction looking at the whole context.

↓

The use of the word 'trust' is not definitive if lacking genuine intention.

↓

No need to use the word 'trust'; informal words and actions are acceptable.

↓

The settlor's conduct alone may show intention.

Figure 1.1: Certainty of intention

CERTAINTY OF SUBJECT MATTER

A trust must have assets; in other words, the trust property or the subject matter. The property subject to the trust must be described with sufficient certainty, otherwise the trust fails, as you can see from **Practice example 1.5**.

> **Practice example 1.5**
>
> A testator's will has the following clause: I leave on trust 'the bulk of my **residuary estate**'. Is there certainty of subject matter?
>
> This phrase was used in the case of *Palmer v Simmonds* [1854] 2 Drew 221, where the court held that the subject matter was insufficiently certain due to the word 'bulk'. There is no valid trust.

> **Key term: residuary estate**
>
> The residue is everything that is left in a deceased's estate after all debts and taxes have been paid and all specific and non-specific gifts have been distributed.

The subject matter of a trust includes both the property subject to the trust and the beneficial entitlement of each beneficiary. For example, if a testator leaves 'All my shares in British Gas on trust for my four children equally'. There is certainty of subject matter because:
- There is certainty of property: the shares in British Gas.
- There is certainty of beneficial interest: each beneficiary is entitled to a quarter share.

Let's consider the consequences where the beneficial interest is uncertain.

Certainty of property without certainty of beneficial interest
The trust fails if there is uncertainty of beneficial interest. The case of *Boyce v Boyce* [1849] 16 Sim 476 is a good example: the testator left two houses to his trustees to hold one for his daughter Maria, 'whichever she may choose' and the other to his daughter Charlotte. Maria died before making her choice. As Charlotte's share was dependent on Maria's choice, Charlotte's beneficial interest was uncertain and the trust failed.

Exam warning
Be aware that the property subject to the trust and the beneficial interests may not always be the same as illustrated in *Boyce v Boyce*. Make sure you know how to identify the trust property as well as the beneficial interest. Start by identifying the trust property; then identify how much each beneficiary is entitled to.

Where appropriate, the court can save the trust if they are able to objectively assess a beneficiary's entitlement.

Objective assessment by the court
It is common practice for a settlor to leave property on trust for their child with a direction that the child is to receive a reasonable income from the property. The property subject to the trust is certain assuming it has been clearly identified. The issue is whether there is certainty of beneficial interest. The child is to receive a 'reasonable income' but the amount was not specified. Is this considered certain?

In *Re Golay's Trust* [1965] 1 WLR 1969, the testator directed that his daughter should enjoy one of his flats during her lifetime and receive a reasonable income from his other properties. The court was willing to accept the words 'reasonable income' as being sufficiently certain as they can make an objective assessment of the amount the beneficiary should receive based on the circumstances of the case.

One final issue to consider is the different degree of certainty required depending on the type of asset.

Tangible assets vs intangible assets
Another area examinable in the SQE is the different degree of certainty required for **tangible** and **intangible assets**.

Key term: tangible assets
Physical property or chattels.

Key term: intangible assets
Non-physical property such as shares, patents, etc.

Tangible assets

If a settlor created a trust of only part of their assets, for example, part of their wine collection, there is no certainty of subject matter unless the tangible assets are clearly identified, usually by segregating them from the larger stock as demonstrated in **Practice example 1.6**.

> **Practice example 1.6**
>
> A customer of a fine wine company just heard that the company has gone into liquidation. The customer is worried about their order of four cases of wine placed and paid for just before the company went into liquidation. Must the customer join the queue as an unsecured creditor or is the customer entitled to their order?
>
> According to the decision in *Re London Wine Co. (Shippers) Ltd* [1986] PCC 21, the answer depends on whether the company had segregated the wine ordered by the customer. It must be clear that the segregated wine was meant for the customer. If so, the customer is entitled to the wine as the actions of the company demonstrated an intention to create a trust and the fact that the wine was kept aside would show certainty of subject matter.
>
> If the order had not been segregated, the customer is considered an unsecured creditor.

Having looked at tangible assets, we will now consider intangible assets.

Intangible assets

Intangible assets are treated differently; provided the assets are similar, there is no need for segregation. **Practice example 1.7** provides a useful illustration.

> **Practice example 1.7**
>
> An employer agreed to give 50 of his 950 shares to his employee. The employer died before he could transfer the shares, nor did he identify the 50 shares. Is the employee entitled to the shares?
>
> This was what happened in the case of *Hunter v Moss* [1994] 1 WLR 452, where the court had to decide whether the employer had the intention to create a trust, and if so whether there was certainty of subject matter. The court held that there was an intention to create

a trust and as the shares were identical to each other, there was no need for segregation and the employee was entitled to the 50 shares.

Summary: Certainty of subject matter	
Certainty of property	The trust property must be certain.
	Different degree of certainty for:
	• Tangible assets
	• Intangible assets
Certainty of beneficial interest	The entitlement of each beneficiary must be certain.
	The court can assist if the beneficial interest can be objectively assessed.

CERTAINTY OF OBJECTS

The objects of a trust are its beneficiaries. A trust without beneficiaries fails. Where there is more than one beneficiary, the **class of beneficiaries** must be ascertainable. The test to determine certainty of objects differ for **fixed trusts** and **discretionary trusts**.

Key term: class of beneficiaries
Where a trust has more than one beneficiary but the settlor has not identified each and every beneficiary but refers instead to a class, such as 'my grandchildren', 'my employees', etc.

Key term: fixed trust
In a fixed trust, each beneficiary is entitled to a specific share of the trust property.

Key term: discretionary trust
In a discretionary trust, the trustees have a discretion on whether or not to pay any member of a defined class of beneficiaries. The beneficiaries have no automatic right to payment, only the right to be considered by the trustees.

Table 1.2 gives some examples of fixed and discretionary trusts.

14 The three certainties

Table 1.2: Examples of fixed and discretionary trusts

Examples of fixed trusts:	Example of a discretionary trust:
a) On trust 'for A for life, remainder to B absolutely' – A has the life interest and B has the remainder interest. b) On trust 'for A, B and C in equal shares' – each beneficiary is entitled to 1/3 of the trust property.	'On discretionary trusts for the grandchildren of Alice' – the trustees may select who to pay out of Alice's grandchildren but have no obligation to pay something to each grandchild, or to pay in equal shares, or even to make any payments.

We will now consider the different requirements to establish certainty of objects for fixed and discretionary trusts. Make sure you pay particular attention to this in your revision as you may encounter a problem-based scenario in the SQE in this area.

Fixed trusts

For fixed trusts, the test for certainty of objects is the class ascertainability test. It must be possible to compile a *complete list* of all beneficiaries.

Practice example 1.8

A testator left a will with a following clause: '£1m on trust for all my grandchildren in equal shares'. Is this a fixed trust? If so, does it meet the test for certainty of objects?

This is a fixed trust as each beneficiary is entitled to a specific share of the trust property. There is certainty of objects as it is possible to compile a complete list of all the beneficiaries.

Discretionary trusts

For discretionary trusts, the test for certainty of objects is the *individual ascertainability test* as explained in the case of *McPhail v Doulton* [1970] 2 All ER 228: the trustees must ask 'can it be said with certainty that any given individual is or is not a member of the class?'.

The test is less stringent than for fixed trusts, as there is no need to draw up a complete list of beneficiaries. **Practice example 1.9** demonstrates the flexibility of this test.

Practice example 1.9

A settlor, who owned a company, established a discretionary trust for the benefit of 'my employees and ex-employees, and any relatives of such persons'. Are the objects of this trust certain?

You have been told that this is a discretionary trust and therefore must apply the individual ascertainability test. All the trustees need to do is apply the test to each person in turn rather than to render a complete list of all beneficiaries falling within the description. As you can see, it is much easier to determine whether an individual was an employee, ex-employee or a relative of such a person. The trust is valid.

Summary	Test for certainty of objects
Fixed trust	Class ascertainability: trustees can compile a complete list of all beneficiaries.
Discretionary trust	Individual ascertainability: can it be said with certainty that any given individual is or is not a member of the class?

Exam warning

If the SQE exam question requires consideration of whether the object of a trust is certain, remember to first check whether the trust is a fixed or a discretionary trust before applying the appropriate test.

Issues arising when ascertaining certainty of objects

There are four important issues to remember when looking at certainty of objects. These are:
- Conceptual uncertainty
- Evidential uncertainty
- Administrative unworkability
- Gifts to individuals answering a particular description: the one-person test.

We will now look at each in turn.

Conceptual uncertainty makes a trust void

There is conceptual uncertainty where the words used by the settlor to describe the beneficiaries are too vague for the courts to apply. Case law provides some guidance on whether the following popular terms are conceptually certain:
- The term 'friends' is considered conceptually uncertain.
- The term 'relatives' is considered conceptually certain. Similarly, the term 'family' is also certain.
- The term 'dependants' is conceptually certain; 'dependants' being persons wholly or in part dependent upon the means of another.

There is no conceptual uncertainty if:
- The settlor gives meaning to phrases so the trustees can identify the class: 'To my trustee to hold on trust for my Facebook friends'.
- The settlor left the discretion to someone to decide who falls within the class: 'To my trustee to hold on trust for my friends as determined in his absolute discretion'.

Evidential uncertainty

If the settlor included a clear description of the beneficiaries, there is conceptual certainty, but if the trustees are unable to determine exactly who fits the description, due to lack of evidence, there is evidential uncertainty. For example, 'to the former employees of my now defunct company' is conceptually certain but may be evidentially uncertain if there are no records of the employees.

Extrinsic evidence is admissible to clear up any evidential uncertainty. So in our example, evidence might include employment contracts, pay slips, etc.

Key term: extrinsic evidence
Facts or information outside of a written document like a will or a trust deed.

Exam warning
Candidates tend to conflate the concepts of conceptual and evidential certainty so make sure you know the difference. Remember that conceptual uncertainty renders a trust void but evidential uncertainty can be remedied by the admission of extrinsic evidence.

Certainty of objects 17

Administrative unworkability

A trust fails for administrative unworkability where the description used by the settlor is clear but the definition of beneficiaries is too wide to form a class.

A good example of this can be found in *R v District Auditor ex Parte West Yorkshire Met County Council* [1986] 26, where a trust for the benefit of the inhabitants of West Yorkshire (population: 2.5m) was held to be void for administrative unworkability.

Gifts to individuals answering a particular description: the one-person test

At times, a testator may include a bequest in their will where each beneficiary is entitled to a similar gift and the number of beneficiaries does not affect the size of each gift. For such bequests, conceptual certainty is not required so long as at least one person meets the criteria.

For example, consider the following clause in a will: '£50 to be paid by my trustees to any of my family or friends who has supported my business over the years'. Every person who meets the description is to be given £50; the number of people who meet the description is irrelevant. For clarification, see **Practice example 1.10**.

> **Practice example 1.10**
>
> A testator's will left paintings for 'any members of my family and any friends of mine who wish to do so' to purchase at a reduced price. Is this valid for certainty of objects?
>
> This was the bequest in *Re Barlow's WT* [1979] 1 WLR 278, which was held to be a series of individual gifts. As such, there was no requirement to establish all the members of the class, only that any person wishing to buy a painting was indeed 'family' or 'friend'. Thus, there was no need to decide if 'friends' was conceptually certain. This gift was valid because any uncertainty regarding the class of beneficiaries does not affect the 'share' of anyone who can prove that they qualify.

Figure 1.2 provides a summary of what happens when each certainty is lacking.

18 The three certainties

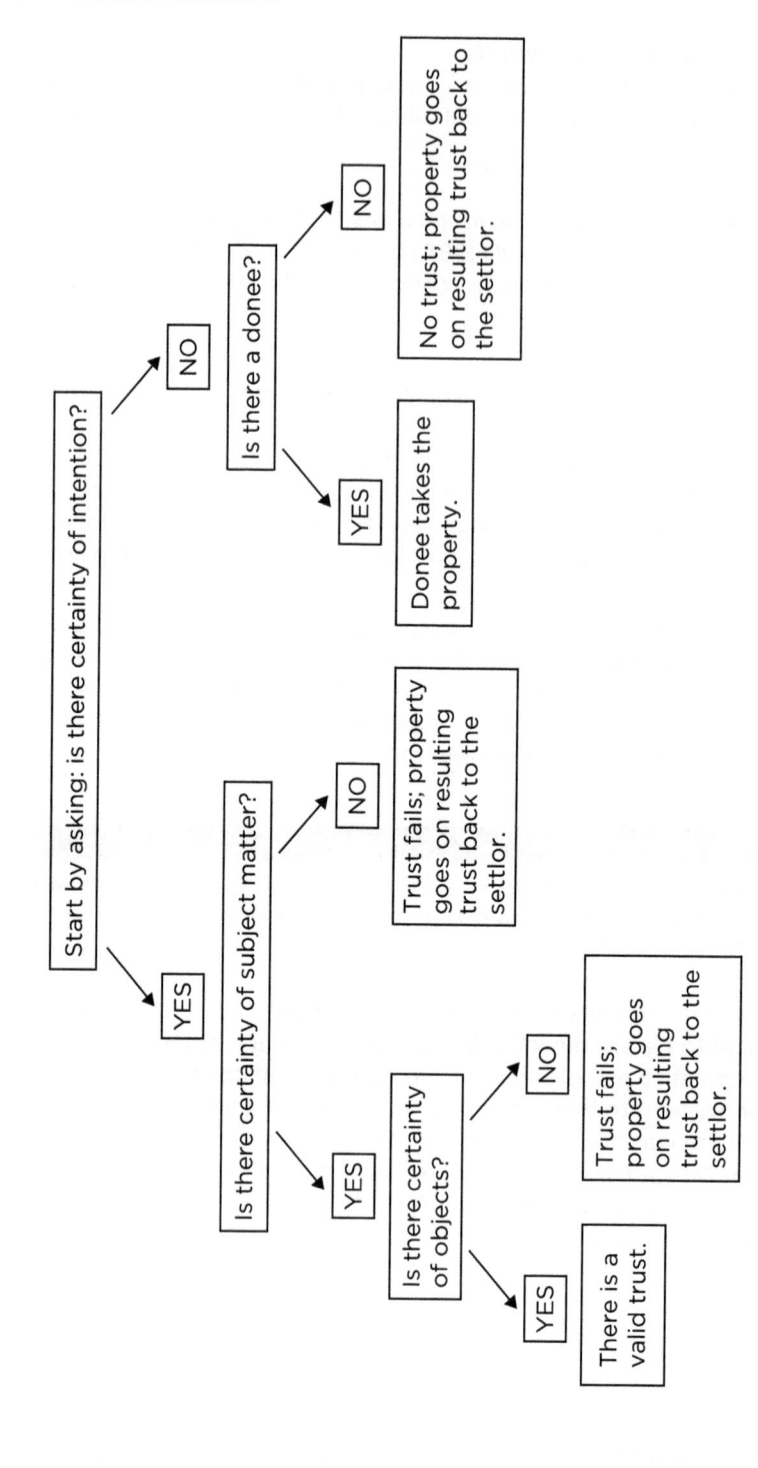

Figure 1.2: When certainty is lacking

■ KEY POINT CHECKLIST

This chapter has covered the following key knowledge points. You can use these to structure your revision around, making sure to recall the key details for each point, as covered in this chapter.
- The validity of an express private trust depends on the three certainties.
- The intention to create a trust can be found by looking at many factors, including the settlor's words, actions and all other relevant factors.
- Certainty of subject matter includes certainty of the trust assets as well as certainty of each beneficiary's entitlement.
- There is certainty of objects if the beneficiaries are ascertainable.
- In a fixed trust, there is certainty of objects if it is possible to produce a complete list of the beneficiaries.
- In a discretionary trust, apply the individual ascertainability test to determine certainty of objects.

■ KEY TERMS AND CONCEPTS
- private trust (**page 3**)
- settlor (**page 3**)
- inter vivos (**page 3**)
- testamentary (**page 3**)
- testator (**page 3**)
- trustees (**page 3**)
- beneficiaries (**page 4**)
- precatory words (**page 5**)
- gift over in default of appointment (**page 6**)
- residuary estate (**page 10**)
- tangible assets (**page 11**)
- intangible assets (**page 11**)
- class of beneficiaries (**page 13**)
- fixed trust (**page 13**)
- discretionary trusts (**page 13**)
- extrinsic evidence (**page 16**)

■ SQE1-STYLE QUESTIONS

QUESTION 1

A company director died leaving a will by which her estate is to be held on trust for her son for life and after his death to be divided between all

20 The three certainties

the present and past employees of her company. The son is concerned that the trust is not workable. He has a complete list of past and present employees but is unsure that all of them can be traced.

Which of the following statements provides the best advice regarding the trust?

A. The trust is valid because the company still exists.
B. The trust is valid because there are a large number of employees who can benefit from it.
C. The trust is valid because there is a complete record of past and present employees.
D. The trust is not valid because a company cannot be a beneficiary.
E. The trust is not valid because the class of beneficiaries is administratively unworkable.

QUESTION 2

A settlor recently transferred £10m to set up a trust with the following clause: 'The trustees shall apply the net income of the fund in making at their absolute discretion payments to any of my relatives or dependants in such amounts, at such times and on such conditions as they think fit'.

Which of the following statements provides the best advice regarding the trust?

A. The trust is not valid due to conceptual uncertainty.
B. The settlor has created a fixed trust.
C. The validity of the trust depends on the trustees being able to draw up a complete list of all the beneficiaries.
D. The beneficiaries of the trust are not entitled to equal shares of the trust income.
E. The trustees must ensure that the beneficiaries receive payment.

QUESTION 3

A client is seeking advice on the following gift in her husband's will: '£500k to my wife, and I am confident that she will make good use of the money to take good care of our children'.

Which of the following statements provides the best advice regarding the gift?

A. The wife holds the money on trust for the children.
B. The husband intended to create a trust.
C. The money will be returned to the husband's estate.
D. The children are entitled to the money absolutely.
E. The wife is entitled to the money absolutely.

QUESTION 4

A testator's will made the following bequest: 'My shares in Energy plc to my cousin from which he must ensure regular payments to his mother, my aunt, to maintain a reasonable standard of living for her'.

Which of the following statements provides the best advice regarding the gift?

A. The gift is void for lack of certainty of subject matter.
B. The gift is void for lack of certainty of objects.
C. The cousin can take the shares absolutely.
D. The aunt is the beneficiary of the trust.
E. The cousin is the beneficiary of the trust.

QUESTION 5

A testator's will contains the following clause: 'The bulk of my residue to be divided amongst all the faithful employees and the dependants of such employees of my former company as my executors think fit'. The testator's company ceased operating a decade ago and the executors are unsure if there are any records left of the employees.

Which of the following statements provides the best advice regarding the gift?

A. The gift is valid because there are a large number of beneficiaries who can benefit from it.
B. The gift is valid because the executors can use extrinsic evidence to identify the beneficiaries.
C. The gift is not valid because the company no longer exists.
D. The gift is not valid because the executors cannot draw up a complete list of all the beneficiaries.
E. The gift is not valid because the subject matter is uncertain.

■ ANSWERS TO QUESTIONS

Answers to 'What do you know already?' questions at the start of the chapter

1) False. An express trust can also be created by considering the settlor's words or conduct.
2) False. There is no need to use the word 'trust' so long as the settlor demonstrated a clear intention to create a trust.
3) False. The courts are unlikely to construe loose conversations as an intent to create a trust.
4) There is certainty of subject matter in (b) as Daisy specified the number of shares she wants to bequeath Billie. Note that as shares are intangible assets, there is no need for Daisy to have segregated the shares. In (a), the use of the word 'majority' meant there was uncertainty of subject matter.
5) The term 'friends' is regarded as conceptually uncertain but there is conceptual certainty in (b) as the settlor provided further explanation of the 'friends' intended to benefit. It is possible for the trustees to draw up a complete list of Facebook friends.

Answers to end-of-chapter SQE1-style questions

Question 1:
   The correct answer was C. This is a fixed trust and certainty of objects is determined by whether the trustees can compile a complete list of all beneficiaries. Options A, B, D and E are wrong because the reasons given do not determine the validity of the trust.

Question 2:
   The correct answer was D. This is a discretionary trust (Option B is wrong), and as such the trustees are under no obligation to ensure payment to all the beneficiaries (not Option E). The test to determine conceptual certainty is the individual ascertainability test, the trustees need not draw up a complete list of the beneficiaries so not Option C. Option A is wrong because the description of the class of beneficiaries is conceptually certain.

Question 3:
   The correct answer was E. 'I am confident' are precatory words, which are not emphatic enough to show certainty of intention to create a trust. As there is no trust, the answer cannot be A, B or D.

The wife (who is the donee) is absolutely entitled to the money so Option C is wrong.

Question 4:
The correct answer was D. There was intention to create a trust with the trustee (the cousin) holding for the benefit of his mother (the testator's aunt), who is the object (Option B is wrong). The subject matter is certain: the shares (Option A is wrong). The beneficial interest ('reasonable standard of living') is certain as the amount can be objective assessed by the court. The cousin is a trustee so he cannot benefit from the shares (so not Options C or E).

Question 5:
The correct answer was E. The subject matter of the gift is uncertain due to the word 'bulk'. There is no valid gift so the answer cannot be A or B. Options C and D are incorrect because the reasons given are not why the gift is invalid.

■ KEY CASES, RULES, STATUTES AND INSTRUMENTS

There are many cases cited in this chapter but they are merely for illustrative purposes. There is no need to memorise any case names.

2

Formalities for the creation of trusts

■ MAKE SURE YOU KNOW

We now know from Chapter 1 that the three certainties are required in the creation of an express private trust. In addition to this, a valid trust must also comply with certain formalities. This chapter explains the formalities required for different types of trusts. You must be familiar with the formalities in order to effectively apply the law to client-based scenarios in your SQE assessment.

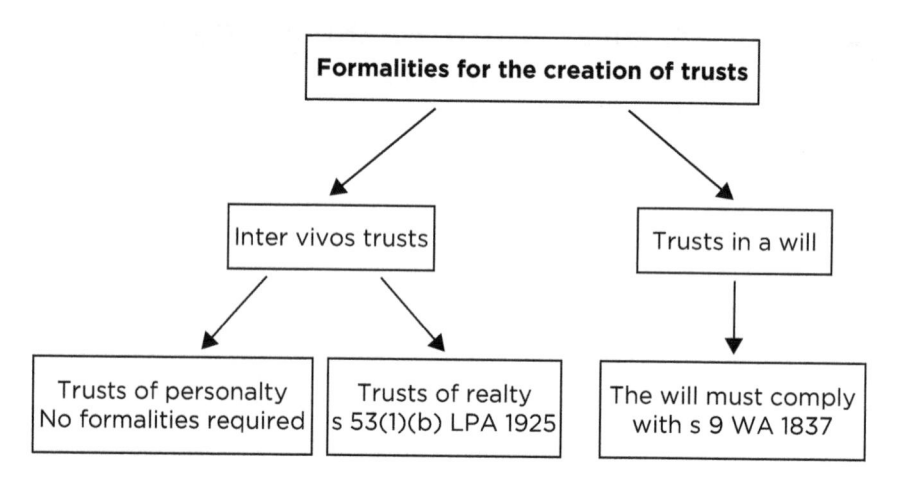

```
                Formalities for the creation of trusts
                       /                    \
              Inter vivos trusts         Trusts in a will
               /           \                   |
    Trusts of personalty   Trusts of realty    The will must comply
    No formalities required  s 53(1)(b) LPA 1925   with s 9 WA 1837
```

As well as the formalities required for the creation of a trust, you must also be familiar with the formality requirements for the transfer of an equitable interest.

■ SQE ASSESSMENT ADVICE

Apart from the three certainties, a settlor creating a trust must also comply with certain formalities as required by the Law of Property Act (LPA) 1925. Please note the SQE1 does not require you to memorise this authority, but it will be useful to be familiar with it.

As you work through this chapter, remember to pay particular attention in your revision to:
- The requirements of s 53(1)(b) LPA 1925 when creating a trust of land and the consequence of non-compliance.
- The requirements of s 53(1)(c) LPA 1925 when disposing of an equitable interest and the consequence of non-compliance.
- Be aware of the types of disposition that must comply with s 53(1)(c).

■ WHAT DO YOU KNOW ALREADY?

Have a go at these questions before reading this chapter. If you find some difficult or cannot remember the answers, make a note to look more closely at that during your revision.

1) What are the formalities required when creating a trust of land?
   [Introduction to formalities, page 26]
2) What are the formalities required when creating a trust of personalty?
   [Introduction to formalities, page 26]
3) True or false: It is possible for a settlor to orally declare a trust of land so long as the settlor ensures that the correct formalities have been met after the declaration.
   [Introduction to formalities, page 26]
4) True or false: If a settlor orally declares a trust of land but later puts it in writing, the date of creation of the trust is the date of the written instrument.
   [Introduction to formalities, page 26]
5) A trust was set up to benefit the settlor's only child, who is an adult. The adult beneficiary decided to transfer her beneficial interest to her best friend. She orally informed the trustees to pay the trust income to her best friend. Was there a valid transfer of her beneficial interest to the friend?
   [Disposition of an equitable interest, page 28]

INTRODUCTION TO FORMALITIES

The focus of this topic is the formalities required to create an **inter vivos** trust and the formalities required in the disposition of an equitable interest. In the case of a testamentary trust, the proper execution of the will in accordance with the Wills Act 1837 ensures automatic compliance with all formalities.

> **Key term: inter vivos**
> During the lifetime of the settlor.

If you recall from the previous chapter, on the three certainties, a settlor may create a trust by manifesting an intention to do so, and by ensuring that the trust property and the beneficiaries are clearly specified.

We will now consider whether any additional formalities are required in creating a valid trust. The formality requirements differ for trusts of **personalty** and trusts of **realty**.

> **Key term: personalty**
> Movable assets; any property other than realty.

> **Key term: realty**
> Real property; land and anything attached to the land, such as buildings.

Inter vivos trusts of personalty

The creation of trusts of personalty requires no special formalities. A good example can be found in the case of *Paul v Constance* [1977] 1 WLR 527. In this case, a man separated from his wife and moved in with his female friend. He opened a bank account in his sole name but with the intention that the woman also benefitted from it. The court held that the man's actions and words demonstrated an intention to create a trust of the money in the account benefitting his female friend. There were no other formalities required for that trust (see **Chapter 1** for the full facts).

Inter vivos trusts of realty

For such trusts, the formality requirements of s 53(1)(b) must be met: 'a declaration of trust respecting any land or any interest therein must be manifested and proved by some writing signed by some person who is able to declare such a trust or by his will'.

The following sets out what you need to remember concerning this provision:
- Evidenced in writing.
- Signed by the settlor.
- If originally oral, the relevant date would be the date of the oral declaration.
- Unenforceable if not complied with (but not void – to prevent the trustee from gaining unjust enrichment).

Exam warning
A common mistake candidates make is to assume that non-compliance with s 53(1)(b) renders the trust void but the trust is merely unenforceable. Consider this: If the settlor transferred land to trustees to hold on trust for a beneficiary but there was no written evidence of the trust, according to s 53(1)(b), the trust is merely unenforceable. This means the beneficiary is not entitled to the trust property and the trustees must hold the land on **resulting trust** for the settlor. If the trust was void, however, the trustees may argue that as they are not *trustees* they can keep the property.

Key term: resulting trust
A type of trust that comes into existence under certain circumstances. In the example above, where the settlor transfers property to trustees on an express trust which has failed, the trustees are said to hold the property on resulting trust back to the settlor (see **Chapter 7**).

Practice example 2.1
According to your client, his aunt made a declaration to the whole family at a Christmas gathering that she intended to hold her Dorset house on trust for him. He also produced a letter from his aunt dated a week later in which she confirmed the trust. What is your advice to him regarding the validity of the trust?

The three certainties have been met: there was a clear intention on her part to create a trust, the subject matter of the trust is the house and the object is your client.

> As for the formality requirements, even if the original declaration was merely oral, when the aunt later wrote to your client, the letter (assuming it was signed) complied with s 53(1)(b) and the trust is valid.

You now know that if a settlor is creating a trust during their lifetime, they must comply with the formality of writing if the trust asset is realty. What about testamentary trusts? This is explained below.

TESTAMENTARY TRUSTS

It is possible to create a trust by will. The will must be validly executed in accordance with the requirements of the Wills Act 1837: it must be in writing signed by the testator and attested by two independent witnesses in the presence of the testator. As you can see in **Practice example 2.2**, compliance with these requirements would mean automatic compliance with s 53(1)(b).

> **Practice example 2.2**
>
> A father wished to set up trusts benefitting his two infant children in the event of his death. He executed a will leaving all his personalty on trust for his daughter and all his realty on trust for his son. Are there any other formalities he must comply with?
>
> So long as the will was properly executed, no other formalities are required. The requirement that the trust of land be evidenced in writing and signed by the testator is met by mere execution of the will.

Once a trust has been created, the beneficiary holds the equitable interest in the trust assets. The remainder of this topic will focus on the formality requirements for the transfer of such equitable interests.

DISPOSITION OF AN EQUITABLE INTEREST

The beneficiary of a trust may wish to transfer their equitable interest to another. The transfer is only valid if the formality requirements of s 53(1)(c) have been met. According to the section, a 'disposition of an equitable interest ... subsisting at the time of the disposition, must be in writing signed by the person disposing of the same, or by his agent thereunto lawfully authorised in writing or by will'.

Here is what you need to remember:
- The disposition is of a **subsisting equitable interest**.
- Applicable to trusts of personalty or realty.
- Before the disposition, the legal and equitable ownership have already been separated.
- Required to be in writing.
- Void if not complied with (outcome: equitable interest remains with the person trying to dispose of it).
- Allows for a signature by an agent if given written authorisation.

> **Key term: subsisting equitable interest**
>
> An equitable interest that has *already* been separated from the legal title.
>
> Note that s 53(1)(c) does not apply to the creation of a trust. On the creation of a trust, the legal and equitable title of the trust property splits, the legal title lies with the trustees and the equitable interest moves to the beneficiary. As you can see, there was no disposition of a *subsisting* equitable interest.

The equitable interest of trust property can be disposed of by the person entitled to it (the beneficiary) in favour of a third party in any one of four different ways:
- Assign to a third party directly
- Direct the trustees to hold the property for a third party
- Contract for valuable consideration to assign the equitable interest
- Declare oneself a trustee of such an interest.

We will now observe each of these methods and consider if each is considered a 'disposition' within s 53(1)(c):

Method 1: assigning to a third party

A beneficiary may wish to transfer their beneficial interest to a third party, but to do this successfully the transfer must comply with the formalities set out in s 53(1)(c). This is illustrated in **Figure 2.1** and **Practice example 2.3**.

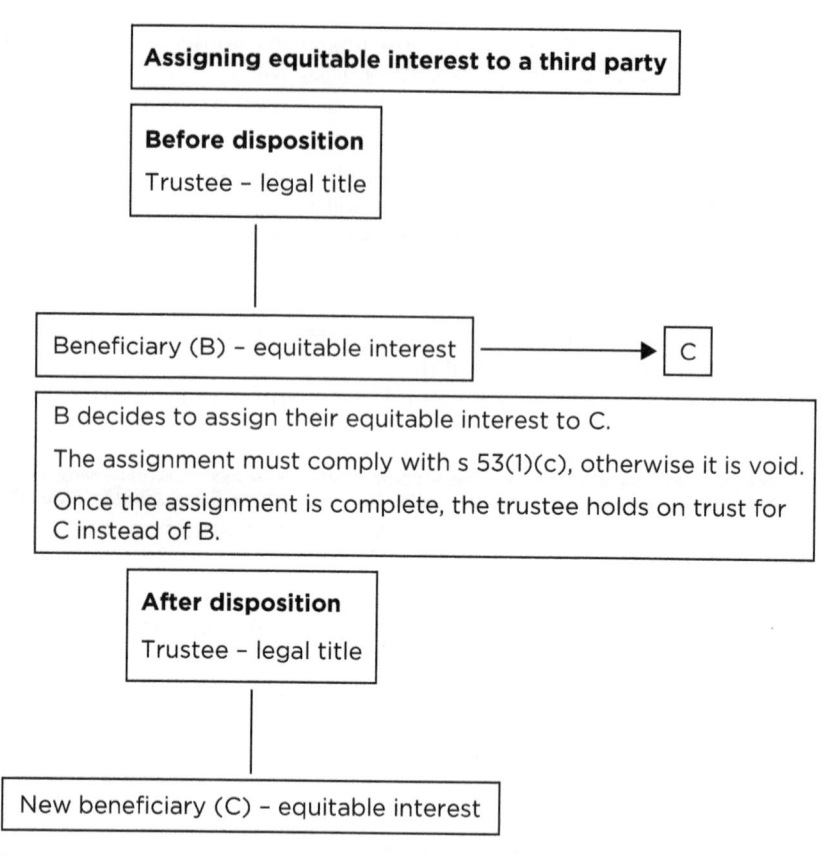

Assigning equitable interest to a third party

Before disposition
Trustee – legal title

↓

Beneficiary (B) – equitable interest → C

B decides to assign their equitable interest to C.

The assignment must comply with s 53(1)(c), otherwise it is void.

Once the assignment is complete, the trustee holds on trust for C instead of B.

After disposition
Trustee – legal title

↓

New beneficiary (C) – equitable interest

Figure 2.1: Assigning equitable interest to a third party

Practice example 2.3

Amal is a beneficiary of a trust created by her parents. Amal does not wish to benefit from the trust and would like to assign her interest to her daughter. What formalities must she comply with to ensure this?

The formalities of s 53(1)(c) must be met as the assignment of Amal's equitable interest to her daughter is a 'disposition' within that section. The transfer must be in writing and signed by Amal (the transferor).

Failure to comply with s 53(1)(c) renders the disposition void. This is to prevent fraudulent hidden oral transactions of equitable interests thereby making it extremely difficult for trustees to ascertain the true beneficiaries.

Method 2: directing the trustees to hold the property for a third party

Here, we are looking at cases where the beneficiary of a **bare trust** directed the trustees to hold the trust property for another. Most of the cases have turned on the meaning of the word 'disposition', and involved an attempt to avoid tax, usually stamp duty. Stamp duty can only be levied on a written instrument transferring stocks and shares. It does not extend to paperless transactions, hence the various attempts to transfer shares orally in the cases below. Please note that there is no need to remember the names of the cases for the purpose of the SQE, focus instead on the different outcomes and make sure you understand the reasons.

> **Key term: bare trust**
>
> In a bare trust, although the assets are held in the name of the trustee, the adult beneficiary has an absolute right to the assets, including the income generated from the assets. The trustee has no say in the distribution of the assets. The beneficiary can instruct the trustees on what to do with the trust assets.

Where the beneficiary directs the trustees to transfer trust property to another

An example can be found in the case of *Vandervell v IRC* [1967] AC 291. Here, Vandervell wished to donate £150,000 to the Royal College of Surgeons (RCS). He directed the trustees who were holding shares on bare trust for him to transfer the shares to the RCS. He also directed the RCS to grant the trustees an option to repurchase the shares for £5,000. Once the shares had been transferred to the RCS, Vandervell declared and paid dividends of £145,000 to the RCS. The RCS then sold the shares back to the trustees for £5,000.

Issue: did the transfer of the shares to the RCS amount to a disposition under s 53(1)(c)?

Held: not a disposition under s 53(1)(c) as the transfer to the RCS moved both the legal and equitable interests that merged when they reached the RCS making them the absolute owner.

32 Formalities for the creation of trusts

Candidates generally find the facts of Vandervell to be complicated so have a look at the simplified diagram in **Figure 2.2**.

Vandervell v IRC

- V wanted to donate money to the RCS. Trustees held shares on bare trust for V.
- V directed trustees to transfer the shares to the RCS.

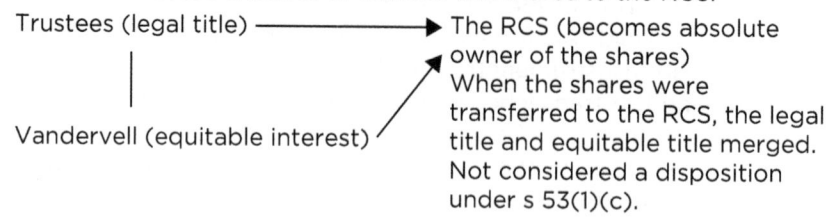

Trustees (legal title) ⟶ The RCS (becomes absolute owner of the shares)

Vandervell (equitable interest)

When the shares were transferred to the RCS, the legal title and equitable title merged. Not considered a disposition under s 53(1)(c).

Figure 2.2: Vandervell v IRC

Where the beneficiary directs the trustees to hold the equitable interest on trust for another

An example can be found in the case of *Grey v IRC* [1960] AC 1. Here, Hunter wished to transfer shares to his six grandchildren, aiming for them to benefit under separate trusts. He created six trusts of nominal value. Then, to avoid stamp duty liability, he created a separate bare trust into which he transferred over 18,000 shares. Hunter declared himself as sole beneficiary, as by retaining the beneficial interest he would not have to pay stamp duty. Hunter subsequently orally directed his trustees to hold the shares on the terms of the six trusts held for his grandchildren. After the oral direction, he and his trustees executed a deed confirming the transfer.

Issue: whether the equitable interest of the shares passed on the oral direction or when the confirmatory deed was executed.

Held: It was clear that when Hunter directed the trustees to hold the shares not for his benefit but for the benefit of the grandchildren there was an attempt to dispose of a *subsisting equitable interest*. Under s 53(1)(c), the oral transfer was void and the confirmatory deed effectively transferred the equitable interest and duty could be levied upon it.

The facts of *Grey* can be complicated so here is a simplified diagram in **Figure 2.3**.

Grey v IRC

Settlor set up six trusts for the benefit of grandchildren (minimal value): Trusts 1–6.

Settlor transferred shares to trustees to hold on trust for himself on a bare trust.

Settlor orally instructed trustees to hold the same shares for the trusts benefitting the grandchildren.

This was considered a 'disposition' of a subsisting equitable interest and must comply with s 53(1)(c).

```
Trustees (legal title)                              Trustees
     |                                                 |
     | (Bare trust)                                    | (Trusts 1-6)
     |                                                 |
Settlor (equitable interest) ─────────────────────▶ Grandchildren
                        Movement of equitable interest
                        from settlor to grandchildren
```

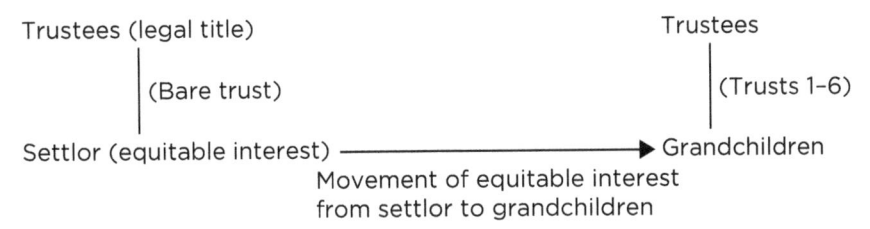

Figure 2.3: Grey v IRC

Exam warning

In deciding whether a disposition must meet the formalities, remember to check whether the equitable interest is moving with the legal title resulting in the two merging (*Vandervell*) or whether the equitable title remains separate from the legal title (*Grey*). The former is not considered a disposition within s 53(1)(c) but the latter is.

Practice example 2.4

A beneficiary under a bare trust directed her trustees to transfer the trust assets to her brother to help him start a business. Must the transfer comply with s 53(1(c)?

The transfer of the trust assets to the brother is not considered a disposition under s 53(1)(c). On the transfer, the equitable interest does not stay separate, instead it merges with the legal title. The brother becomes the absolute owner.

Method 3: entering into a contract for valuable consideration to assign the equitable interest

Here, we are looking at the scenario where a beneficiary entered into a contract with another to assign their equitable interest to the other party in exchange for consideration. Is this agreement a 'disposition' which must comply with s 53(1)(c)?

To answer the question, we consider the case of *Oughtred v IRC* [1960] AC 206.

Mrs Oughtred owned 72,700 shares in a company. Another 200,000 shares were held on trust for Mrs Oughtred for life, remainder to her son Peter (Mrs O had the **life interest** and Peter had the **remainder interest**). Under this arrangement, on Mrs Oughtred's death, the 200,000 shares would pass to Peter absolutely but would be subject to a hefty **death duty**. In order to save on death duty, Peter orally agreed with his mother that he should exchange his remainder interest in the 200,000 shares as consideration for her 72,700 shares. This resulted in the mother being the sole beneficiary of the 200,000 shares and Peter owning the 72,700 shares absolutely. To achieve this, a deed of release was executed.

Issue: whether the oral contract effectively transferred Peter's remainder interest to his mother and the deed of release was merely confirmation of the contract, or whether the 'disposition' of Peter's interest was only effective on execution of the deed. If the deed was merely confirmatory, no stamp duty is payable.

Held: there was a disposition of the son's equitable interest in the shares to the mother which must comply with s 53(1)(c). Accordingly, stamp duty was levied on the deed of release. So, as you can see, while the parties may have saved on death duty, they could not escape having to pay stamp duty.

> **Key term: life interest**
>
> A beneficial interest that only lasts during the lifetime of the beneficiary. The beneficiary is not entitled to the property, only to the income generated by the property, if any; or if the property is land, to enjoy the property during their lifetime.

> **Key term: remainder interest**
>
> A beneficial interest that follows a life interest. The beneficiary with the remainder interest is only entitled to take ownership once the life interest has ended.

> **Key term: death duty**
> A tax payable on the assets of someone who has died. It is now called inheritance tax.

In summary, even entering into a valid oral contract with consideration will not exempt the requirement of s 53(1)(c). The most important question you need to ask is whether the equitable interest moved from one person to another. If the answer is yes, the disposition is void unless the formalities have been met. For the SQE assessment, there is no need to remember the case name, just the principle.

Method 4: declaring oneself a trustee of one's equitable interest

Here we are looking at the scenario where a beneficiary decides to declare a trust of their equitable interest for the benefit of a third party, in effect, creating a sub-trust. A genuine sub-trust is not considered a disposition as the beneficiary retains their beneficial interest and effectively creates a new sub-interest. However, if the sub-trust was not a genuine trust, it must comply with s 53(1)(c). Have a look at **Figure 2.4**.

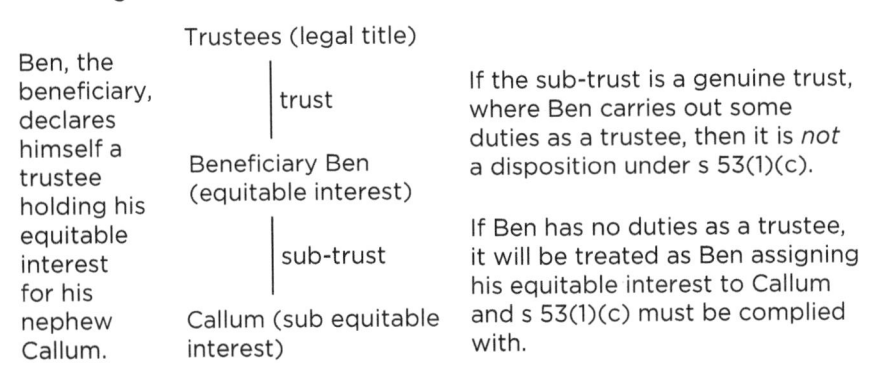

Declaring oneself a trustee holding the equitable interest for another:

| Ben, the beneficiary, declares himself a trustee holding his equitable interest for his nephew Callum. | Trustees (legal title)
trust
Beneficiary Ben (equitable interest)
sub-trust
Callum (sub equitable interest) | If the sub-trust is a genuine trust, where Ben carries out some duties as a trustee, then it is *not* a disposition under s 53(1)(c).

If Ben has no duties as a trustee, it will be treated as Ben assigning his equitable interest to Callum and s 53(1)(c) must be complied with. |

Figure 2.4: Declaring oneself a trustee holding the equitable interest for another

Practice example 2.5 provides clarification.

> **Practice example 2.5**
> Dele, an adult beneficiary of a substantial trust, orally declared a trust of his equitable interest for the benefit of his infant child. Dele

set up several investment accounts for his child and all payments received from the trustees were placed into these accounts. Dele plays an active role in deciding which account to invest in. Has Dele disposed of his equitable interest to his child?

This appears to be a genuine sub-trust as Dele plays an active role as a trustee. Dele retains his equitable interest and he holds it on trust for his child, who has a sub-interest. Compliance with s 53(1)(c) is not required.

Exam warning

Whether a sub-trust is genuine or not is a question of fact for the court to determine. If the sub-trust is a sham, the beneficiary is considered to have assigned their interest to the third party as explained in **Method 1** above (see **Figure 2.1**). In the SQE assessment, check if the beneficiary has an active role as trustee of the sub-trust.

Below are other ways to effectively dispose of an equitable interest without the need to comply with s 53(1)(c).

Other means of 'disposing' of an equitable interest (no need for s 53(1)(c))

Where an equitable interest is disclaimed

A beneficiary disclaiming their beneficial interest is not considered a disposition – see **Practice example 2.6**.

Practice example 2.6

Your client is a beneficiary of a trust created by their parents. Your client does not wish to benefit from the trust and wants to disclaim their interest. Must they comply with the formality requirements of s 53(1)(c)?

A disclaimer is not considered a disposition of an equitable interest and there is no need to comply with s 53(1)(c). The client may disclaim orally.

Nominations under a pension fund

An employee with a pension must nominate people to receive their benefits on their death. Such nominations are not regarded as 'dispositions' under s 53(1)(c). The same reasoning would apply to nominations under an insurance policy.

Finally, you should be aware of the exception in s 53(2) LPA 1925 which states that s 53(1)(b) and s 53(1)(c) do not apply to implied, resulting and constructive trusts. There is no need to consider these trusts here. They will be explained in detail in **Chapter 7** and **Chapter 9**.

■ KEY POINT CHECKLIST

This chapter has covered the following key knowledge points. You can use these to structure your revision around, making sure to recall the key details for each point, as covered in this chapter.

- In addition to the three certainties, the requirements of s 53(1)(b) must be met when creating a trust of realty.
- Non-compliance with s 53(1)(b) makes the trust unenforceable.
- Trusts of personalty have no additional formality requirements apart from the three certainties.
- Once a trust has been created, a beneficiary who wished to transfer their interest to another must do so in compliance of s 53(1)(c).
- There is a disposition of an equitable interest which must comply with s 53(1)(c) if the subsisting equitable interest is being moved independently of the legal title.
- Non-compliance with s 53(1)(c) renders the disposition void and the equitable interest remains with the person who attempted the transfer.

■ KEY TERMS AND CONCEPTS

- inter vivos (**page 26**)
- personalty (**page 26**)
- realty (**page 26**)
- resulting trust (**page 27**)
- subsisting equitable interest (**page 29**)
- bare trust (**page 31**)
- life interest (**page 34**)
- remainder interest (**page 34**)
- death duty (**page 35**)

38 Formalities for the creation of trusts

■ SQE1-STYLE QUESTIONS

QUESTION 1

A woman was granted shares in a private company in her divorce settlement and decided to hold the shares on trust for her only son. The woman announced her intention at a family gathering and later left a voicemail to the son confirming her decision.

Which of the following statements best summarises the outcome of the woman's actions?

A. There is no valid declaration of trust as the woman did not execute a trust deed.

B. There is no valid declaration of trust as the woman did not complete the share transfer forms.

C. There is no valid declaration of trust as there was nothing in writing confirming the woman's statement.

D. There is no valid declaration of trust as the woman did not appoint a trustee.

E. There is a valid declaration of trust.

QUESTION 2

A father is the beneficiary of a trust and wishes to transfer the benefits under the trust to his infant daughter. He informed the trustees orally of his intention to create a trust of his equitable interest for his daughter, after which he ensures that all payments received from the trustees are paid into investment accounts he set up for his daughter. He reviews the investments regularly and makes changes where necessary.

Which of the following statements best summarises the outcome of the father's actions?

A. There is a valid trust as the father is an active trustee.

B. There is no valid trust as the father should have executed a trust deed.

C. There is no valid trust as the father should have assigned his equitable interest to the daughter in writing.

D. There is no valid trust as the father should have appointed a trustee.

E. There is no valid trust as a beneficiary cannot also be a trustee.

QUESTION 3

A will trust contains the following provision: 'All my investments to be held on trust for my son until he turns 25; he is to be paid the income before then'. The testator has just died and the son, who is aged 19, met with the trustees and informed them that he does not wish to take any benefit from his father's estate. According to the will, the testator's daughter is the residuary legatee.

Which of the following statements best describes the effect of the son's actions?

A. The trustees continue to hold the property on trust for the son.
B. The trustees must pay any income to the son.
C. The investments belong to the daughter.
D. The son's actions have no legal effect, he should have disclaimed in writing.
E. The son's actions have no legal effect, he should have disclaimed by deed.

QUESTION 4

At a family dinner celebrating her son's 18th birthday, the mother announced that, as a birthday present for the son, she intends to hold her apartment in London on trust for him. She then wrote the same on a birthday card which she signed. A month later, the mother and son had an argument and are no longer on speaking terms. The son seeks advice on his rights to the apartment.

Which of the following statements best describes the outcome of the mother's actions?

A. There is no valid declaration of trust as the mother should have executed a trust deed.
B. There is no valid declaration of trust as the mother did not appoint trustees.
C. There is no valid declaration of trust as she should have conveyed the apartment to him by deed.
D. There is a valid enforceable declaration of trust.
E. There is a valid declaration of trust provided the son can show that he is not a volunteer.

QUESTION 5

Under a settlement, trustees are holding trust assets worth £50,000 on a bare trust for a man. The man wished to transfer his benefit to his grandchildren without incurring stamp duty. He set up a trust benefitting his grandchildren with the same trustees and orally directed the trustees to hold the investments for the benefit of the second trust.

Which of the following statements best summarises the outcome of the man's actions?

A. The oral direction is effective to transfer the interest to the grandchildren regardless of whether the trust assets are personalty or realty.

B. The oral direction is effective to transfer the interest to the grandchildren provided the trust assets are pure personalty.

C. The oral direction is effective to transfer the interest to the grandchildren as both trusts have the same trustees.

D. The oral direction is not effective because the grandchildren are volunteers.

E. The oral direction is not effective as it should have been done in writing.

■ ANSWERS TO QUESTIONS

Answers to 'What do you know already?' questions at the start of the chapter

1) According to s 53(1)(b) LPA 1925, the creation of a trust of land must be evidenced in writing and signed by the settlor.

2) There are no formalities required when creating a trust of personalty, apart from the requirement of the three certainties.

3) True. The settlor can orally declare a trust of realty so long as they follow up later with written evidence complying with s 53(1)(b) LPA 1925.

4) False. The date of creation is the earlier date of declaration.

5) The beneficiary was attempting to transfer her equitable interest to her best friend. There was no valid transfer as the requirements of s 53(1)(c) LPA 1925 have not been met. The trustees continue to hold on trust for the beneficiary.

Answers to end-of-chapter SQE1-style questions

Question 1:
The correct answer was E. There are no formality requirements for the creation of trusts of personalty so long as the three certainties are met. This means that there is no requirement to execute a trust deed (so Option A is wrong) and there is no requirement for the trust to be evidenced in writing (so Option C is wrong). Option B is incorrect because the issue is whether the woman has validly *declared* the trust; the requirement for a share transfer form is a constitution requirement, which is a separate matter. Option D is incorrect because the woman made a self-declaration of trust.

Question 2:
The correct answer was A. The father has created a valid sub-trust with his daughter as the beneficiary where he is an active trustee. As the father has not dropped out of the picture entirely, there is no need to comply with the formality requirements that the disposition must be in writing and signed (so Option C is wrong). The father has made a self-declaration of trust (so Option D is wrong) and there is no requirement for a trust deed (therefore Option B is wrong). Option E is incorrect because a beneficiary can be a trustee.

Question 3:
The correct answer was C. The son's oral disclaimer is valid because a disclaimer is not a disposition requiring written evidence or deed (so Options D and E are wrong). The legal effect of the disclaimer is that the investments will fall into the residue and pass to the daughter (therefore Options A and B are wrong).

Question 4:
The correct answer was D. The oral declaration of trust over land was followed by evidence of trust by signed writing in the card and therefore this is a valid declaration of trust. There is no requirement for a trust deed to comply with the statutory formalities (so Option A is wrong). Option B is wrong because the mother made a self-declaration of trust. Option C is incorrect because the need for a deed of conveyance is a constitution requirement, separate to the formality requirements. Option E is wrong because it is irrelevant whether the son is a volunteer or not.

Question 5:
The correct answer was E. There is movement of a subsisting equitable interest from the bare trust to the trust benefitting the grandchildren. This requires compliance with the statutory formalities

that the declaration of trust must be in writing and signed. Options A–D are wrong because they ignore the fact that the disposition was not made in writing.

■ KEY CASES, RULES, STATUTES AND INSTRUMENTS

Please note that there is no need to memorise the statutory provisions or cases. Focus instead on the necessary formality requirements and the different examples from the cases and consider when the formality requirements are applicable.

3

Constitution of trusts

■ MAKE SURE YOU KNOW

This chapter will cover the final requirement of an express private trust, which is the constitution of the trust. This is done by ensuring that the trustees have the legal title to the trust property.

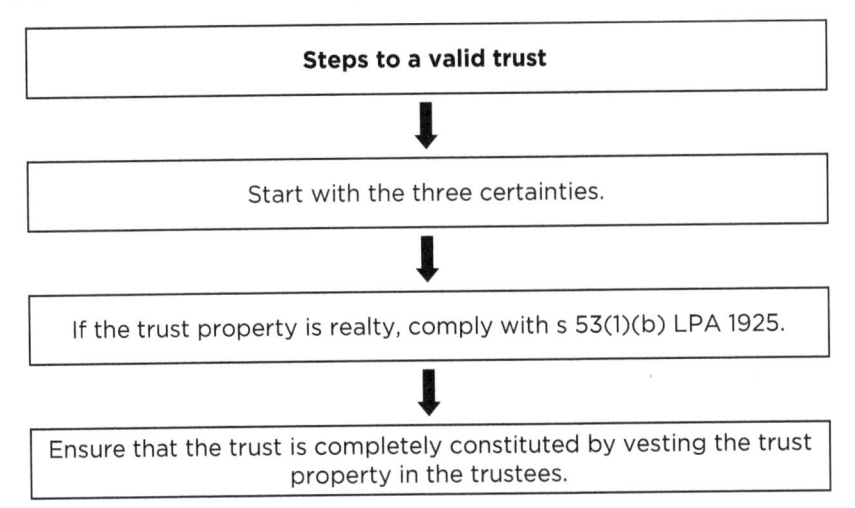

Steps to a valid trust

⬇

Start with the three certainties.

⬇

If the trust property is realty, comply with s 53(1)(b) LPA 1925.

⬇

Ensure that the trust is completely constituted by vesting the trust property in the trustees.

■ SQE ASSESSMENT ADVICE

The topic of constitution of trusts requires understanding of the steps that a settlor must take to ensure that the trust is valid and enforceable. You will likely encounter scenarios in the SQE assessment requiring an understanding of the impact of an incompletely constituted trust. Familiarising yourself with the different formalities for transferring the various types of property will greatly help with your understanding.

As you work through this chapter, remember to pay particular attention in your revision to:
- How to identify an incompletely constituted trust.

- Whether the beneficiaries of an incompletely constituted trust have any rights.
- Who is the trustee? In creating a trust, a settlor can choose to act as the trustee or to appoint others as trustee. In the former, the trust is completely constituted; but in the latter, to constitute the trust, the settlor must first transfer the property to the trustees.
- The different methods of transferring different types of property.

■ WHAT DO YOU KNOW ALREADY?

Have a go at these questions before reading this chapter. If you find some difficult or cannot remember the answers, make a note to look more closely at that during your revision.

1) Who is a volunteer and why is it important in the context of an incompletely constituted trust?
   [Introduction to constitution of trusts, page 45]

2) True or false: Once a settlor has declared a trust of personalty complying with the three certainties, the beneficiaries become absolutely entitled to the trust property and the settlor is bound by the terms of the trust.
   [Introduction to constitution of trusts, page 45]

3) In which of the following has the trust been completely constituted?
   a) A settlor declared herself a trustee holding her shares in British Gas plc on trust for her son.
   b) A settlor executed a trust instrument appointing trustees T1 & T2, instructing them to hold the settlor's shares in British Gas plc on trust for the son.
   [Introduction to constitution of trusts, page 45]

4) Which of the following scenarios results in the creation of a valid trust and why?
   Scenario 1: Lee was in the pub when he heard the good news that he has become a first-time grandfather. He turned to his drinking buddy Don and said, 'I have 300 shares in BT, I would like you to hold them on trust for my granddaughter'.
   Scenario 2: Lee was in the pub when he heard the good news that he has become a first-time grandfather. He turned to his drinking buddy Don and said, 'I have 300 shares in BT, I would like to hold them on trust for my granddaughter'.
   [Introduction to constitution of trusts, page 45]

5) True or false: In a covenant to settle, the beneficiaries can only enforce the covenant if they have provided consideration.
   [Introduction to constitution of trusts, page 45]

INTRODUCTION TO CONSTITUTION OF TRUSTS

In previous chapters we established that a valid trust must meet certain requirements. The constitution of trust is the final requirement. After declaring a trust that complies with the three certainties and all the necessary formalities, the settlor must **vest** the property in the trustees. Once vested, the trust is 'completely constituted' and binding on the settlor.

> **Key term: vest**
> To vest the property in the trustees is to transfer the legal title of the property to the trustees using the proper formalities.

A trust is described as being incompletely constituted if the trust property is not vested in the trustees. Beneficiaries who have not provided consideration for the trust are **volunteers**. Volunteer beneficiaries cannot enforce an incompletely constituted trust. The relevant equitable maxims are:
- Equity will not perfect an imperfect gift
  An imperfect gift could mean an invalid attempt to make a gift to another or an incompletely constituted trust. In both instances, the court will not assist the recipient of the imperfect gift or the beneficiary of the incompletely constituted trust to obtain the property.
- Equity will not assist a volunteer
  A volunteer who was the recipient of an incomplete gift or the beneficiary of an incompletely constituted trust will not receive assistance from the court to obtain the property.

> **Key term: volunteer**
> A person who has not provided consideration (money or money's worth).

However, beneficiaries who have given consideration can rely on the maxim 'equity deems as done that which ought to be done'. This means that the recipient of an imperfect gift or the beneficiary of an incompletely constituted trust who has provided consideration can enforce the obligation, generally through the grant of an order of specific performance for the property.

Constitution of trusts

> **Revision tip**
>
> Do not forget that a valid trust (one that meets the three certainties, all necessary formalities and is properly constituted) is binding on the settlor. The beneficiaries are entitled to the trust property without having to prove that they have given consideration.

You can test your understanding of constitution of trusts by reading **Practice example 3.1**.

> **Practice example 3.1**
>
> Anna just bought 2,000 shares in Nowflix Inc. She would like the shares to benefit her infant grandson Matthew. She executed a trust deed specifying the shares as the trust property, naming Matthew as the sole beneficiary and appointing her best friends Beth and Callie as trustees.
>
> Is there anything else Anna needs to do?
>
> **To ensure that the trust is completely constituted, Anna must vest the shares in the trustees Beth and Callie. To transfer legal title to shares, Anna must complete the stock transfer form and send the completed form to the company so that the registrar can change the names of the legal owners.**
>
> As the shares have not been vested in the trustees, the trust is incompletely constituted (imperfect) and Matthew has no rights. He is a volunteer and the gift cannot be perfected.

The choice of trustees

When creating a trust, a settlor can do one of two things: they can choose to be the trustee or they can name another as trustee.

The settlor as trustee

Assuming the three certainties are present and all requisite formalities have been met, the trust is completely constituted. The settlor already holds the legal title to the trust property and on creation of the trust, the equitable interest separates from the legal title and moves to the beneficiary. See **Example 1** in **Figure 3.1**.

Someone else as trustee

Assuming the three certainties are present and all requisite formalities have been met, the trust is not yet completely constituted. The settlor

Introduction to constitution of trusts   47

must transfer the legal title to the trustees in whatever is the appropriate manner for that type of property. Once this has been done, the trust is completely constituted and the trustee holds the legal title of the property on trust for the beneficiary who has the equitable interest. See Example 2 in **Figure 3.1**.

Example 1:
Settlor declares a trust with herself as trustee.
The trust is completely constituted as the settlor already has the legal title to the property. On declaration of the trust, the equitable title splits from the legal title and moves to the beneficiary.

→ Settlor holds as trustee (legal title)
  |
  Beneficiary (equitable interest)

Example 2:
Settlor declares a trust where T is the trustee. The trust is incompletely constituted until legal title to the trust property is transferred to the trustee, T.

→ Settlor transfers legal title to T) → T is the trustee (legal title)
  |
  Beneficiary (equitable interest)

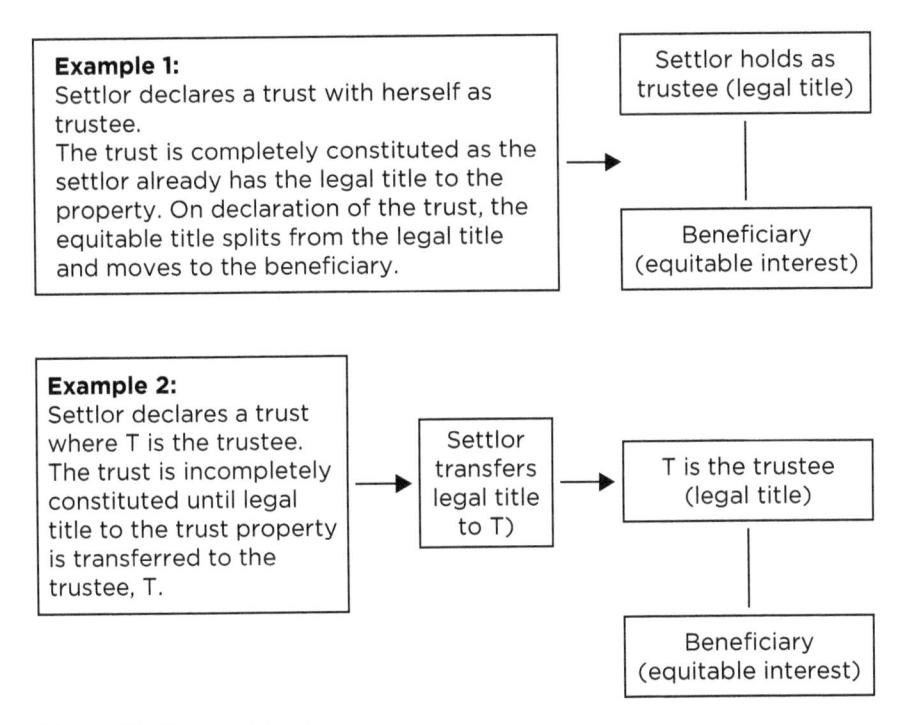

Figure 3.1: Choice of trustees

To summarise, if your aim is to benefit another through a gift or trust, you must do everything necessary to ensure that the property has been properly vested in the right person.

Exam warning

If you are told in an SQE question that a settlor has executed a trust deed specifying the trust assets, the trustees and the beneficiaries, do not assume that the trust is constituted. The presence of a trust deed does not automatically lead to a valid and enforceable trust.

So far, we have looked at how a settlor can benefit another by creating a trust and we now know what the settlor needs to do to ensure that the trust is valid. Another way to benefit someone is to make an outright gift of the property to them. Let's consider and compare the three methods whereby a **donor** can benefit a **donee** as explained in **Table 3.1**.

Table 3.1: Ways to benefit another

Method 1	The owner of property transfers the property to the donee.	This is a straightforward transfer where the legal and equitable title move together to the donee.	This is a gift.
Method 2	The owner of property creates a trust where they hold the property as trustee for the beneficiary.	The owner is both the settlor and the trustee holding the legal title; the separated equitable interest passes to the beneficiary.	This is a trust.
Method 3	The owner of property creates a trust with trustees holding the property for the beneficiary.	The owner is the settlor and they must transfer the legal title to the trustees; the equitable interest passes to the beneficiary.	This is a trust.

> **Key term: donor**
> The donor is the person giving the gift. In a trust, the donor is the settlor.

> **Key term: donee**
> The donee is the recipient of the gift. In a trust, the donee is the beneficiary.

If it is clear that the donor intended to use a particular method but the transfer was imperfect, equity will not perfect the gift by assuming that a different method was intended.

A good example can be found in the case of *Jones v Lock* [1865] LR 1 Ch App 25, where the court refused to construe a void gift as a declaration of trust. A father had placed a cheque payable to him in the hands of his infant son with the words, 'I give this to baby for himself'. He later took the cheque and declared, 'I am going to put it away for him'. It was argued unsuccessfully that the latter statement demonstrated an intention to create a trust with himself holding the cheque for his son. The son was a volunteer and the gift was imperfect. Do you remember the relevant maxims? You can remind yourself by looking back at the opening to this chapter.

Practice example 3.2 provides further illustration.

Practice example 3.2

George decided to reward his son Xander, who has just graduated from university with a degree in law, by transferring his apartment in London to him. George took the land certificate and title deeds from his safe and posted them together with a letter to Xander saying, 'Dear Xander, I am very proud of you. I am giving you my London apartment. Love, Dad'.

A month later, George and Xander fell out when George found out that Xander intended to pursue a career in acting. George demanded that Xander return the title documents and told Xander that he is no longer welcome to stay in the apartment and must move out.

Advise the parties:
a) Was there a valid gift of the apartment to Xander?
b) Did George create a valid trust whereby he is a trustee holding the apartment on trust for Xander?

Part (a)
George should have conveyed the apartment to his son by deed. In the absence of a deed, the gift is imperfect. Xander is not entitled to the apartment.

Part (b)
From the facts, it is clear that George's intention was to make a gift of the apartment to Xander but the gift was imperfect. The court will not help Xander by construing George's actions as an attempt to create a trust (which would have been a valid trust with George holding the land as trustee for Xander as beneficiary). Xander is a volunteer and the court will not assist in perfecting the gift.

50 Constitution of trusts

Clearly, where a settlor chooses to appoint another as trustee, they must constitute the trust by vesting the trust property in the trustee. The following table explains the relevant formalities for transferring different types of property.

Formalities for transferring the different types of property

There are a number of formalities for transferring different types of property. These are summarised in **Table 3.2**.

Table 3.2: Formalities for property transfer

Land (freehold/leasehold)	s 52(1) Law of Property Act 1925: all conveyances of land or an interest in land must be made by deed.
	The deed must be written, make it clear on its face that it is intended to be a deed, signed by the parties to the deed and their signatures witnessed: s 1 Law of Property (Miscellaneous Provisions) Act 1989.
Shares	The owner of the shares must complete a stock transfer form which is sent to the company so that the registrar of the company can cancel the original share certificates and issue new ones reflecting the change in ownership: Stock Transfer Act 1963.
Chattels	**Chattels** can be transferred by actual physical delivery of the chattel to the donee or by deed. The act of delivery must be unequivocal, demonstrating a transfer of possession to the donee.
	The deed must follow the form prescribed in s 1 LP(MP)A 1989.
Equitable interests	s 53(1)(c) LPA 1925 (see **Chapter 2**).
Choses in Action	A **chose in action** can be assigned to another by giving written notice of the assignment to the debtor: s 136 LPA 1925.
Cheques	Provided the cheque is not an 'account payee only' cheque, it can be transferred to another by endorsing the cheque. This requires the endorser to sign the back of the cheque: s 32 Bills of Exchange Act 1882.

Key term: chattel

Tangible moveable personal property such as furniture, jewellery, etc.

Key term: chose in action

A chose in action is a right which can only be enforced by taking action. Example: a debt.

Practice example 3.3 shows what happens if the correct formalities have not been followed.

Practice example 3.3

The owner of leasehold premises attempted to gift the lease to the donee (E) by endorsing on the lease 'This deed and all thereto belonging I give to E from this time forth ...' The document was delivered to E's mother on his behalf. The mother is seeking your advice on the validity of this transaction.

These are the facts of *Richards v Delbridge* [1874] LR 18 Eq 11, where the Court of Appeal held that there was a clear intention to make an outright gift of the lease to E but the gift was incomplete. As there was no express declaration of trust, the gift cannot be saved by holding the intended transfer to operate as a declaration of trust, 'for then every imperfect instrument would be made effectual by being converted into a perfect trust'.

Remember the formalities to transfer land as required by s 52(1) LPA 1925; merely endorsing the leasehold document is insufficient.

In case you were confused about the formalities applicable to transferring a chose in action, **Practice example 3.4** should help.

Practice example 3.4

Kelly owes Harold £3,000. Harold found out that his brother Ken has just lost his job and would like to help him out. Harold would like Kelly to pay the money she owed him to Ken instead.

What should Harold do to ensure this?

A debt is a chose in action and is assignable to another. In order to assign (transfer) the chose in action, Harold must give notice in writing to Kelly to pay the money to Ken.

In conclusion, remember that the volunteer donee of an imperfect gift and the volunteer beneficiary of an incompletely constituted trust cannot enforce the gift/trust.

Next, we need to consider covenants to settle as a type of incompletely constituted trust.

Covenants to settle

As you know, a settlor can create a trust by executing a trust deed, appointing the trustees and naming the beneficiaries. In the same trust deed, the settlor may have covenanted with the trustees that they will transfer property to the trustees at a later date. If the settlor has entered into a **covenant** to transfer property to the trustees, but not performed the covenant, the issue is whether either the beneficiaries of the intended **settlement**, or the trustees, can enforce the covenant.

Exam warning

Remember that in a covenant to settle, the settlor has merely covenanted (promised by deed) that they would settle (transfer) the property onto the trustees. This means that until the settlor effects the transfer, the trust is incompletely constituted.

Key term: covenant

A promise made by deed. (The person who makes the promise is the covenantor and the person to whom the promise is made is the covenantee.)

Key term: settlement

The term can be used interchangeably with 'trust'. To settle property is to place the property on trust. A covenant to settle is a promise to place property on trust.

As you are now aware, a covenant to settle is an incompletely constituted trust and the usual maxims apply so that a volunteer beneficiary cannot enforce the trust. However, there is a type of consideration called a **marriage consideration** and the beneficiaries who fall within it are not considered volunteers and can enforce the covenant.

Key term: marriage consideration

A type of consideration recognised in equity.

Introduction to constitution of trusts 53

Beneficiaries who have given marriage consideration

Such beneficiaries may enforce the covenant and in the case of a **marriage settlement** the parties to the marriage and the children of the marriage are all within the marriage consideration.

> **Key term: marriage settlement**
>
> A trust established on the occasion of a marriage. Generally, the beneficiaries of the settlement are the parties to the marriage and their issue (children). These beneficiaries are considered to have given marriage consideration.

The case of *Pullan v Koe* [1913] 1 Ch 9 provides a useful illustration of how this issue could arise in an SQE question. The wife (who was a party to the marriage settlement) covenanted to settle **after-acquired property** on the settlement. The wife later received some money which was invested in bearer bonds. The trustees of the marriage settlement sought an order of specific performance to obtain the bonds for the settlement.

The court held that as the beneficiaries of the marriage settlement had all given marriage consideration, they were not volunteers and were able to enforce the covenant. The bonds belong to the settlement.

> **Key term: after-acquired property**
>
> Property which the covenantor does not yet own at the date of the covenant but is due to acquire or inherit at some later date.

> **Exam warning**
>
> Remember that only the parties to the marriage and their issue are deemed to have provided marriage consideration. If the covenant to settle includes other beneficiaries, these persons remain volunteers as they cannot be said to have provided marriage consideration.

Practice example 3.5 explains the position of persons falling outside the marriage consideration.

> **Practice example 3.5**
>
> A wife covenanted to transfer after-acquired property to her marriage settlement. She subsequently acquired some property which she never transferred to the settlement. The wife's next of kin (not the children of the marriage but the nephews and nieces) sought to enforce the covenant. What is your best advice for the nephews and nieces regarding their right to enforce the covenant?

> These are the facts of *Re Plumptre's Marriage Settlement* [1910] 1 Ch 609, where the court explained that as the trust was a marriage settlement, only the parties to the marriage and their children were considered to have provided consideration. The nephews and nieces fell outside the marriage consideration and were volunteers. They had no right to enforce the covenant.

Next, we will consider beneficiaries who have provided no consideration but have signed the deed containing the covenant and are therefore parties to the covenant. The parties to a trust settlement are usually the settlor and the trustees, but sometimes the beneficiary may have signed the deed and, by doing so, becomes a party to the covenant.

Beneficiaries who are parties to the covenant

Such beneficiaries may sue on the covenant at common law for damages. A covenant is treated like a contract and anyone privy to the contract can sue on it.

Exam warning

If it is clear from the SQE question that the beneficiary is a party to a covenant to settle, remember that this beneficiary is only entitled to sue on the covenant and claim damages. They are considered a volunteer in equity and cannot enforce the covenant using specific performance.

This is illustrated in **Practice example 3.6**.

Practice example 3.6

A father covenanted to settle after-acquired property on a trust benefitting his daughter. The daughter was a party to the covenant. The father later acquired the property but refused to settle it. What is the daughter's entitlement? Can she enforce the covenant?

These are the facts of *Cannon v Hartley* [1949] Ch 213, where the daughter was able to sue for breach of covenant and claim damages. She could not enforce the covenant as that would have required an order of specific performance, which is an equitable remedy. She was a volunteer and, as you know, equity would not assist her.

> **Exam warning**
> Remember that the remedy of damages *is the only common law remedy*. Other remedies such as specific performance and injunction are equitable remedies (see **Chapter 12**).

So far, we have considered the entitlement of beneficiaries in a covenant to settle. Next, we will explore whether the trustees can sue the settlor for breach of covenant on behalf of the beneficiaries.

Action by the trustees
Finally, we need to consider the volunteer beneficiaries who are not parties to the covenant. What is their recourse? Do you think the trustees can sue on their behalf? After all, the trustees are parties to the covenant.

It has been held that such beneficiaries may not compel the trustees to sue on the covenant and that the court will direct the trustees not to sue. To allow otherwise would mean that beneficiaries are able to indirectly obtain relief which they could not obtain directly.

Summary: Type of consideration	Recognised in equity? Remedy: specific performance	Recognised at law? Remedy: damages
Money or money's worth	Yes	Yes
Covenant in a deed	No	Yes
Marriage settlement	Yes	No

■ KEY POINT CHECKLIST
This chapter has covered the following key knowledge points. You can use these to structure your revision around, making sure to recall the key details for each point, as covered in this chapter.
- Where the settlor is also the trustee, the trust is completely constituted.
- When the settlor appoints others as trustees, the settlor must vest the trust property in those trustees to completely constitute the trust.

- An imperfect gift includes a failed attempt at a gift, an incompletely constituted trust or a covenant to settle where the promised property has not been transferred to the trustees.
- You must remember the different formalities required to transfer different types of property.
- Be aware of the different types of consideration and how this affects an imperfect gift.
- In a covenant to settle, consider the rights of the beneficiaries as well as the role of the trustees.

■ KEY TERMS AND CONCEPTS

- vest (**page 45**)
- volunteer (**page 45**)
- donor (**page 48**)
- donee (**page 48**)
- chattel (**page 51**)
- chose in action (**page 51**)
- covenant (**page 52**)
- settlement (**page 52**)
- marriage consideration (**page 52**)
- marriage settlement (**page 53**)
- after-acquired property (**page 53**)

■ SQE1-STYLE QUESTIONS

QUESTION 1

A man bought a house and furnished it lavishly with expensive furniture. He took his new wife to the house for the first time, telling her to close her eyes. He opened the front door and told her to open her eyes, assuring her that everything she sees belongs to her. The man later became bankrupt and the trustee in bankruptcy is claiming the furniture. The wife claims that the furniture was a gift to her.

Which of the following statements best describes the position with regard to the furniture?

A. There was a valid gift of the furniture to the wife.
B. The man holds the furniture on trust for his wife.
C. The trustee in bankruptcy can claim the furniture.

D. The wife can claim the furniture as she has provided marriage consideration.
E. The wife can sue for breach of covenant and claim damages equivalent to the value of the furniture.

QUESTION 2

According to the terms of a settlement signed by the settlor and his trustees, the trustees are to hold property on trust for the settlor's daughter until she turns 25. The settlement includes a covenant by the settlor to settle all the property he is due to inherit from his mother's estate. Two months ago, his mother's personal representatives conveyed her house to him in accordance with the terms of her will. The settlor died last week without having transferred the house to the trustees.

Which of the following statements provides the best advice to the daughter?

A. The daughter can claim the house by specific performance.
B. The daughter can claim damages equivalent to the value of the house.
C. The daughter can sue the trustees for damages equivalent to the value of the house.
D. The trustees can sue on the daughter's behalf and claim the house by specific performance.
E. The daughter has no cause of action.

QUESTION 3

A man declared a trust whereby his brother is to hold the man's house on trust for the brother's daughter. The man wrote, 'My brother is the trustee of my house and his daughter is the beneficiary' on a piece of paper which he signed. He gave the paper and the deeds of his house to his brother. The man died leaving his entire estate to charity.

Which of the following statements provides the best advice regarding the house?

A. The house will pass to the charity.
B. The brother holds the house on trust for his daughter.
C. The brother can claim the house for his daughter by specific performance.

D. The brother is entitled to damages to the value of the house for his daughter.
E. The daughter can claim the house by specific performance.

QUESTION 4

A woman met her friend for coffee. The friend admired the bracelet the woman was wearing. She took the bracelet off and fastened it on her friend's wrist, saying, 'It looks good on you, you should have it'. As they were leaving the coffee shop, the woman took the bracelet back, saying that her outfit is incomplete without it. She died a week later. According to her will, all her jewellery is to be given to her sister.

Which one of the following statements best describes the claim to the bracelet?

A. The friend can sue for the value of the bracelet.
B. The sister will inherit the bracelet.
C. The bracelet belongs to the friend.
D. The woman holds the bracelet on trust for her friend.
E. The sister holds the bracelet on trust for the friend.

QUESTION 5

A husband covenanted to settle after-acquired property from his father's estate to his marriage settlement. The beneficiaries of the settlement are the married couple, their children and the couple's two nieces. The husband later inherited some shares from his father but he and his wife died in a car accident before he could transfer the shares to the settlement. The husband and wife have no children.

Which one of the following statements best explains the nieces' claim to the shares?

A. The nieces can claim the shares by specific performance.
B. The nieces can sue for breach of covenant and claim damages to the value of the shares.
C. The nieces have no claim to the shares.
D. The nieces can compel the trustees to sue on their behalf.
E. The nieces can sue the trustees for damages to the value of the shares.

◼ ANSWERS TO QUESTIONS

Answers to 'What do you know already?' questions at the start of the chapter

1) A volunteer is a person who has not provided consideration. Once a trust is completely constituted, it is binding on the settlor and the beneficiary (whether a volunteer or not) can enforce the trust. If the trust is incompletely constituted, the volunteer beneficiary cannot enforce it as equity will not assist a volunteer to perfect an imperfect gift.
2) Whether the answer is true or false depends on who the trustee is. If the settlor is also the trustee, the trust is completely constituted as the property is already vested in the trustee. If the settlor named another as trustee, the trust is not constituted until the settlor has transferred the legal title of the trust property to the trustee.
3) The trust in part (a) is completely constituted as the legal title to the shares is already vested in the trustee, who is also the settlor. In part (b), the trust deed may meet the three certainties but the trust remains incompletely constituted until the legal title of the shares has been transferred to the trustees.
4) There is a valid trust in **Scenario 2** as Lee declared a trust with himself as trustee holding the shares for his granddaughter. The trust is completely constituted. On his declaration, the legal title remains with him but the equitable title passes to his granddaughter.

   In **Scenario 1**, the trustee is Don and in order to constitute the trust, Lee must take the further step of vesting the shares in Don.
5) True. A covenant to settle is a type of incompletely constituted trust and volunteer beneficiaries cannot enforce the trust.

Answers to end-of-chapter SQE1-style questions

Question 1:
  The correct answer was C. There has been no valid delivery (by deed) of the furniture to the wife (so not Option A). He did not declare a trust of the furniture with his wife as the beneficiary so Option B is wrong. There was no covenant to benefit the wife, so Options D and E are wrong.

Question 2:
  The correct answer was E. The daughter was a volunteer and not entitled to an order of specific performance (so Option A is wrong).

60 Constitution of trusts

She was not a party to the settlement and cannot sue for damages (so Options B and C are incorrect). The trustees will not be allowed to sue on her behalf (so Option D is wrong).

Question 3:

The correct answer was A. The trust was incompletely constituted as a deed of conveyance/transfer form is required to convey land. The daughter (beneficiary) is a volunteer and has no claim to the house. As the trust has not been constituted, and the daughter is a volunteer, Options B–E are wrong.

Question 4:

The correct answer was B. The facts suggested an attempted inter vivos gift of the bracelet to the friend, but the gift was imperfect as the woman did not part with possession of the bracelet (she took it back). Option A is wrong as the friend is a volunteer. Option C is wrong due to the imperfect delivery of the bracelet. Options D and E are wrong as there is no indication of an intention to create a trust on the part of the woman.

Question 5:

The correct answer was C. Only the parties to the marriage and their children have marriage consideration. The nieces are volunteers. They have no right to specific performance or damages (so Options A, B, D and E are incorrect).

■ KEY CASES, RULES, STATUTES AND INSTRUMENTS

The SQE1 Assessment Specification does not require you to remember the names of the cases cited in this chapter, but the principles that they lay down are important. You also do not need to memorise the statutory provisions cited in this chapter, just remember the relevant law.
Good to know: s 52(1) LPA 1925.

4

Exceptions to the maxim that equity will not assist a volunteer

■ MAKE SURE YOU KNOW

This chapter will explain the exceptions to the maxim 'equity will not assist a volunteer to perfect an imperfect gift', which you are required to understand in order to apply to the problem-based SQE assessments.

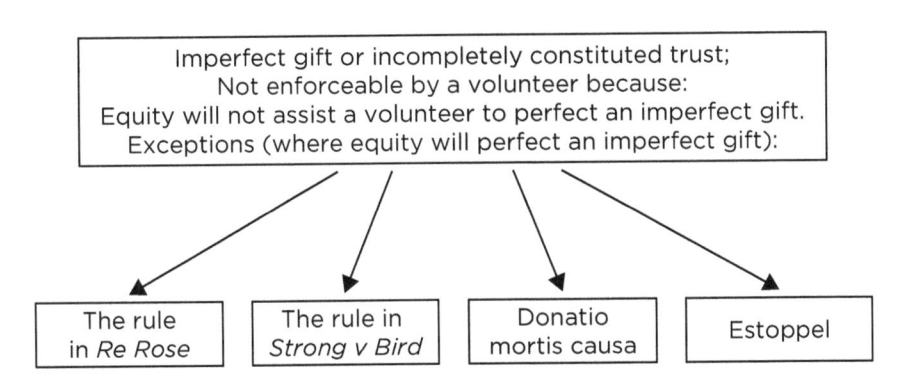

Imperfect gift or incompletely constituted trust;
Not enforceable by a volunteer because:
Equity will not assist a volunteer to perfect an imperfect gift.
Exceptions (where equity will perfect an imperfect gift):

- The rule in *Re Rose*
- The rule in *Strong v Bird*
- Donatio mortis causa
- Estoppel

62   Exceptions to the maxim that equity will not assist a volunteer

■ SQE ASSESSMENT ADVICE

As you work through this chapter, remember to pay particular attention in your revision to:
- The rule in *Re Rose*
- The rule in *Strong v Bird*
- The requirements of donatio mortis causa
- The requirements of estoppel.

■ WHAT DO YOU KNOW ALREADY?

Have a go at these questions before reading this chapter. If you find some difficult or cannot remember the answers, make a note to look more closely at that during your revision.

1) How does the rule in *Re Rose* assist a beneficiary of an incompletely constituted trust?

   [The rule in *Re Rose*, page 63]

2) True or false: the rule in *Strong v Bird* only applies to unpaid debts.

   [The rule in *Strong v Bird*, page 65]

3) True or false: donatio mortis causa is applicable whenever an old and frail donor makes an imperfect gift.

   [Donatio mortis causa, page 67]

4) True or false: the doctrine of proprietary estoppel can only be used as a defence.

   [Estoppel, page 71]

5) A woman executed a trust deed appointing her brother as trustee holding her 5,000 shares in British Gas for the benefit of her son. The woman completed the share transfer forms confirming a transfer of the shares to her brother. As she was in a hurry to get to work, she gave the envelope containing the completed forms and her old share certificates to her brother, telling him to post it for her. He agreed.
   On her way to work, the woman's car was in an accident and she was killed.
   Is there a valid trust of the shares for her son?

   [The rule in *Re Rose*, page 63]

INTRODUCTION TO THE EXCEPTIONS

Remember the maxim that 'equity will not assist a volunteer to perfect an imperfect gift'? This means that a donee of an imperfect gift is not entitled to the gift or that a beneficiary of an incompletely constituted trust is not entitled to the trust property (see **Chapter 3**).
There are exceptions to this maxim. The exceptions are:
- The rule in *Re Rose*
- The rule in *Strong v Bird*
- The doctrine of donatio mortis causa
- Estoppel

We will consider each of these exceptions in turn.

THE RULE IN *RE ROSE*

According to the rule in *Re Rose*, provided the transferor has done all in their power to transfer title to the property, equity will regard the transfer as effective, although some action by a third party is required to complete the transfer of the legal title.
Consider the facts of *Re Rose* (1952) Ch 499:

The donor wished to make a gift of some shares to his wife. He completed the share transfer forms and posted the forms and share certificates to the company on 30 March 1943. The transfer was registered by the company three months later on 30 June 1943. The donor died in 1947. The transfer would have been subject to estate duty if it took place after 9 April 1943. Since action by a third party was required to complete the transfer of legal title and the donor had done all he could to divest himself of the title, the court accepted that the gift had been completed in March.

Practice example 4.1 shows an illustration of the rule.

Practice example 4.1

Arun decided to transfer his house to his son. He executed a deed of transfer, then handed the documents to his son. All that the son needed to do was to have the transfer stamped and registered. Before the son could do so, they had a falling out. Is it possible for Arun to retract the gift?

These are the facts of *Mascall v Mascall* [1985] 49 P & Cr 119, where the court held that the property belonged to the son in equity.

> The father had done everything in his power to make the transfer effective, and all other steps could be carried out by another. Even though legal title had not passed to the son, following the rule in *Re Rose*, the gift was perfected and the equitable title had passed to the son. Arun can no longer retract the gift.

The rule in *Re Rose* was generously extended in the case of *T Choithram International SA v Pagarani* [2000] UKPC 46:

TC was a businessman who had terminal cancer. He executed a trust deed on his deathbed to establish a trust to act as an umbrella organisation for a number of charities he had established during his lifetime. TC was one of the trustees of the trust. After signing the deed, he orally declared that all his wealth now belongs to the trust. The directors of his four companies passed a resolution confirming that the companies' shares would be held on trust by the trustees of the foundation. When TC died, the shares had not been transferred to the trustees (the trust was incompletely constituted).

The court applied *Re Rose* and held that as the settlor (TC) was one of the trustees, he had done everything necessary to create the trust and it was completely constituted.

It is arguable that the settlor had not done everything in his power to transfer the property to the other trustees but the court generously agreed that *Re Rose* could be applied considering he was on his deathbed and the fact that he clearly intended to transfer all his worldly goods to the charity.

> **Revision tip**
>
> Remember that *Re Rose* is applied to complete a gift or a trust. So, there must first be an imperfect gift or an incompletely constituted trust but the facts show that the donor/settlor has done everything necessary and anything else needed to be done can be carried out by another. If so, the court will assist the volunteer donee/beneficiary to perfect the gift.

It is important to have a good understanding of the rule in *Re Rose*, as it could well feature in the SQE. **Figure 4.1** provides a summary to help remember the necessary steps to recall.

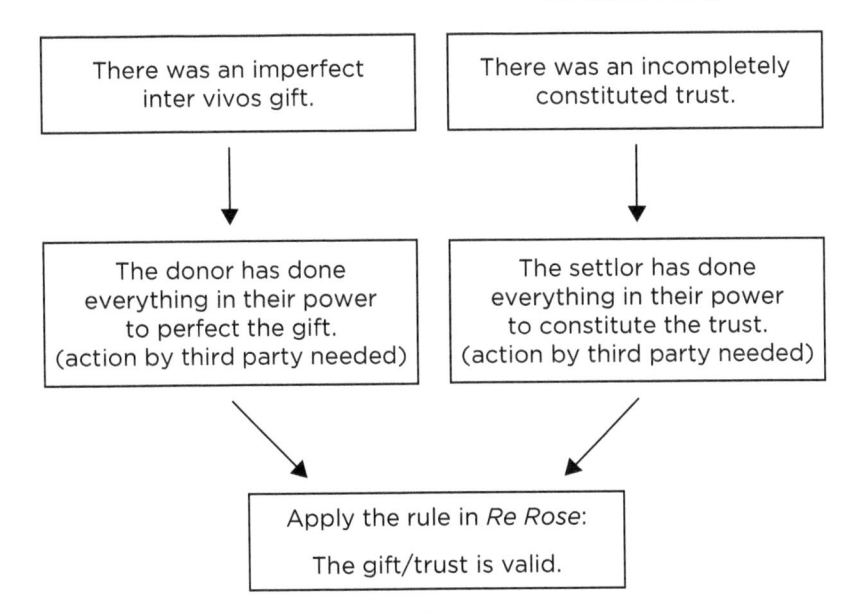

```
┌─────────────────────┐         ┌─────────────────────┐
│ There was an        │         │ There was an        │
│ imperfect inter     │         │ incompletely        │
│ vivos gift.         │         │ constituted trust.  │
└──────────┬──────────┘         └──────────┬──────────┘
           │                               │
           ▼                               ▼
┌─────────────────────────┐     ┌─────────────────────────┐
│ The donor has done      │     │ The settlor has done    │
│ everything in their     │     │ everything in their     │
│ power to perfect the    │     │ power to constitute the │
│ gift. (action by third  │     │ trust. (action by third │
│ party needed)           │     │ party needed)           │
└───────────┬─────────────┘     └────────────┬────────────┘
            │                                │
            └──────────────┐   ┌─────────────┘
                           ▼   ▼
                 ┌─────────────────────────┐
                 │ Apply the rule in       │
                 │ Re Rose:                │
                 │ The gift/trust is valid.│
                 └─────────────────────────┘
```

Figure 4.1: Summary of the rule in Re Rose

THE RULE IN *STRONG V BIRD*

According to the rule, if a donor makes an imperfect lifetime gift and the intended donee becomes the donor's **executor** or **administrator** on their death, the gift is perfected, provided the donor had a continuing intention to make the gift up until their death.

In *Strong v Bird* [1874] Lr 18 Eq 315, a man borrowed £1,100 from his stepmother who lived in his house and paid him rent. She agreed to pay a reduced rent (by way of him repaying the debt) but only did so twice. She paid the full rent thereafter and died with his debt still amounting to £900. He was appointed her executor. It was held that her continuing intention until death that he should be released from the debt coupled with the fact that he was appointed as her executor would result in the debt being forgiven.

> **Key term: executor**
> The person appointed by the testator in the will to administer the testator's estate.

> **Key term: administrator**
> The person appointed by the court to administer the deceased's estate where there is no executor.

Practice example 4.2 emphasises the requirements of the rule.

> **Practice example 4.2**
> Anya is seeking your advice on the following: Her mother had wanted Anya, who is illegitimate, to inherit the house but was under the mistaken belief that she could not leave the house by will to Anya due to her illegitimacy. The mother wrote a cheque for the value of the house to Anya and placed the cheque in an envelope but never gave it Anya. After her mother died, Anya was appointed as the administrator of her mother's estate and she found the envelope containing the cheque among her mother's papers. Can Anya claim the house using the rule in *Strong v Bird*?
>
> *Strong v Bird* is inapplicable as there was no continuing intention on the mother's part that the house should go to Anya (as evidenced by the cheque). Unfortunately, the cheque became useless on the mother's death. Anya cannot claim either the house or the money.

The rule has been extended and applied to cases where a settlor covenants to settle property and the property becomes vested in the trustees in some different capacity. An example of this can be found in *Re Ralli's WT* [1964] Ch 288:

A settlor, Helen, covenanted with her trustee to settle property which she was due to inherit under her father's will. The father's will left property to Helen's mother for life, the remainder to Helen. Helen predeceased her mother and so she died without transferring the property to the trustee. However, the trustee happened to be the executor of the father's will and was holding the legal title to the promised property. The court held that Helen's trust was completely constituted and enforceable by the beneficiaries. It was irrelevant that the trustee received the property in a different capacity, what mattered was that the trust property was already vested in him. As you can see, luck played a role in completing the trust created by Helen.

Exam warning

If you are told in an SQE question that the donee of an imperfect lifetime gift has been appointed as the donor's **personal representative**, this is a clue to consider whether the gift can be perfected by applying the requirements of *Strong v Bird*.

Key term: personal representative

A general term referring to either the executor or administrator.

It is important that you have a good understanding of the rule in *Strong v Bird* and the steps are summarised in **Figure 4.2**.

```
The donor made an imperfect
inter vivos gift.
         ↓
The donor's intention to make the
gift continued until their death.
         ↓
The donee was appointed as the
donor's executor or administrator.
         ↓
Apply the rule in Strong v Bird to
perfect the gift.
```

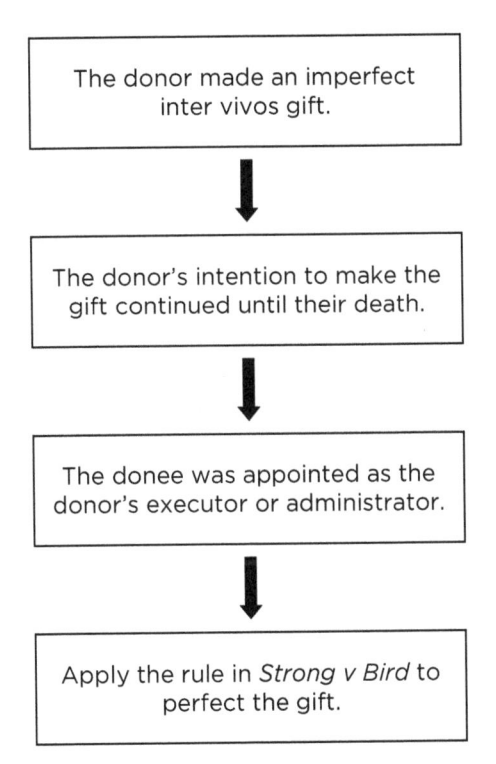

Figure 4.2: Summary of the rule in Strong v Bird

DONATIO MORTIS CAUSA

In the SQE assessment, you may come across a scenario where a donor makes an imperfect inter vivos gift but dies soon after. Donatio mortis

causa (DMC) is a special type of gift made during the donor's lifetime but is not effective until their death (conditional upon their death). The following requirements must be met:
- The gift must be made in contemplation of death from some particular cause, although it does not matter if death actually occurs due to some other cause. For example, in *Wilkes v Allington* [1931] 2 Ch 104, the donor made the gift knowing that he was suffering from cancer and believing that he would die soon. He died a month later from pneumonia unrelated to the cancer but the court upheld the gift.
- The intention is that the gift is conditional upon the donor's death.
- The subject matter of the gift must be delivered to the donee and the property must be capable of passing by donation.

We will now consider each requirement in turn:

In contemplation of death
For DMC to apply, the donor had to be contemplating their own death from a known cause. An elderly donor approaching the end of their natural life span does not meet the requirement.

This was confirmed in *King v Chiltern Dog Rescue* [2016] 2 WLR 1, where an aunt's will left her estate to several animal charities. When she became elderly and frail, her nephew moved in to care for her. She later gave him the title deeds to her house saying, 'This will be yours when I go'. During the six months before she died, she signed three separate documents purporting to leave her property to him. Unfortunately, none of the documents were validly executed wills. On her death, the original will took effect. In considering the nephew's claim of the house based on DMC, the court held that the aunt was not contemplating her death when she gave him the deeds (imperfect gift). In fact, her various attempts to execute a will negated an intention to make a lifetime gift. The house passed to the charities.

The requirement that the donor must be contemplating their death leads us to the next requirement.

The gift is conditional upon the donor's death
DMC only applies if it is clear that the donor only intended to give the gift if they actually die. The donor can revoke during their lifetime and it is automatically revoked if the donor recovers.

The subject matter of the gift must be delivered to the donee and the property must be capable of passing by DMC

The final requirement of DMC is that the subject matter of the gift must be delivered to the donee and the property must be capable of passing by DMC. Delivery includes an actual physical delivery of the gift, handing over of the means of obtaining the gift, or handing over of the 'essential evidence of title' as proof that the donor has relinquished control over the property.

The type of delivery depends on the gift. Let's consider the various types of property in relation to a DMC scenario that you may encounter in the SQE assessment.

Chattels
This includes actual physical delivery of the chattel or delivery of a means of obtaining it, like a key. For example, in *Re Lillingston* [1952] 2 All ER 184, the donee was given keys to a trunk containing the key to a safe deposit box at Harrods, which contained some jewellery as well as the key to a city safe deposit box that contained more of the donor's jewellery. The court held that there was an effective DMC of all the jewellery to the donee.

What about car keys? Do you think their delivery is sufficient to pass the car to the donee? According to the case of *Woodard v Woodard* [1995] 3 All ER 980, where a father gave his car keys to his son, there was a successful gift of the car as the father's actions clearly showed that he intended to pass over control of the car to his son.

Money
If the donor had the money with them, then just giving the money to the donee is effective delivery provided all the other requirements of DMC have been met.

Savings in a bank account can also be the subject of a DMC; older case law confirmed that delivery of a bank passbook or a Post Office savings book are sufficient as essential evidence of title. There is no authority as yet on whether delivery of a bank card and PIN code would suffice.

Land
In *Sen v Headley* [1991] 2 All ER 636, the court held that the delivery of the title deeds to a house plus the house keys amounted to a valid DMC of the house.

> **Exam warning**
>
> The house in *Sen v Headley* was unregistered land. There is no authority on whether registered land can pass by DMC. In registered land, 'evidence of title' is the entry in the Land Registry. We await a court judgment on this issue.

Shares

Although there is no definitive case law confirming that shares can be the subject of DMC, it is arguable that share certificates are the 'essential evidence of title' and their delivery to the donee could be a valid DMC of the shares.

Cheques

A cheque drawn on the donor's own bank account cannot pass by DMC because it does not constitute as property in itself but as an instruction to the donor's bank, which is revoked on the donor's death. However, cheques drawn by third parties are capable of passing by DMC as illustrated in **Practice example 4.3**.

> **Practice example 4.3**
>
> Mo was driving home from a party and swerved to avoid a pothole. Her car overturned and drifted to the edge of the road, teetering over a sheer drop into the valley below. Her friend Idris, who was following in the car behind, tried to help but everything he did caused the car to slide further over the edge. Mo was certain she would fall to her death.
>
> She told Idris that it was hopeless, reached in her pocket and pulled out a cheque for £5,000 from her employer. She passed the cheque to him and said, 'It is yours'. He tried to reach for her hand but only managed to grab the cheque when the car fell into the valley killing her instantly. Is Idris entitled to the £5,000?
>
> **All the requirements of DMC were met and as the cheque was drawn by another (not the donor), it is capable of passing by DMC and Idris is entitled to the money.**

The SQE assessment could feature a question on DMC and it is important for you to remember the requirements. **Figure 4.3** summarises the essentials.

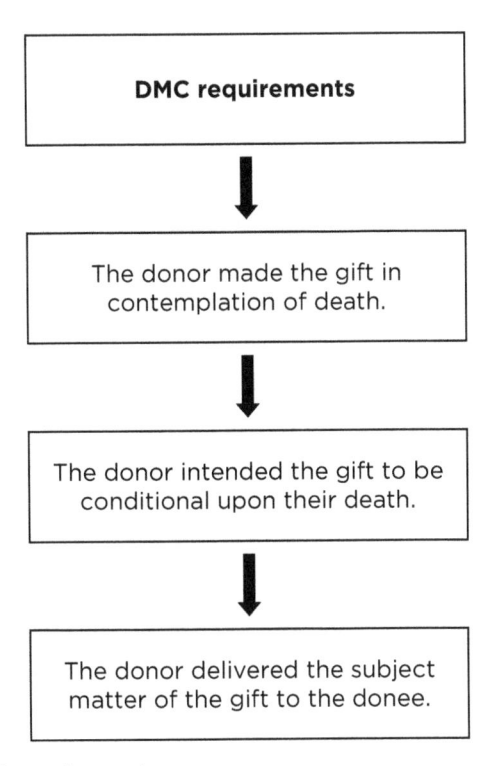

```
┌─────────────────────────┐
│    DMC requirements     │
└─────────────────────────┘
             ↓
┌─────────────────────────┐
│ The donor made the gift │
│ in contemplation of death. │
└─────────────────────────┘
             ↓
┌─────────────────────────┐
│ The donor intended the gift to be │
│ conditional upon their death. │
└─────────────────────────┘
             ↓
┌─────────────────────────┐
│ The donor delivered the subject │
│ matter of the gift to the donee. │
└─────────────────────────┘
```

Figure 4.3: DMC requirements

ESTOPPEL

The doctrine of **estoppel** prevents someone from acting in a manner inconsistent with their representations to another in reliance on which that other has acted to their detriment. There are two types of estoppel, promissory estoppel and proprietary estoppel.

The topic of promissory estoppel is dealt with in contract law; the topic of proprietary estoppel will be dealt with later in **Chapter 8**.

> **Key term: estoppel**
> A principle that prevents someone from asserting a claim that contradicts what they have previously promised.

72   Exceptions to the maxim that equity will not assist a volunteer

For now, you only need to remember that when a **promisor** has made a promise to another coupled with an imperfect gift, the promisee may rely on estoppel to perfect the gift if the **promisee** has suffered detriment in reliance on the promise.

Key term: promisor
The person making the promise.

Key term: promisee
The person to whom the promise was made.

Practice example 4.4 shows estoppel in action.

Practice example 4.4

Noah turned 80 and asked his nephew Ethan to move into his cottage with him and be his caregiver. Noah assured Ethan that in exchange for his care, Noah would leave the cottage to Ethan in his will. Noah gave Ethan the title deeds to the cottage. Ethan worked from home as a composer but no matter how busy he was, he always made sure that his uncle ate well, took his medication and that the cottage was clean. Noah died last month and his will left his whole estate to a local homeless shelter. Is Ethan entitled to the cottage?

There was an imperfect gift of the cottage to Ethan; Noah should have conveyed the cottage to him by deed (not merely passing the title deeds to him) or left him the cottage by will. However an estoppel arises as there was a promise made by the uncle and Ethan suffered detriment (looking after the uncle) in reliance on the promise. The gift is perfected and Ethan is entitled to the cottage.

You may encounter a question on estoppel in the SQE assessment and so it is important that you know the requirements, as summarised in **Figure 4.4**.

```
┌─────────────────────────┐
│  Estoppel requirements  │
└─────────────────────────┘
             ↓
┌─────────────────────────────┐
│ The donor made an imperfect │
│ lifetime gift or promise.   │
└─────────────────────────────┘
             ↓
┌─────────────────────────────┐
│ The donee relied on the     │
│ donor's promise of the gift.│
└─────────────────────────────┘
             ↓
┌─────────────────────────────┐
│ The donee suffered detriment│
│ as a result.                │
└─────────────────────────────┘
             ↓
┌─────────────────────────┐
│ The gift is perfected.  │
└─────────────────────────┘
```

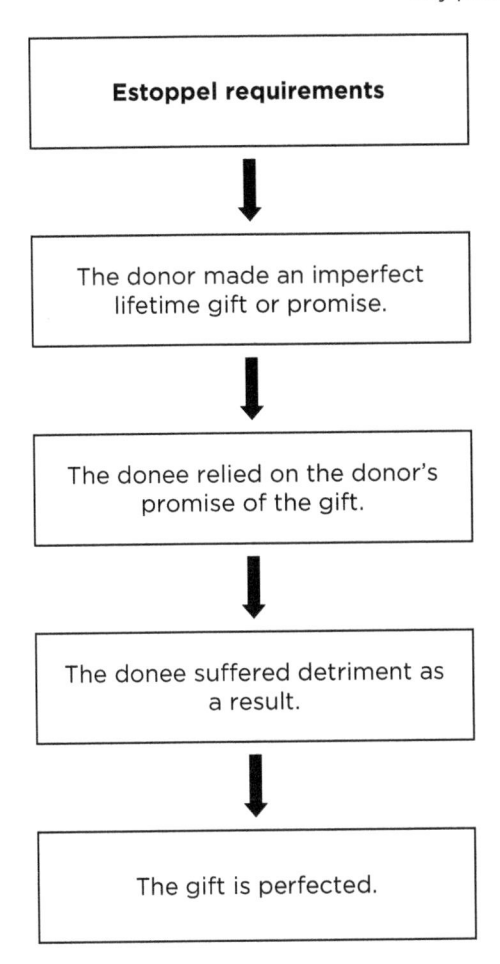

Figure 4.4: Estoppel requirements

■ KEY POINT CHECKLIST

This chapter has covered the following key knowledge points. You can use these to structure your revision around, making sure to recall the key details for each point, as covered in this chapter.
- The exceptions are applicable to assist a volunteer to perfect a gift or to complete a trust.
- The rule in *Re Rose* requires proof that the donor has done everything necessary to perfect the gift.

74 Exceptions to the maxim that equity will not assist a volunteer

- The rule in *Strong v Bird* requires proof of continuing intention by the donor plus the donee's appointment as the donor's personal representative.
- DMC applies to conditional imperfect lifetime gifts made in contemplation of death where the subject matter of the gift has been delivered.
- Estoppel applies where the donor made an imperfect lifetime gift (or promised a gift) which the donee relied upon to their detriment.

■ KEY TERMS AND CONCEPTS

- executor (**page 65**)
- administrator (**page 66**)
- personal representative (**page 67**)
- estoppel (**page 71**)
- promisor (**page 72**)
- promisee (**page 72**)

■ SQE1-STYLE QUESTIONS

QUESTION 1

A woman worked abroad and visited her grandfather twice a year. During one such visit, her grandfather informed her that he did not expect to live long enough for her next visit. He gave her the deeds to his house and told her, 'I want you to have the house; you have your own set of keys'. The woman's grandfather died a month later. His will left his whole estate to a local children's charity.

Which of the following statements best describes the woman's the entitlement to the house?

A. The house will pass to the charity.
B. The woman can claim the house by estoppel.
C. The woman can claim the house by relying on donatio mortis causa.
D. There was an inter vivos gift of the house to the woman.
E. There is a valid trust of the house benefitting the woman.

QUESTION 2

A decade ago, the testator made a will leaving her entire estate to several animal charities. Two years ago, she suffered a stroke and her nephew decided to move in with her as her caregiver. Last year, she presented him with the deeds to her house, telling him that the house is his when she dies. A month ago, they both signed a document purporting to be a deed leaving the house to the nephew. There was no other signature on the document. The testator died last week. Her will appointed her nephew as the executor.

Which of the following best describes the entitlement to the house?

A. The nephew can claim the house as there was a deed of conveyance in his favour.
B. The nephew can claim the house as he is the executor of the estate.
C. The nephew can claim the house by donatio mortis causa as there was delivery of the title deeds to him.
D. The nephew can claim the house as she had done everything in her power to transfer the house to him.
E. The nephew can claim the house using estoppel.

QUESTION 3

A man turned 80 last month, his only surviving next of kin are his daughter and her son. The man wanted to ensure that they should have some security in the event of his passing. He gave the title deeds to his house to his daughter, saying, 'I want you to hold my house for your son'. He then wrote, 'This house is for my grandson', on the back of the one of the deeds which he signed, saying, 'There, now it is official'. The man died last week. His will, which was executed in 1980, appointed his best friend as his executor and left his entire estate to charity.

Which of the following statements best describes the entitlement to the house?

A. The daughter holds on trust for the grandson as there was a continuing intention to benefit the grandson and the gift was perfected on the man's death.
B. Donatio mortis causa applies and the daughter holds on trust for the grandson.
C. The man's personal representatives hold the house on trust for the grandson.
D. The grandson is not entitled to the house.
E. The daughter holds on trust for the grandson as the man had done everything in his power to transfer the house to her.

76 Exceptions to the maxim that equity will not assist a volunteer

QUESTION 4

A woman has two children: a son from a brief relationship with a man who died before they could marry, and a daughter from her marriage. When the woman turned 80, she decided to execute a will but mistakenly assumed that any gift left in the will to her son would be invalid due to his illegitimacy. The woman's will names her son as her executor and left her whole estate to her daughter. Later that same day, she told her son that the house belongs to him. She passed the title deeds of the house to him together with a note saying, 'The house is yours. Love, Mum'. The next day, worried that she may not have properly conveyed the house to him, she wrote a cheque for the value of the house to him. No one else knew about the cheque and on her death, the cheque was found stapled to the will.

Which of the following statements best describes the entitlement to the house?

A. The daughter inherits the whole estate including the house.
B. The son is entitled to the house as he is the executor of the estate.
C. The son is not entitled to the house but he can claim the value of the house as represented by the cheque.
D. The son can claim the house by relying on donatio mortis causa.
E. The daughter holds the house on trust for the son.

QUESTION 5

Fifteen years ago, a man and a woman started a relationship and she moved in with him. The man was the sole owner of the house in which they lived and he paid the mortgage instalments. The couple never married but had two children together. Five years ago, the man fell in love with his personal assistant and moved in with her. Before he moved out, he told the mother of his children not to worry as the house was now hers. He told her where the title deeds to the house were kept. She started paying the mortgage instalments and spent a lot of money and effort installing a new fitted kitchen. The man is now seeking to evict the woman and their children from his house.

Which of the following statements best describes the woman's entitlement to the house?

A. The woman is not entitled to the house as there is nothing in writing to support her claim.

B. The woman is not entitled to the house as she has provided no consideration.
C. The woman is entitled to the house as the man had done everything in his power to transfer it to her.
D. The woman is entitled to the house by relying on donatio mortis causa.
E. The woman is entitled to the house by estoppel.

■ ANSWERS TO QUESTIONS

Answers to 'What do you know already?' questions at the start of the chapter

1) In an incompletely constituted trust, the settlor has not vested the trust property in the trustees. However, if the settlor has done everything in their power to vest the property and anything else that needed to be done can be carried out by a third party, the rule in *Re Rose* applies and the trust is deemed to be completely constituted.

2) False. Although the imperfect gift in *Strong v Bird* concerns the forgiving of an unpaid debt, the rule is applicable to all imperfect gifts if the requirements are met.

3) False. Donatio mortis causa is only applicable where the gift was made in contemplation of death. The fact that the donor is old and frail is in itself not regarded as 'contemplation of death'.

4) False. Proprietary estoppel can be used either as a cause of action or as a defence.

5) When the woman died, the trust property was not vested in the trustee (her brother). The trust is prima facie incompletely constituted and her son cannot benefit from it. However, using the exception in *Re Rose*: if the settlor (the woman) had done everything in her power to vest the trust property and some action by a third party/s (her brother the trustee and the registrar of the company) is required to complete the transfer of title, equity will perfect the gift. All the trustee needed to do was to post the envelope and on receipt of the documents, the registrar of the company will register the change in ownership. The trust is valid.

Answers to end-of-chapter SQE1-style questions

Question 1:
The correct answer was A. There was an imperfect lifetime gift of the house to the woman but none of the exceptions are applicable to

78 Exceptions to the maxim that equity will not assist a volunteer

perfect the gift. It is not Option B because the elements of estoppel were not present. It is not Option C because the donor was not anticipating death from a known cause. It is not Option D because he did not convey the house to her by deed. It is not Option E because he had no intention to create a trust.

Question 2:

The correct answer was B. The document they signed is neither a deed nor a will (lacking proper formalities) so not Option A. There was an imperfect lifetime gift of the house to the nephew but her intention to make the gift continued up to her death. As he was appointed her executor, all the requirements of *Strong v Bird* have been met and the gift is perfected. Option E is wrong because even though the nephew may have suffered detriment in having to look after his aunt, he did so voluntarily, not because she promised him the house. There was no evidence that she was contemplating her death so Option C is wrong. She has not done everything possible to transfer the house so Option D is wrong.

Question 3:

The correct answer was D. The man had intended to create a trust of the house with his daughter as trustee holding for the benefit of her son, but the trust was incompletely constituted as he failed to vest the legal title to the house on the daughter. None of the exceptions are applicable to perfect the trust (so all the other options are wrong).

Question 4:

The correct answer was A. There was an imperfect lifetime gift of the house to the son. Although he was appointed as the executor of his mother's estate, the rule in *Strong v Bird* is inapplicable as there was no continuing intention on the mother's part to give him the house (the cheque negated continuing intention) so Options B and C are wrong. There was no evidence that she was contemplating her death so Option D is wrong. There was no intention to create a trust so Option E is wrong.

Question 5:

The correct answer was E. The man made a promise to the woman that the house was hers and in reliance on his promise, she suffered detriment (paying mortgage instalments, installing fitted kitchen) thus perfecting the gift. The promise need not be made in writing so Option A is wrong. So long as she can prove all the elements of estoppel, consideration is not required, so Option B is wrong. None of the other exceptions are applicable so Options C and D are wrong.

■ KEY CASES, RULES, STATUTES AND INSTRUMENTS

You must know the following two cases as they established the two rules which are exceptions to the maxim:
- *Re Rose* [1952] Ch 499.
- *Strong v Bird* [1874] Lr 18 Eq 315.

The following two cases illustrate extensions to the rules in *Re Rose* and *Strong v Bird*, so they are helpful for you to know but there is no need to remember their names:
- *T Choithram International SA v Pagarani* [2000] UKPC 46.
- *Re Ralli's WT* [1964] Ch 288.

5

Beneficial entitlement

■ MAKE SURE YOU KNOW

In a trust, the legal title to the trust property is held by the trustees; the beneficiaries hold the equitable title and have certain entitlements. Beneficial entitlements differ depending on the terms of the trust and on the type of trust created. This chapter will explain the different beneficial interests and rights. You must learn to identify the relevant beneficial entitlements from the client-based scenarios in your SQE assessment in order to provide the best advice to your client.

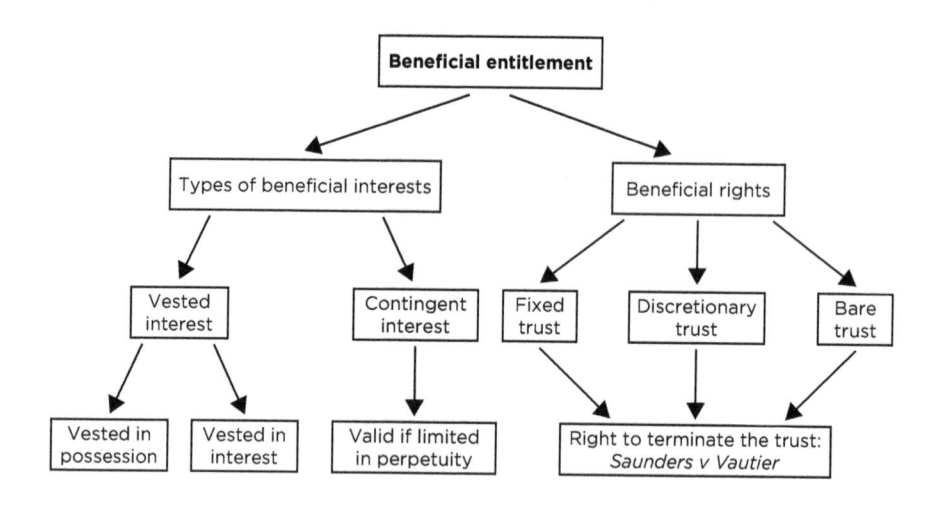

```
                    Beneficial entitlement
                    /                    \
    Types of beneficial interests      Beneficial rights
         /           \              /        |        \
    Vested      Contingent       Fixed  Discretionary  Bare
    interest     interest        trust     trust       trust
    /    \           |                \      |      /
Vested in Vested in  Valid if limited   Right to terminate the trust:
possession interest  in perpetuity           Saunders v Vautier
```

■ SQE ASSESSMENT ADVICE

As you work through this chapter, remember to pay particular attention in your revision to:
- How to identify the different types of beneficial interests: vested or contingent.
- The fact that a vested interest can take effect in possession or in remainder.

Beneficial entitlement 81

- The beneficiary's entitlement if they have a vested interest.
- What a contingent interest is and how a contingent interest becomes vested.
- The different types of trusts which determine the different beneficial rights.
- The beneficiary's right to terminate a trust and the relevant requirements.

■ WHAT DO YOU KNOW ALREADY?

Have a go at these questions before reading this chapter. If you find some difficult or cannot remember the answers, make a note to look more closely at that during your revision.

1) True or false: Property is held on trust for P for life, remainder to Q absolutely. P claims to be entitled to the capital.
   [Types of beneficial interests, page 82]

2) True or false: Property is held on trust for P for life, remainder to Q absolutely. Q predeceased P. Q's estate cannot benefit from the trust.
   [Types of beneficial interest, page 82]

3) True or false: Property is held on trust for A, B, C and D jointly. A and B are adults but C and D are aged 16 and 17 respectively. The beneficiaries claim that as they are all in agreement, they can compel the trustees to transfer the trust assets to them thereby terminating the trust.
   [Beneficiaries' rights, page 87]

4) A trustee is holding £150,000 on bare trust for X, who is 21. X would like the trustee to invest the entire sum according to an investment plan drawn up by X. The trustee refuses to do so as they have their own investment plan. Must the trustee comply with X's investment plans?
   [Beneficiaries' rights, page 87]

5) Settlement 1: 'Trustees are to hold my shares in Google Inc on trust for my son S until he turns 25, at which time, the trustees must transfer the shares to S absolutely'.
   Settlement 2: 'All my shares in BT plc on trust for my son S if he qualifies as a solicitor'.
   S has just turned 18; can he use the rule in *Saunders v Vautier* to compel the trustees of both settlements to transfer the shares to him absolutely?
   [Beneficiaries' rights, page 87]

BENEFICIAL INTERESTS AND RIGHTS

We know that a private trust must have beneficiaries (the certainty of objects). In this chapter, we focus on the beneficiaries. We will need to consider:
- The different types of beneficial interests.
- The beneficiary's rights in different types of trusts.

> **Revision tip**
>
> In revising for the SQE, and in the assessment itself, you may come across different terms describing the beneficiary's interest, such as equitable title, equitable interest or beneficial interest. Remember that they mean the same thing.

TYPES OF BENEFICIAL INTERESTS

A beneficiary's interest can be *vested* or *contingent* depending on their entitlement under the trust.

Vested interests

A beneficiary with a vested interest has a rightful claim to the trust assets. The vested interest can take effect in possession or in remainder.

To help you distinguish between an interest in possession and an interest in remainder, have a look at the following example:

'Trustees are holding property on trust for A for life, then to B absolutely'. **Table 5.1** sets out the nature of each beneficiary's interest and entitlement.

Table 5.1: Types of vested interests

A's interest and entitlement:	B's interest and entitlement:
A has a life interest and A's interest is **vested in possession**.	B has a remainder interest in the capital and B's interest is **vested in interest**.
A has an immediate right to the income.	B has a right to the capital that vests in possession on A's death. If B predeceased A, their entitlement will pass to their estate on A's death.

> **Key term: vested in possession**
> An interest that is vested in possession is a present right to present enjoyment.

> **Key term: vested in interest**
> An interest that is vested in interest is a present right to future enjoyment.

To determine whether an interest is vested or not, the conditions of vesting are:
- The beneficiaries must be ascertained or ascertainable.
- They must be ready to take possession; but may be prevented from doing so due to the existence of a prior interest.

If either requirement is not met, the interest cannot be a vested interest.

> **Exam warning**
> Remember that once a beneficiary's interest is vested, even if it is a future interest, that beneficiary becomes rightfully entitled. The interest cannot be lost. If the beneficiary dies before the interest becomes vested in possession, it will pass to their estate at the relevant time. Bear this in mind as this is the type of SQE scenario you may encounter.

Contingent interests

If the beneficiary must meet a condition before they can benefit from the trust, the beneficiary has a **contingent interest**. This type of interest gives no rights to the beneficiary until the condition is met. Once the condition is met, the interest becomes a vested interest.

> **Key term: contingent interest**
> An interest that is contingent upon an event taking place. The settlor may impose a condition which the beneficiary must meet before they become entitled to the trust property. If the beneficiary dies before meeting the condition, the interest is lost.

An example of a contingent interest can be found in **Practice example 5.1**.

Beneficial entitlement

> **Practice example 5.1**
>
> In a settlement, the trustees hold '£100,000 on trust for the first child of A to reach the age of 21'. A has three daughters, aged 20, 17 and 15 respectively. The 20-year old wishes to claim the money. What is your advice to her?
>
> This is an example of a contingent interest. The contingency is turning 21. A's children are all under 21, none are entitled to the interest as the contingency has not been met. The first child to turn 21 has a vested interest and is entitled to the money. The eldest daughter must meet the contingency before she can claim the money.

It is sometimes difficult to distinguish between a vested interest and a contingent interest. It is a matter of construction for the courts. Have a look at **Table 5.2** for further clarification.

Table 5.2: Vested or contingent?

Vested interest:	Contingent interest:
An interest is vested if it is clear from the words used that the beneficiary is entitled to the trust assets even though the enjoyment is postponed to a future date.	A contingent interest is dependent on the fulfilment of a condition. The beneficiary is not entitled to benefit unless the condition is met.
For example: 'Trustees to hold shares on trust for my son until he turns 25, at which time, they must transfer the shares to him'.	For example: 'Trustees to hold shares on trust for the first of my children to reach 25'.
It is clear that the settlor intended the son to benefit from the shares and his entitlement is merely postponed until he turns 25.	It is clear that no beneficiary can be said to be entitled to the shares until one has met the condition.
Usually, in a vested interest, there is no gift over.	The settlor would normally include a gift over in a contingent gift, such as: 'In the event none of my children shall meet the contingency, the shares are to be divided amongst my nieces and nephews equally'.

Contingent interests must be limited in perpetuity. This means that the interest must vest within the perpetuity period. We will now consider the rule against perpetuities.

The rule against perpetuities
A settlement with future interests tying up property may make the property **inalienable** for years. Take, for example, a settlement where the trustees must hold land on trust for the first of the settlor's great-grandchildren to reach the age of 25. If the settlor is childless at the date of the settlement, the trustees will be holding on to the land for a long time waiting for the rightful beneficiary to meet this contingency. The purpose of the rule is to void any gifts that tie up property for longer than the **perpetuity period**.

Key term: inalienable
Tied up; not freely transferable.

Key term: perpetuity period
The perpetuity period is 'lives in being' plus 21 years. The period is calculated thus: all the lives in being must have died, and 21 years is added on after the death of the last surviving life in being.

The lives in being may be expressed or implied. The following examples will explain the difference.

Example of express lives in being:
The settlor may expressly name people to act as lives in being; these people are the express lives in being. The settlement may expressly nominate 'Queen Elizabeth II and her descendants to act as lives in being'. If so, the express lives in being are the Queen, her children, grandchildren and great-grandchildren alive at the date of the grant. This means the perpetuity period is 21 years after the last person from this group of people has died. Express lives in being need not do anything, they are merely there so that the trustees are able to measure the perpetuity period.

Example of implied lives in being:
If the settlor did not specify express lives in being, they may be implied from the settlement. The implied lives in being are everyone who is alive at the date of the settlement *and* has been implicated in the settlement.

Let us now consider the following examples of contingent gifts; we will learn how to identify the implied lives in being and whether the gifts are valid or void for perpetuities.

Example 1: 'to the first child of Eve to reach the age of 21'.
Eve has two children and is six months pregnant at the date of the grant. Eve is the implied life in being.
The perpetuity period ends 21 years after Eve's death.
Conclusion: the gift is valid as her children will reach the age of 21 within that period. It does not matter which child meets the condition. Note that the perpetuity period includes a gestation period so the child Eve is carrying becomes entitled to the property on reaching 21 if their two elder siblings die before meeting the contingency.
Remember that it is irrelevant that all her children may predecease her and the gift will never vest; what matters is that if they do outlive her, the gift must vest within the perpetuity period.

Example 2: 'to the first grandchild of A to reach the age of 21'.
A is alive and has two children, B and C, at the date of the grant but no grandchildren.
The implied lives in being are A, B and C.
The perpetuity period is 21 years after the death of the last survivor between A, B and C.
Conclusion: the gift is void as B and C may predecease A; and A may have another child, D. Should A die in childbirth, the perpetuity period only has 21 years left to run. It will take more than 21 years for D to then have a child (i.e. a grandchild) who must reach 21 for the gift to vest.
Note that the common law is concerned with possibilities (worst-case scenario) and is not concerned with whether A is fertile or not.

The Perpetuities and Accumulations Act 1964, s 3 makes it possible to wait and see whether or not an interest actually vests within the period. This means that rather than declaring the grant as void by applying the worst-case scenario, the trustees can now wait for the length of the perpetuity period for the gift to vest. In most cases, there is no need to wait for the full period as the gift would vest much sooner.

Under the Perpetuities and Accumulations Act 2009, a settlor can choose to bypass the perpetuity period test by expressly specifying a period of up to 125 years. When the settlor has specified a perpetuity period, all contingent gifts are deemed valid and will be paid to the relevant beneficiary who meets the contingency within that period. If the contingency has not been met at the end of the period, the gift fails and the property will go back to the settlor's estate or be paid to those entitled in a gift over.

Revision tip

The issue of perpetuities can be confusing but the SQE assessment is unlikely to focus on this area. All you need is the basics so that you can understand this requirement in the following chapter on purpose trusts.

Summary: types of beneficial interests

Interest is vested in possession	Beneficiary is entitled.
Interest is vested in interest	Beneficiary is entitled but must wait until the interest vests in possession.
Contingent interest	Beneficiary is not entitled unless and until the contingency is met. The contingent interest is void if not limited in perpetuity.

BENEFICIARIES' RIGHTS

In a valid and constituted trust, the beneficiary has an equitable interest in the trust property. This equitable interest gives rise to certain rights within the trust. The rights may differ depending on the type of trust created. We will now consider each type of trust and the corresponding beneficial rights.

Fixed trust

In a fixed trust, the beneficial interest of each beneficiary is fixed and they have an automatic right to payment in accordance with the terms of the trust. The beneficiary has an equitable proprietary interest in the property, which they can enforce against anyone who comes into possession of it through the mechanism of a constructive trust or through the process of tracing. The topics of constructive trust and tracing will be dealt with in later chapters (**Chapters 9** and **12**).

Discretionary trust

Unlike in a fixed trust, the beneficiaries of a discretionary trust do not have an automatic right to payment. They have no proprietary interest in the trust assets unless and until the trustees decide to distribute. In a discretionary trust, the beneficiaries' only right is to be considered by the trustees in the exercise of their discretion.

> **Exam warning**
>
> In the SQE assessment, remember that in a discretionary trust, the beneficiaries may never benefit. They cannot compel the trustees to decide in their favour. However, they may be able to terminate the trust.

Bare trust

A bare trust arises where trustees are holding property for the sole benefit of an adult beneficiary. The beneficiary has full control over the actions of the trustees in relation to the trust property. The trustees must comply with the beneficiary's instructions, including how to invest the assets, how much to pay the beneficiary or even terminating the trust and transferring the legal title to the beneficiary if so ordered.

Summary: beneficiaries' rights	
Fixed trust	Beneficiary has a right to payment in accordance with the terms of the trust.
Discretionary trust	Beneficiary has no right to payment, only the right to be considered by the trustees in the exercise of their discretion.
Bare trust	Beneficiary has full control over the actions of the trustees in relation to the trust property.

Having looked at the rights of beneficiaries under the various types of trust, we will now consider whether the beneficiaries have the right to bring the trust to an end.

Terminating the trust

In *Saunders v Vautier* [1841] 4 Beav 115, the court ruled that a sole beneficiary who is **sui juris** and is absolutely entitled to the whole beneficial interest may compel the trustees to transfer the legal title to them thereby terminating the trust.

> **Key term: sui juris**
>
> Of full age and under no disability.

Practice example 5.2 explains how the rule can be used.

Practice example 5.2

A father's will left his shares in a company on trust for his son, with the instruction that the trustee is to hold the shares on trust until the son turns 25 years old, at which time the trustee must transfer the shares to the son, thereby terminating the trust. The son has just turned 18 and wants the trustee to transfer the shares to him, thus bringing the trust to an end. Is this possible?

These are the facts of *Saunders v Vautier*. The son is an adult who is the sole beneficiary absolutely entitled to the whole of the beneficial interest; provided he is under no disability, he can bring the trust to an end. The trustee must transfer the legal title of the shares to the son. Once this is done, the son becomes the absolute owner.

The rule in *Saunders v Vautier* has since been extended to apply to a group of beneficiaries. If all the beneficiaries are adults, under no disability and together are absolutely entitled, they may agree to bring the trust to an end by calling on the trustees to transfer the legal title to them.

Practice example 5.3 demonstrates the rule in practice where there is more than one beneficiary.

Practice example 5.3

A trustee is holding property on trust for X for life, remainder to Y absolutely. X and Y have decided that they would like the trust to be terminated and the property to be transferred to them jointly. Can they compel the trustee to do so?

Separately, neither X nor Y are absolutely entitled to the whole of the beneficial interest. X is entitled to the life interest and Y is entitled to the remainder interest. Together, however, both are entitled to the whole and so long as they are both sui juris, they may use the rule in *Saunders v Vautier* to terminate the trust.

Clearly, the rule applies to a fixed trust where the beneficiaries have a vested interest in the trust assets. What about discretionary trusts? As you know, the beneficiaries of such a trust are wholly dependent on the trustees exercising the discretion in their favour and have no real claim to the property until then. If all the beneficiaries are sui juris, can they use the rule to terminate the trust and share the trust assets?

90 Beneficial entitlement

The court in *Re Smith* [1928] Ch 915 confirmed that the rule is applicable to discretionary trusts where the trustees are required to distribute the whole of the trust fund but they have a discretion as to who should benefit and how much to pay. In such instances, it is possible to treat all the beneficiaries as though they were one person. This means that so long as all the beneficiaries are sui juris, they are treated as one person who can then compel the trustees to transfer the property to them.

> ### Exam warning
> Whilst the rule in *Saunders v Vautier* may sound like an easy solution to terminate a trust, remember that where you have a group of beneficiaries, all the beneficiaries must be adults, under no disability, are all in agreement and together are absolutely entitled to the whole of the beneficial interest. If some of the beneficiaries are still minors, the rule is inapplicable. Bear this in mind when considering whether a group of beneficiaries can terminate a trust in the SQE assessment.

To remind yourself of the requirements of the rule, have a look at **Figure 5.1**.

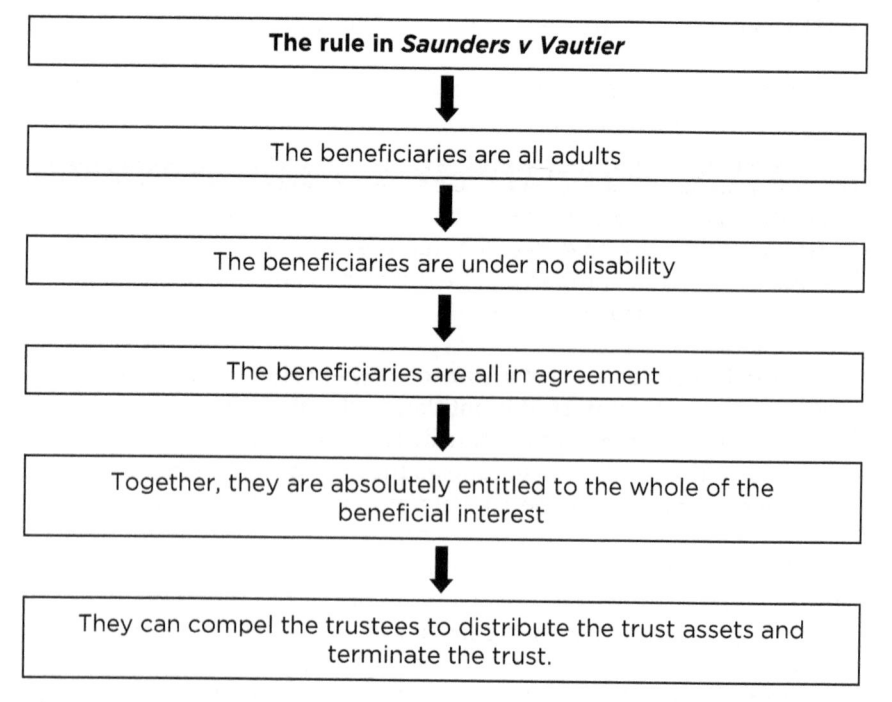

```
The rule in Saunders v Vautier
            ↓
The beneficiaries are all adults
            ↓
The beneficiaries are under no disability
            ↓
The beneficiaries are all in agreement
            ↓
Together, they are absolutely entitled to the whole of the
            beneficial interest
            ↓
They can compel the trustees to distribute the trust assets and
            terminate the trust.
```

Figure 5.1: The rule in Saunders v Vautier

■ KEY POINT CHECKLIST

This chapter has covered the following key knowledge points. You can use these to structure your revision around, making sure to recall the key details for each point, as covered in this chapter.
- Make sure you know how to identify the different types of beneficial interests.
- An interest vested in possession gives the beneficiary an immediate claim to the trust assets in accordance with the terms of the trust.
- An interest vested in interest also gives the beneficiary a rightful claim to the assets but the right is postponed until the interest is vested in possession.
- A contingent interest means that there is a condition which must be met before the interest vests. The beneficiary has no right to the trust assets until the condition is met.
- Contingent interests must be limited in perpetuity.
- The beneficiaries of a fixed trust have a right to payment in accordance with the terms of the trust.
- The beneficiaries of a discretionary trust have no right to payment, only the right to be considered by the trustees.
- The beneficiary of a bare trust has full control over the running of the trust.
- The rule in *Saunders v Vautier* can be used by beneficiaries to terminate the trust provided the beneficiaries are sui juris and together are absolutely entitled to the whole beneficial interest.

■ KEY TERMS AND CONCEPTS
- vested in possession (**page 83**)
- vested in interest (**page 83**)
- contingent interest (**page 83**)
- inalienable (**page 85**)
- perpetuity period (**page 85**)
- sui juris (**page 88**)

■ SQE1-STYLE QUESTIONS

QUESTION 1

A testator's will contains the following provision:
'My house to be held on trust to allow my mother to live in the house during her lifetime and after her death to be held on trust for such of my

niece and nephew as survive my mother and reach the age of 21 years in equal shares'. The niece is now 18 and the nephew is 22.

Which of the following statements best describes the parties' beneficial interests?

A. They all have vested interests.
B. They all have contingent interests.
C. The mother and the nephew have vested interests, but the niece has a contingent interest.
D. The mother has a contingent interest, but the niece and nephew have vested interests.
E. The mother has a vested interest, but the niece and nephew have contingent interests.

QUESTION 2

A man dies and is survived by his wife and a son who is aged 27 years. The man's will leaves his residuary estate on trust 'to pay the income to my wife for her life and after her death to my son if he survives my wife and attains the age of 25 years but if he does not so survive then to my brother absolutely'. The wife wishes to bring the trust to an end.

Whose consent is required to bring the trust to an end?

A. The wife.
B. The wife and the son.
C. The wife, the son, and the brother.
D. The wife and the brother.
E. The son and the brother.

QUESTION 3

A settlor recently transferred £10m to set up a trust with the following clause: 'The trustees shall apply the net income of the fund in making at their absolute discretion payments to any of my relatives in such amounts, at such times and on such conditions as they think fit'. The settlor has a large family, but the trustees are able to draw up a complete list of all his relatives, at least a dozen of whom are minors. As the list is complete, the relatives want to bring the trust to an end and the money to be divided equally between themselves.

Which of the following best represents the beneficiaries' position regarding termination of the trust?

A. The trust can be terminated because there is a complete list of all beneficiaries.
B. The trust can be terminated because the beneficiaries are all in agreement.
C. The trust can be terminated because the beneficiaries all have vested interests.
D. The trust cannot be terminated because the beneficiaries are not all adults.
E. The trust cannot be terminated because not all the beneficiaries have met the contingency.

QUESTION 4

A woman settled property on trust for her husband for life, remainder to her daughter for life, remainder to her grandson absolutely. The husband and grandson are still alive, but the daughter has just died.

Which statement best describes the beneficiaries' entitlement?

A. On the husband's death, the property will pass to the grandson.
B. On the husband's death, the property will pass to the daughter's estate.
C. On the husband's death, the property will pass to the grandson provided he is still alive.
D. On the husband's death, the property will go on resulting trust back to the settlor's estate if the grandson is dead.
E. On the husband's death, the property will pass to the husband's estate.

QUESTION 5

A man has settled property on trust for his son for life, then to his granddaughter if she qualifies as a solicitor. Both beneficiaries are adults. The granddaughter has not yet qualified as a solicitor.

94 Beneficial entitlement

Which statement best describes the beneficiaries' interests?

A. Both have vested interests.
B. The son's interest is vested, but the granddaughter's interest is contingent.
C. Both have contingent interests.
D. The son's interest is contingent, but the granddaughter's interest is vested.
E. On the son's death, the property will pass to the granddaughter.

■ ANSWERS TO QUESTIONS

Answers to 'What do you know already?' questions at the start of the chapter

1) False. P has a life interest in the trust assets and is entitled to the income generated by the assets during P's lifetime. Q's interest is vested in interest and Q becomes entitled to the capital on P's death.

2) False: Q has a remainder interest in the trust assets. This is a vested interest that entitles Q to benefit even if they died before they could take possession of the property. On P's death, the property passes to Q's estate.

3) False. According to the rule in *Saunders v Vautier*, all the beneficiaries must be adults, under no disability and are absolutely entitled before they can terminate the trust. A, B, C and D together are absolutely entitled to the trust assets but not all are adults. They cannot bring the trust to an end until C and D turn 18.

4) As the trustee is holding on a bare trust, the adult beneficiary has full control over the trustee's actions in relation to the trust property. The trustee must comply.

5) S has vested interest in Settlement 1. As he is an adult and is absolutely entitled to the whole beneficial interest, the rule in *Saunders v Vautier* is applicable and the trustees must comply with his wish.

Settlement 2 imposes a condition that S must meet before he is entitled to the trust property. Assuming he has not qualified as a solicitor, this is a contingent interest and therefore S is not absolutely entitled to the beneficial interest. *Saunders v Vautier* cannot be used to terminate this trust.

Answers to end-of-chapter SQE1-style questions

Question 1:
   The correct answer was E. The mother has an interest that is vested in possession as she is able to enjoy the house now. The niece and nephew have contingent interests, the contingency being twofold, that they survive the mother and reach the age of 21. The nephew has only met one of the conditions, so his interest remains contingent. All other options are therefore incorrect.

Question 2:
   The correct answer was C. To bring the trust to an end, the rule in *Saunders v Vautier* applies. All the beneficiaries (whether they have a vested or contingent interest) must be adults, in agreement and together are absolutely entitled. Option C is the only choice featuring all three beneficiaries; therefore all other options are incorrect.

Question 3:
   The correct answer was D. To compel the trustees to terminate the trust and distribute the money, the beneficiaries must use the rule in *Saunders v Vautier*. The rule is only applicable if all the beneficiaries are adults. Option A is incorrect because it is irrelevant whether a complete list is available. Option B is incorrect because the agreement of all beneficiaries is not sufficient; all beneficiaries must also be adults. Option C is incorrect as this is a discretionary trust. Option E is incorrect because the trust did not impose a contingency.

Question 4:
   The correct answer was A. The husband and daughter both have a life interest in the property. The daughter's entitlement is lost on death, meaning that her estate cannot claim the property (so Option B is wrong). As the grandson is a remainder person, the property will not pass to the husband's estate (so Option E is wrong). So, on the husband's death, the property will pass to the grandson. While the husband is alive, the grandson's interest is vested in interest but becomes vested in possession when the husband dies. Options C and D are wrong because if the grandson is dead the property will pass to the grandson's estate.

Question 5:
   The correct answer was B. The son has a vested interest, but the granddaughter must meet a condition before becoming entitled so her interest is contingent. Given that the granddaughter has not

yet met the condition, her interest remains contingent (therefore Options A, C and D are wrong). Option E is incorrect as the granddaughter must meet the contingency before she can claim the property.

■ KEY CASES, RULES, STATUTES AND INSTRUMENTS

- *Saunders v Vautier* [1841] 4 Beav 115.

This is the only case you need to remember as it introduced the rule allowing beneficiaries to terminate a trust.

6

Purpose trusts

■ MAKE SURE YOU KNOW

Purpose trusts are created for a purpose or purposes rather than to benefit ascertainable persons. There are two types of purpose trusts to consider, the non-charitable purpose trust and the charitable trust. You may be required to distinguish a non-charitable purpose trust from a charitable trust in the SQE.

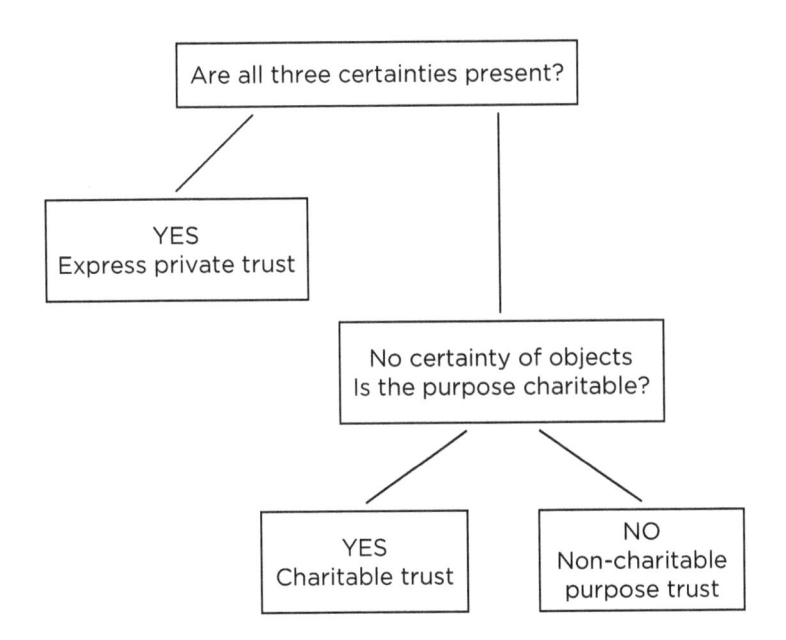

```
                Are all three certainties present?
                  /                    \
        YES                              
   Express private trust                 
                                         
                         No certainty of objects
                         Is the purpose charitable?
                           /              \
                     YES                    NO
               Charitable trust        Non-charitable
                                        purpose trust
```

■ SQE ASSESSMENT ADVICE

This chapter deals with the two types of purpose trusts: the non-charitable purpose trust and the charitable trust. As you work through this chapter, remember to pay particular attention in your revision to:
- The beneficiary principle, which applies to all private trusts. This means that a private trust without beneficiaries is generally void (see **Chapter 1**).
- The fact that non-charitable purpose trusts are an exception to the beneficiary principle. Such trusts are only valid if they meet the requirements explained below.
- The requirements of a charitable trust. Charitable trusts are public trusts enforced by the Attorney-General.
- The differences between the non-charitable and the charitable trusts.

■ WHAT DO YOU KNOW ALREADY?

Have a go at these questions before reading this chapter. If you find some difficult or cannot remember the answers, make a note to look more closely at that during your revision.

1) True or false: A non-charitable purpose trust with no beneficiaries is void.
   [Non-charitable purpose trusts, page 99]
2) True or false: Private purpose trusts can continue indefinitely.
   [Non-charitable purpose trusts, page 99]
3) A settlor has just died leaving a will in which £5,000 is to be held on trust for the maintenance of her two pet rabbits. Is this trust valid?
   [Non-charitable purpose trusts, page 99]
4) A settlor has just died leaving land and money on trust with instructions to his trustees to maintain the land as an open space for the public to enjoy. Is this trust valid? If so, how long can this trust last?
   [Charitable trusts, page 104]
5) A trust has been set up by the director of a large multinational company the purpose of which is to provide undergraduate scholarships for the children of the employees of the company. Is this a valid charitable trust?
   [Charitable trusts, page 104]

INTRODUCTION TO PURPOSE TRUSTS

A purpose trust has no beneficiaries; the trust is created for a purpose rather than for the benefit of identified persons. This chapter will consider the two types of purpose trusts: the non-charitable purpose trusts and the charitable trusts. Non-charitable purpose trusts are private trusts but charitable trusts are public trusts. It is important that you learn the differences between the two types of trusts as well as the requirements for both. We will consider the requirements of a non-charitable trust first, followed by the requirements of a charitable trust. Finally, we will examine the differences between the two.

NON-CHARITABLE PURPOSE TRUSTS

As a general rule, all private trusts must have objects. Why the need for beneficiaries? In a valid trust, it is the beneficiaries who benefit from the trust assets. Without beneficiaries, there is no one to enforce the terms of the trust and the trustees' actions remain unchecked. Private trusts without beneficiaries are generally void, as we can see from **Practice example 6.1**.

> **Practice example 6.1**
>
> A testator in his will left his substantial shareholding in a newspaper company on trust for the 'maintenance ... of good understanding ... between nations, the preservation of independence and integrity of newspapers, the control publication ... financing or management of any newspapers'. The executor of the will seeks your advice on the validity of this trust.
>
> These were the purposes set out in *Re Astor's ST* **[1952] Ch 534**, where the court held that as the purposes were not charitable, the trust remained a private trust without beneficiaries. The lack of beneficiaries meant that the court could neither enforce the trust nor control the trustees' execution of the trust. This trust is void.

You can see from **Practice example 6.1** that a trust for a purpose is void unless the purpose is charitable. However, there are exceptions to this rule. The courts have allowed limited categories of non-charitable purpose trusts (private purpose trusts) to exist as a concession to human sentiment. These trusts are valid if they meet the following three conditions:
- The purposes fall within a category previously upheld by the court in *Re Endacott* [1960] Ch 232.

- The trust is limited in perpetuity.
- There is someone willing to carry out the purpose – this final requirement is a question of fact. It is for the trustee or executor to indicate that they are willing to follow the testator's instructions.

Before considering the *Re Endacott* categories, here is a quick recap of the rule against perpetuities as it pertains to non-charitable purpose trusts:
- The perpetuity period is lives in being plus 21 years. This means that the purpose must vest within this period and once vested, the purpose cannot continue for longer than this period.
- The lives in being may be express or implied.
- To ensure that the purpose trust continues for as long as possible, a testator is free to specify express lives in being (see **Chapter 5**).
- The implied lives in being are normally the persons implicated in the gift but as a purpose trust has no human beneficiaries, there is no one to act as the implied life in being.
- This means that non-charitable purpose trusts have a perpetuity period of 21 years.
- The testator's right to set a perpetuity period of 125 years is inapplicable to purpose trusts: s 18 Perpetuities and Accumulations Act 2009.
- For a non-charitable purpose trust to be valid, the testator must expressly limit the trust in perpetuity. Failure to do so may not always be fatal; the trust may yet be valid with the court's assistance.

We will now consider the *Re Endacott* categories plus the requirement that such trusts must be limited in perpetuity.

The *Re Endacott* categories and the perpetuity period
There are three main categories:

Trusts for the erection or maintenance of tombs/monuments
Generally, trusts set up to pay for the upkeep of a religious building and its grounds are considered charitable. This means that if the tomb/monument is on church (or other religious) grounds, the purpose is likely to be charitable provided it meets the requirements of a charitable trust. However, a purpose to erect a tomb/monument anywhere else is considered a private purpose. Where the purpose is merely to erect tombs/monuments, it is impliedly limited in perpetuity. There is no need to include an express perpetuity clause as the court assumes that the tomb/monument would be erected within 21 years. However,

where the purpose is for the *upkeep* of a tomb/monument, which could theoretically go on for many years, the trust must be expressly limited in perpetuity.

Practice example 6.2 illustrates the different approach by the courts to the two purposes.

Practice example 6.2
A testator in their will left £10,000 on trust 'to be applied in the erection of a monument to X' and a further £8,000 'the interest of which was to be applied in keeping up the monument'. The executor of the will is willing to carry out the testator's wishes but before doing so they require advice on the validity of both dispositions.

The testator in *Musset v Bingle* [1876] WN 170 left similar dispositions in his will and the court confirmed the first purpose was valid despite the fact that it had not been limited in perpetuity. The assumption was that the monument will be built within 21 years. The second purpose was void for perpetuity.

Exam warning
Remember that if the purpose is to erect a tomb/monument, there is no need to include a perpetuity period. The court assumes that the action will be carried out within 21 years.

A purpose to *maintain* the tomb/monument is only valid if expressly limited in perpetuity.

Examples of acceptable phrases you may encounter in the SQE include: 'to last for the perpetuity period', 'for so long as the law allows' or 'for the next 21 years'.

Trusts for the saying of masses
A testator may leave a sum of money in their will for the purpose of the saying of masses in church. If the mass is open to the public, it is considered charitable, but if the mass is private it becomes a private purpose trust. Such trusts must be expressly limited in perpetuity.

Trusts for the maintenance of pets
Testators very frequently leave legacies for the maintenance of their pets. If you were wondering why such trusts are considered purpose

trusts when the pets are the beneficiaries, it is because the law requires the object of a trust to be human.

Trusts for the maintenance of pets must be expressly limited in perpetuity. However, the courts have stepped in to save trusts not limited in perpetuity by taking **judicial notice** of the fact that the pet will not live beyond the perpetuity period (see **Practice example 6.3**).

> **Key term: judicial notice**
>
> This is a rule in the law of evidence that allows a fact to be introduced without proof if the truth of that fact is so well known that it cannot be doubted.

> **Practice example 6.3**
>
> A testator left a sum of money in his will for the maintenance of his cat. There was no other clause in the will referring to the perpetuity period. Is the executor allowed to use the money for the cat?
>
> **As this is a non-charitable purpose trust, it is void unless the testator has made it clear that it will not last beyond the perpetuity period. However, the court may take judicial notice of the fact that the cat cannot live for longer than 21 years. The court saved the trust in** *Re Haines* **[1952] 11 WLUK 23 by doing just that.**

> **Exam warning**
>
> Although judicial notice may seem like a useful tool to save a purpose trust benefitting pets, be aware that it can only be used for certain animals. It may not be suitable for animals that are notoriously long-lived, like tortoises. It may depend on the age of the animal at the date of the grant.

In summary, if the purpose is a *Re Endacott* category, is limited in perpetuity and there is someone willing to carry it out, the trust is valid. However, to remind us that such trusts are anomalous and the question of their validity is at the discretion of the court, consider the decision in *Re Endacott*, where the testator had left £20,000 to a parish council for the 'purpose of providing some useful memorial to myself'. The trust failed as it was uncertain what the testator had meant by 'useful memorial' and the court felt that the sum of money was too large and therefore wasteful.

What if the purpose is not one listed in *Re Endacott*? Is the trust automatically void? Not according to the court in *Re Denley's Trust Deed* [1969] 1 Ch 373, which confirmed that a purpose trust is valid if:
- It is directly or indirectly for the benefit of an individual or individuals, provided the individuals are ascertainable, and
- the trust is expressly limited in perpetuity.

To further your understanding, have a look at **Practice example 6.4**.

> **Practice example 6.4**
>
> A testator in his will settled land on trustees to be maintained and used for the purpose of a sports ground for the employees of a named company. The will also contained a clause naming several people as express lives in being and specified that the land is to be used for that purpose 'until the expiration of the period of 21 years from the death of the last survivor' of the lives in being. The trustees are seeking advice on the validity of the settlement.
>
> **Although the trust is expressed as a purpose trust, it is valid following *Re Denley* as it benefits ascertainable individuals (the employees) and is expressly limited in perpetuity.**

Figure 6.1 provides a summary of the law on non-charitable purpose trusts.

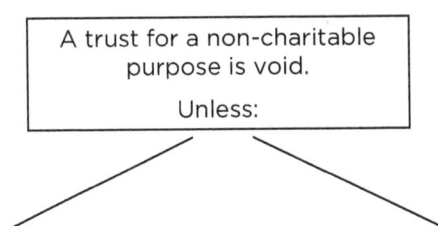

```
                    A trust for a non-charitable
                         purpose is void.
                             Unless:
                   ┌───────────┴───────────┐
The trust meets 3 requirements:     The requirements of Re Denley
                                              apply:
• The purpose is listed in Re
  Endacott (tomb/monuments,        • The trust has ascertainable
  the saying of masses, pets).       beneficiaries, and
• The trust is limited in          • The trust is limited in
  perpetuity.                        perpetuity.
• There is someone willing to
  carry out the purpose.
```

Figure 6.1: Summary of the law on non-charitable purpose trust

Having considered private purpose trusts, we will look next at charitable trusts:

CHARITABLE TRUSTS

Charitable trusts are a type of purpose trust set up for a charitable purpose. Unlike non-charitable purposes trusts, which are a type of private trust, charitable trusts have public purposes.

The law on charitable trusts is governed by the Charities Act 2011, a consolidating statute that brought together several different pieces of legislation on charity.

The Charities Act 2011, s 1 defines a 'charity' as an 'institution' established for 'charitable purposes' only. An 'institution' is defined in s 9 to include companies, unincorporated institutions and trusts. A valid charitable trust must have a charitable purpose (see s 3 below) and be for the 'public benefit'.

Below is the list of charitable purposes listed in s 3:
- The prevention or relief of poverty
- The advancement of education
- The advancement of religion, which includes a religion which involves belief in more than one god, and a religion which does not involve belief in a god
- The advancement of health or the saving of lives
- The advancement of citizenship or community development
- The advancement of the arts, culture, heritage or science
- The advancement of amateur sport
- The advancement of human rights, conflict resolution or reconciliation or the promotion of religious or racial harmony or equality and diversity
- The advancement of environmental protection or improvement
- The relief of those in need because of youth, age, ill-health, disability, financial hardship or other disadvantage
- The advancement of animal welfare
- The promotion of the efficiency of the armed forces of the Crown or of the efficiency of the police, fire and rescue services or ambulance services
- Any other purposes including recreational trusts or purposes recognised as being similar to another charitable purpose.

The requirements of charity

From the statutory provisions above, we can conclude that a trust is deemed a charity under s 1 if it meets two requirements:
- the purpose of the trust must be exclusively charitable under s 3, and
- it is for the public benefit.

We will now consider the requirements.

Charitable purpose

The meaning of charity has been considered in various cases long before the Charities Act came into force. From the high extent of case law in this area, we can deduce that the court takes a broad approach to charity. For example:
- Trusts for the prevention or relief of poverty could benefit not just the destitute but could also be used to prevent persons who are not poor from becoming poor.
- Trusts for the advancement of education include a wide range of purposes such as the provision of scholarships or school equipment, the maintenance of the educational buildings or grounds, etc.
- Trusts for the advancement of religion would similarly include purposes such as maintenance of the religious buildings and grounds. A legacy to a person by virtue of their religious office is deemed to be charitable. (eg '£10,000 to the vicar of my local church'). This is not considered a personal gift to the vicar but is charitable. The vicar must use the money for the advancement of religion.

> **Exam warning**
>
> A trust for animal welfare is charitable and not to be confused with a non-charitable trust where a testator has left money for the upkeep of their pet. The latter is a type of private trust as the benefit is targeted to named and identified animals.

The Act does not include a definition for 'public benefit'. Instead, the meaning of 'public benefit' is derived from case law.

Public benefit

This requirement has two aspects: public and benefit.
- The *public* aspect means that it must benefit either the general public or a sufficient section of the public, and the class of possible beneficiaries must not be connected by a personal nexus.

- The *benefit* aspect means that the benefit must be identifiable or tangible and any detriment that results from the purpose must not outweigh the benefit.

For an example of the *public* aspect of public benefit, consider **Practice example 6.5**.

> **Practice example 6.5**
>
> A settlement directed the trustees to apply income 'in providing for ... the education of children of employees or former employees' of a company. The employees numbered over 110,000. The trustees are seeking your advice on whether this is a valid charitable trust.
>
> **The facts came from the case of *Oppenheim v Tobacco Securities Trust* [1951] AC 297, where the House of Lords held that although the group of possible beneficiaries was numerous, the nexus between them was employment by a particular employer, and accordingly the trust did not satisfy the test for public benefit and failed as a charitable trust.**

The following explains the *benefit* aspect of public benefit.

You may be wondering how a trust for the advancement of animal welfare benefits the public. According to case law, being kind to animals benefits us by elevating our humanity and morality.

However, the advancement of animal welfare must not outweigh a more tangible public benefit. For example, in *National Anti-Vivisection Society v IRC* [1948] AC 31, it was held that the benefit of vivisection to medical science outweighs the benefit of promoting our humanity.

Another example of the requirement that the benefit be tangible can be found in the case of *Gilmour v Coats* [1949] AC 426, where the House of Lords held that a trust for the benefit of a priory where the nuns were cloistered and did not engage with the outside community is not charitable. The nuns' prayers were considered too intangible to satisfy the requirement of public benefit.

One final aspect of public benefit involves trusts with a political element. Case law dealing with this issue agrees that trusts with a political agenda do not necessarily benefit the public.

Politics and charity

As a general rule, a trust set up for a purely political purpose cannot be charitable. However, provided the main purpose of the trust is charitable, ancillary political activities that advance the main charitable purpose will not defeat the trust.

An example of an ancillary purpose is where an animal charity creates a social media campaign to educate the public on the realities of intensive animal farming without actually asking the public to lobby for a change in the law. Similarly, a settlor leaving money on trust to educate the public on the facts of climate change and on the solutions without urging the public to take political action could be considered charitable under the advancement of education.

Having looked that the requirements of charitable trust, we now consider the benefits enjoyed by such trusts.

The benefits of charitable trusts

Charitable trusts enjoy certain advantages over private trusts as explained below:
- Charitable trusts are exempt from the beneficiary principle, the objects of a charitable trust need not be certain.
- Charitable trusts are not subject to the rule against perpetuities. This means that a charitable trust can go on indefinitely.
- Charitable trusts are exempt from certain taxes.

By now, you know some of the differences between charitable trusts and non-charitable trusts. Below are a few more.

Differences between a charitable trust and a non-charitable trust

Apart from the benefits outlined above, there are further differences which set the charitable trust apart from the non-charitable purpose trust, as shown in **Table 6.1** (overleaf).

Table 6.1: Differences between a charitable trust and a non-charitable trust

Charitable trust	Non-charitable purpose trust
Charitable trustees can act by majority.	Trustees must act unanimously.
Charitable trusts are enforced by the Attorney-General.	Usually, a private trust in enforced by its beneficiaries but a non-charitable purpose trust has no beneficiaries, which is why such trusts are anomalous.
Charitable trusts can continue indefinitely.	Non-charitable purpose trusts must be expressly limited in perpetuity.
On the failure of a charitable trust, the trust assets can be saved by applying the **cy-près doctrine**.	On the failure of a non-charitable purpose trust, the trust assets revert to the settlor on resulting trust.

Key term: cy-près doctrine

The doctrine applies where the purpose of a charitable trust has failed or where there is a surplus after the charitable purpose had been carried out. The doctrine enables the court or charity commissioners to establish a scheme for the application of the trust property for other charitable purposes as near as possible to those intended by the donor.

Revision tip

The charity commission is an independent non-ministerial government department responsible for regulating charities. For more information, visit www.gov.uk and search for 'The Charity Commission'.

In summary, remember the two types of purpose trusts: the private purpose trust and the charitable trust. For the purposes of the SQE, you are required to understand the differences between them so that you are able to apply this knowledge in the assessment.

■ KEY POINT CHECKLIST

This chapter has covered the following key knowledge points. You can use these to structure your revision around, making sure to recall the key details for each point, as covered in this chapter.
- A purpose trust has no beneficiaries.
- The validity of a purpose trust depends on the purpose.

- If the purpose is private, the trust is only valid if the purpose is listed in *Re Endacott*, the trust is limited in perpetuity and there is someone willing to carry out the purpose.
- To determine whether a purpose is charitable, refer to s 3 CA 2011 for the list of charitable purposes.
- A trust is considered charitable if the purpose is exclusively charitable and benefits the public.
- Be aware of the distinction and the differences between non-charitable purpose trusts and charitable trusts.

■ KEY TERMS AND CONCEPTS
- judicial notice (**page 102**)
- cy-près doctrine (**page 108**)

■ SQE1-STYLE QUESTIONS

QUESTION 1

A testator has died leaving her whole estate on trust for the purpose of providing scholarships for the children of the employees of her company and the children of her friends. Her trustees require advice on the validity of the trust.

Which of the following provides the best advice regarding the trust?

A. The testator created a valid private purpose trust.
B. The testator created a valid charitable trust for the advancement of education.
C. The testator created a valid express private trust.
D. The testator created an invalid charitable trust due to the lack of public benefit.
E. The testator created an invalid charitable trust due to the lack of conceptual certainty in its description of the beneficiaries.

QUESTION 2

A man died and his will left '£15,000 on trust, the income of which to be used to maintain my baby tortoise, Methuselah'. His executors and trustees require advice on the validity of this legacy. They are willing to care for the tortoise if required.

Purpose trusts

Which of the following provides the best advice regarding the legacy?

A. The legacy is a valid express private trust as the object of the trust is the tortoise.
B. The legacy is a valid charitable trust for the advancement of animal welfare.
C. The legacy is void as it had not been expressly limited in perpetuity.
D. The legacy is a valid private purpose trust.
E. The legacy has a charitable purpose but fails due to the lack of public benefit.

QUESTION 3

A woman has died and her will left a legacy of £10,000 on trust 'to the bishop of my church for the saying of masses for my soul for so long as the law allows; the masses are to be attended by my immediate family only'. The bishop is happy to hold the masses. Her executors and trustees require advice on the validity of this legacy.

Which of the following best describes the legacy?

A. The legacy is a valid private purpose trust.
B. The legacy is a valid charitable trust for the advancement of religion.
C. The legacy is a valid express private trust as the beneficiaries are the testator's immediate family.
D. The legacy is void as an express private trust due to the lack of conceptual certainty.
E. The legacy is void as a private purpose trust for offending the rule against perpetuities.

QUESTION 4

A woman died and her will left a legacy of £10,000 to be held on trust 'the income from which is to be paid annually to the vicar of my local church to be used for the purposes of a summer holiday for the next 10 years'. Her executor and trustees require advice on this trust.

Which of the following best describes the legacy?

A. The legacy is valid.
B. The legacy is a valid charitable trust for the advancement of religion.

C. The legacy is void as a private purpose trust as the purpose is not an acceptable purpose.
D. The legacy is void as a private purpose trust for offending the rule against perpetuities.
E. The legacy is a void as an express private trust as there are no named beneficiaries.

QUESTION 5

A man died leaving a will containing the following: '£3,000 on trust to place a park bench in the village green in my name; and another £3,000 on trust to maintain the park bench'.
Her executor and trustees require advice on the validity of the trusts. They are happy to comply with the man's requests if required.

Which of the following provides the best advice regarding both trusts?

A. Both trusts are void.
B. Both trusts are valid as private purpose trusts.
C. Both trusts are valid as charitable trusts.
D. The trust for the placing of a park bench is void but the trust for the maintenance of the bench is valid.
E. The trust for the placing of a park bench is valid but the trust for the maintenance of the bench is void.

■ ANSWERS TO QUESTIONS

Answers to 'What do you know already?' questions at the start of the chapter

1) False. Although the general rule is that all private trusts must have beneficiaries, private purpose trusts are an exception. Such trusts are valid if they meet certain requirements.
2) False. Private purpose trusts are an exceptional category of trusts that must meet certain conditions, one of which is that the trust be limited in perpetuity. Normally, this means that the trust can only last for 21 years.
3) This is a purpose trust as there are no human beneficiaries. The purpose is private (not charitable). Generally, such trusts are void.

Purpose trusts

However, this trust may be valid as the purpose of providing for pets is an exceptional category recognised by the courts. The other two requirements are that the trust is limited in perpetuity and there is someone willing to look after the rabbits.

4) This is clearly a purpose trust. The purpose appears to be charitable as a recreational trust and so long as it benefits the public, the trust is charitable. Charitable trusts can continue indefinitely.

5) This is not a valid charitable trust. Although the advancement of education is a charitable purpose under the Charities Act 2011, the purpose must benefit the public. As all the possible beneficiaries are connected by a personal nexus (the company), they cannot be considered a section of the public.

Answers to end-of-chapter SQE1-style questions

Question 1:
The correct answer was D. Whilst the purpose may be charitable, the potential beneficiaries are all connected by a personal nexus and cannot be considered a section of the public sufficient for a charitable trust (so Option B is incorrect). Option A is wrong because the trust does not meet the necessary requirements for a valid private purpose trust. Option C is wrong because of the objects have not been described with conceptual certainty due to the word 'friends'. Option E is wrong because charitable trusts do not require beneficiaries, so the issue of conceptual certainty is not relevant.

Question 2:
The correct answer was C. Private purpose trusts benefitting pets are exceptionally valid provided they have been limited in perpetuity or if the animal in question would not live beyond the perpetuity period. Neither is applicable here (therefore Option D is wrong). Option A is wrong because the objects of a private trust must be human. The purpose is to benefit a specific animal and therefore is not charitable (therefore Options B and E are wrong).

Question 3:
The correct answer was A. The purpose may be charitable but lacked public benefit as it was only open to family members (therefore Option B is incorrect). The trust has been set up for a specific purpose, so it is clearly not an express private trust (therefore Options C and D are wrong). Option E is incorrect as the woman limited the trust for 'so long as the law allows' meaning that it does not offend the perpetuities rule.

Question 4:
The correct answer was A. Whilst the trust is a private purpose trust, it is valid as it benefits an ascertainable individual (the vicar) and the trust is limited in perpetuity (10 years). Option B is wrong as there is no 'public' recognised for it to be charitable. Option C is wrong as the purpose is acceptable within the limited exceptions recognised in law (see *Re Denley*). Option D is wrong as the trust is limited by 10 years (well within the perpetuity period) and Option E is wrong as this is not a private trust.

Question 5:
The correct answer was E. Both are private purpose trusts which must be limited in perpetuity. The first trust is impliedly limited in perpetuity as the court assumes that the bench will be put up within 21 years (therefore Option A is wrong). The second is void as it was not expressly limited in perpetuity (therefore Options B and D are wrong). Option C is wrong as this is not a charitable trust.

■ KEY CASES, RULES, STATUTES AND INSTRUMENTS

The SQE1 Assessment Specification does not require you to remember the names of the following two cases, but the principles that they lay down are important.

- *Re Endacott* [1960] Ch 232 is important as it lists the categories of non-charitable purposes which may be valid if the trust is limited in perpetuity.
- *Re Denley's Trust Deed* [1969] 1 Ch 373 is important as it provides an exception to the beneficiary principle.

7

Resulting trusts

■ MAKE SURE YOU KNOW

Previous chapters have explored trusts created from the expressed intention of a settlor. This chapter deals with trusts implied through a set of circumstances without reference to the settlor's expressed intention. We will cover the main aspects of resulting trusts that you will need to know, and *be able to apply to client scenarios, problems and situations*, for the SQE1 assessment.

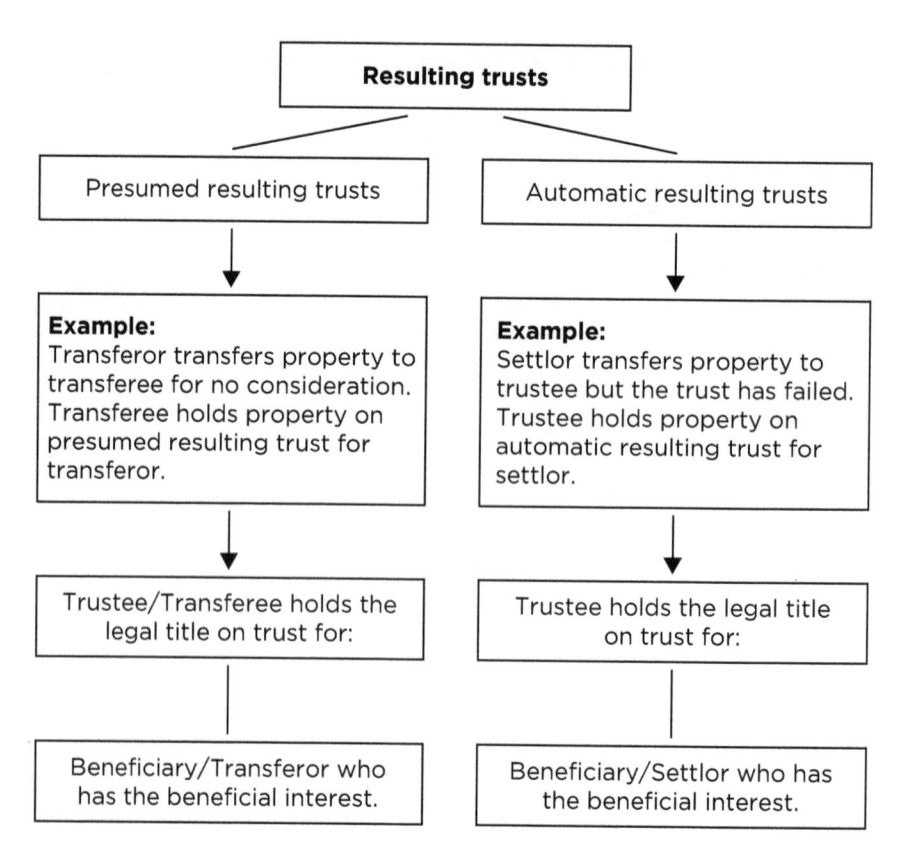

```
                    Resulting trusts
                   /               \
      Presumed resulting trusts    Automatic resulting trusts
                ↓                              ↓
      Example:                        Example:
      Transferor transfers            Settlor transfers property to
      property to transferee          trustee but the trust has failed.
      for no consideration.           Trustee holds property on
      Transferee holds property       automatic resulting trust for
      on presumed resulting           settlor.
      trust for transferor.
                ↓                              ↓
      Trustee/Transferee holds        Trustee holds the legal title
      the legal title on trust for:   on trust for:
                |                              |
      Beneficiary/Transferor who      Beneficiary/Settlor who has
      has the beneficial interest.    the beneficial interest.
```

■ SQE ASSESSMENT ADVICE

A resulting trust arises from a set of circumstances as opposed to being intentionally created by a settlor. In the SQE assessment, you may be expected to identify whether a resulting trust has arisen in a given scenario. As you work through this chapter, remember to pay particular attention in your revision to:
- The two types of resulting trusts: the presumed resulting trust and the automatic resulting trust.
- The circumstances giving rise to a presumed resulting trust and the evidence required to rebut the presumption.
- The circumstances giving rise to an automatic resulting trust.

■ WHAT DO YOU KNOW ALREADY?

Have a go at these questions before reading this chapter. If you find some difficult or cannot remember the answers, make a note to look more closely at that during your revision.

1) True or false: A resulting trust is only valid if the three certainties are present.
   [Introduction to resulting trusts, page 116]
2) True or false: The trustee of a resulting trust is not liable for breach of trust.
   [Introduction to resulting trusts, page 116]
3) A couple decided to buy a house and move in together. They each contributed half the purchase price and the title to the house was conveyed to them jointly. Does this give rise to a presumed resulting trust?
   [Presumed resulting trusts, page 116]
4) A testator in her will left her residue on trust to her niece for life, the remainder to the niece's children equally. The niece died childless a week after the testator. What happens to the residue?
   [Automatic resulting trusts, page 122]
5) A father transferred his flat in London to his son on the day of the son's graduation. Is the son holding the flat on presumed resulting trust for his father?
   [Presumed resulting trusts, page 116]

INTRODUCTION TO RESULTING TRUSTS

You will recall that an express trust requires intention on the part of the settlor to create the trust (see **Chapter 1**). The creation of an implied trust, on the other hand, is not dependent on the settlor's intention. This chapter explains how a resulting trust (which is a type of implied trust) can arise where property has been transferred by one person to another and due to an accepted set of circumstances, the transferee ends up holding the property on a resulting trust for the transferor. In other words, the beneficial interest in the property returns (or *results* back) to the transferor.

> **Exam warning**
>
> In a resulting trust, the transferee holds the property on resulting trust for the transferor. The basic structure of the trust remains the same as an expressly created trust. The transferee is the trustee holding the legal title on trust for the transferor, who has the beneficial interest. When preparing for your SQE assessment, remember that even in a resulting trust, the transferee owes a duty of care to the transferor just like any other trustee.

Resulting trusts can be divided into two categories:
- Presumed resulting trusts
- Automatic resulting trusts

We will now consider each category in more detail.

PRESUMED RESULTING TRUSTS

A presumed resulting trust arises due to the presumed intention of the transferor. When someone transfers property to another for no consideration, equity presumes that the transferor does not do so for selfless reasons. The presumption is that the transferor does not intend to lose their beneficial interest in the property so the transferee holds it on trust for the transferor.

Table 7.1 sets out the scenarios where a resulting trust is presumed.

Table 7.1: Types of presumed resulting trusts

Scenario 1: Voluntary transfer of property to another	A transfers property to B for no consideration.	B holds the property on presumed resulting trust for A.
Scenario 2: Purchase in the name of another	A pays for property but the property is in B's name.	B holds the property on presumed resulting trust for A.
	A contributes to the purchase price of property in B's name.	B holds the property for himself and A in shares proportionate to their respective contribution.

We will now consider the two scenarios outlined in the table in more detail.

Voluntary transfer of property to another

Where a person voluntarily transfers property to another for no consideration, the application of presumed resulting trust principles depends on the type of property.

Realty

In a voluntary transfer of land, s 60(3) of the Law of Property Act 1925 states that there should be no automatic presumption of resulting trust in favour of the transferor. Although this provision appears to have abolished the presumption of resulting trust for transfers of land, case law suggests otherwise. This means that the presumption of resulting trust continues to apply in a voluntary transfer of land as illustrated in **Practice example 7.1.**

> ### Practice example 7.1
> A house owner transferred her house to her lodger on the oral condition that she would be the beneficial owner. The lodger intends to sell the house and keep the money for himself. Is he entitled to do so?
>
> **There was a voluntary transfer of the house for no consideration giving rise to a presumed resulting trust. The lodger holds the house as trustee for the transferor; he is not entitled to it. These were the facts of *Hodgson v Marks* [1971] 2 All ER 682, where the lodger actually sold the house to another and the court held that the purchaser had to transfer the house back to the original owner.**

Personalty

A voluntary transfer of personalty (such as shares) to another for no consideration gives rise to a presumed resulting trust.

In summary, where there is a voluntary transfer of either realty or personalty without consideration, equity presumes that the transferor does not intend to lose their benefit in the property and there is a presumed resulting trust in their favour.

What if the transfer was made for an illegal purpose? Would equity be willing to presume a resulting trust?

Illegal purposes

According to the Supreme Court in *Patel v Mirza* [2016] UKSC 42, in deciding whether the integrity of the legal system would be harmed by taking an illegal purpose into consideration, the court should take a threefold approach by taking the following into account:
- the purpose of the transgressed prohibition and whether that purpose would be enhanced by the denial of the claim,
- any other public policy that would be affected by a denial of the claim, and
- whether denial of the claim is a proportionate response to the illegality.

In other words, the court should consider the reason for the illegal conduct, the policies that would be affected by denying the claim (of resulting trust) and whether denial of the claim is proportionate to the illegal purpose. The Supreme Court also highlighted factors that would be relevant when applying the test: the seriousness of the illegal conduct, whether it was central to the contract, the extent to which each party was culpable and whether there was knowing illegality. Take a look at **Practice example 7.2** for clarification.

Practice example 7.2

The claimant paid the defendant £620,000 under an agreement where the defendant would bet on the price of some shares (using insider information, which is an offence under s 52 of the Criminal Justice Act 1993). The scheme was not carried out as the insider information was inaccurate. The claimant sued for breach of contract and for recovery of his money. The defendant argued that as the contract was illegal, the claim would be precluded by the principle of *ex turpi causa non oritur actio* (from a dishonourable cause an action does not arise). Is there a presumed resulting trust in the claimant's favour allowing him to recover the money?

These are the facts of *Patel v Mirza* where the Supreme Court applied the threefold approach outlined above and allowed the claimant to recover the money from the defendant. An order for the return of the money would not give effect to the illegal act, it would simply restore the parties to their original position.

Purchase in the name of another

Where one person has paid for property in the name of another, there is a presumed resulting trust in favour of the real purchaser. This presumption applies to all types of property (refer back to **Table 7.1** for examples).

> **Revision tip**
> Remember that all presumptions are rebuttable by evidence to the contrary.

Rebutting the presumption of resulting trust

The presumption can be rebutted by evidence to the contrary. Acceptable evidence to the contrary includes proving that the transfer was a gift or using the counter presumption of advancement. Let's look at each in turn:

- The presumption can be rebutted by evidence that the transfer was intended as an outright gift, as shown in **Practice example 7.3**:

> **Practice example 7.3**
> An aunt, who did not have children of her own, purchased a flat in London in the name of her only nephew when she found out that he was being evicted by his landlord. She told her immediate family and the nephew that she wanted him to have a place to call home. Is there a resulting trust in favour of the aunt?
>
> The aunt purchased property in the name of her nephew which prima facie raises the presumption of resulting trust in the aunt's favour. However, the nephew has evidence (from the aunt's

declarations) that she intended it as a gift to him, thus rebutting the presumption. The flat belongs to the nephew, he does not hold on resulting trust for his aunt.

The presumption can also be rebutted by the counter presumption of advancement.

The presumption of advancement applies where a person transfers property or contributes to the purchase price of property to another, and due to their relationship it is presumed to be a gift. The presumption applies to gifts from father to child (or someone to whom he is **in loco parentis**).

Although no such presumption exists between a mother and child, in *Bennett v Bennett* [1879] 10 Ch D 474, it was accepted that it is easier to prove a gift from a mother to her child than that in the case of a stranger.

Key term: in loco parentis
In the place of a parent.

In practice, this means that when a father pays for property in the child's name, it is treated as a gift to the child. Have a look at **Practice example 7.4**.

Practice example 7.4
A father purchased several properties, which were placed in the joint names of himself and his eldest son. The father died recently and his will left the same properties to his youngest son. The youngest son is seeking possession of the properties on the basis that as the father had paid the full purchase price, the eldest son held the properties on resulting trust for the father's estate.

There is a presumption of advancement between the father and the eldest son, which displaces the presumption of resulting trust. The properties belong to the eldest son; there is no presumption of resulting trust. The properties did not form part of the father's estate and cannot pass under his will.

Exam warning
s 199 of the Equality Act 2010 abolished the presumption of advancement but this provision is not yet in force.

Admissible evidence

The basic principle to remember here is that once property has been transferred, subsequent acts and declarations by the transferor are viewed with mistrust by the courts and cannot be used as evidence to prove that the transferor never intended to make the gift. For example: if you have transferred property to another and later changed your mind, you can hopefully rely on the presumption of resulting trust to claim back the property but you cannot rely on anything you said or did after the transfer as evidence that you never intended to make the transfer.

Have a look at **Table 7.2** for clarification.

Table 7.2: What evidence is admissible?

Act and declarations of the parties	Admissibility	In practice
Before or at the time of the transfer (or immediately after the transfer provided it was part of the transaction).	Admissible as evidence for or against the transferor.	If appropriate, can be used by the transferor to prove a presumed resulting trust or by the transferee to prove presumption of advancement.
Subsequent to the transfer.	Admissible only against the transferor.	Cannot be used by the transferor to prove a presumed resulting trust but if appropriate, can be used by the transferee to prove presumption of advancement.

Revision tip

The presumption of advancement is based on the relationship of father and child and only works one way. In other words, there is no such presumption if a child transferred property to their father.

Before we consider the second type of resulting trust, **Figure 7.1** gives a summary of the principles of the presumed resulting trust.

```
┌─────────────────────────────────────┐
│ Presumed resulting trusts           │
│                                     │
│ 2 types:                            │
│                                     │
│ 1. Voluntary transfer of property   │
│ 2. Purchase in the name of another  │
└─────────────────────────────────────┘
                  ↓
┌─────────────────────────────────────┐
│ Rebutting the presumption           │
│                                     │
│ 2 types:                            │
│                                     │
│ 1. Evidence of outright gift        │
│ 2. Presumption of advancement       │
└─────────────────────────────────────┘
```

Figure 7.1: Summary of the principles of the presumed resulting trust

The second category of resulting trust is the automatic resulting trust.

AUTOMATIC RESULTING TRUSTS

Unlike the presumed resulting trust, the law on automatic resulting trust is straightforward. As you will see, an automatic resulting trust arises where the beneficial interests have not been exhausted by the express trust. **Table 7.3** outlines the circumstances which can bring about an automatic resulting trust.

Table 7.3: Types of automatic resulting trusts

	Example	Outcome
Failure of beneficiaries	Settlor created a trust 'to A for life, then to A's children absolutely'. A died childless.	The property is held by the trustees on automatic resulting trust back to the settlor (if alive) or their estate (if settlor has died).
Partially expressed trust	Settlor created a trust 'to A for life' and made no other provision on A's death.	On A's death, the trustees hold the property on automatic resulting trust for the settlor or their estate.

Table 7.3: (contined)

	Example	Outcome
Trust is void as it goes **against public policy** or for offending the perpetuity rule	Settlor created a trust 'to maintain a monument forever'.	The property is held on automatic resulting trust for the settlor or their estate.
Surplus funds	Settlor created a valid express trust that subsequently fails and there is no provision for what should be done with any surplus funds. Example: '£5,000 on trust to maintain my cat'; the cat dies leaving a surplus of £4,000.	The property is held on automatic resulting trust for the settlor or their estate.

Key term: trusts against public policy

Trusts with illegal or immoral objectives are contrary to public policy. Such trusts are void.

Example: A settlor creating a trust benefitting his children provided they never marry or a settlor dictating who their children should or should not marry, etc.

Of all the events giving rise to an automatic resulting trust set out in **Table 7.3**, the one that may be subject to ambiguity is where there are surplus funds after the terms of a trust have been carried out. The following two practice examples provide an illustration of this issue.

Practice example 7.5

The testator's will left money on trust for his two sisters who both suffered from hearing impairments. On the trustee's death, it was discovered that all the money had been spent. An appeal was launched for donations for the sisters. Several people came forward to help and a large sum was raised but there was a surplus when the sisters died. Should the money pass to the sisters' estates or go on automatic resulting trust back to the donors?

The facts are from *Re The Trusts of the Abbott Fund* [1900] 2 Ch 326, where the court held that the surplus should go on automatic resulting trusts back to the people who contributed.

Despite the decision in the case above, surplus funds do not always go on resulting trust back to the settlor. The court may find that there was no failure but rather that there was an absolute gift to the donees. This is a question of construction for the courts. Have a look at **Practice example 7.6**.

Practice example 7.6
A gift was made to a testator's widow 'for her maintenance and for the training of my daughter up to university grade and for the maintenance of my aged mother'. The mother predeceased the testator, the widow died and the daughter completed her university training. What should the trustees do with the surplus funds?
According to the court in *Re Osoba* [1979] 2 All ER 393, there was no need to impose an automatic resulting trust as the daughter was entitled to the money. The reference to purpose was merely to explain the motive to an outright gift. The testator's intention was to make an outright gift to the daughter.

Summary: automatic resulting trusts	
The trusts arises:	When there has been a failure of beneficiaries.
	If the trust was only partially expressed.
	If the trust is void.
	If there is a surplus of funds after the trust has been performed.

As you now know, an automatic resulting trust can arise from the events set out in the summary. You need to remember them as one or more of these scenarios may be assessed in the SQE.

■ KEY POINT CHECKLIST

This chapter has covered the following key knowledge points. You can use these to structure your revision around, making sure to recall the key details for each point, as covered in this chapter.
- A presumed resulting trust arises on a voluntary transfer of property.
- A presumed resulting trust arises when a person pays for property (either in full or in part) in another's name.

- A presumed resulting trust is based on the presumption that the transferor does not wish to lose their interest in the property. The presumption is rebuttable.
- Evidence to the contrary can rebut a presumed resulting trust. Contrary evidence includes the intention of the transferor to make an outright gift and the presumption of advancement.
- Be aware of the court's approach to a voluntary transfer for an illegal purpose.
- An automatic resulting trust arises where the beneficial interest of an express trust have not been exhausted. Familiarise yourself with the various scenarios giving rise to it.

■ KEY TERMS AND CONCEPTS
- in loco parentis (**page 120**)
- trusts against public policy (**page 123**)

■ SQE1-STYLE QUESTIONS

QUESTION 1

A woman paid for the full purchase price of a flat but the title was conveyed to her boyfriend. There was no evidence that the flat was a gift to him. They moved in together but separated after five years. The boyfriend sold the flat and refused to share the proceeds of sale with the woman.

Which of the following is most likely to happen to the proceeds of sale?

A. As the legal owner, the boyfriend is entitled to keep the proceeds.

B. The boyfriend and the woman are entitled to equal shares in the proceeds.

C. The woman is entitled to the proceeds.

D. The boyfriend is entitled to a larger share of the proceeds as he was the legal owner.

E. The woman is entitled to a larger share of the proceeds as she paid the purchase price.

QUESTION 2

Last year, a father bought a house that was conveyed to his son, who had just graduated from university with a degree in medicine. The father

126 Resulting trusts

and son had a falling out last month as the son decided that he wanted to be a professional gamer instead of a doctor. The father wants the house back and is seeking your advice.

Which of the following statements provides the best advice?

A. The son is not entitled to keep the house.
B. The house belongs to the father as he paid for it.
C. The son is holding the house on presumed resulting trust for the father.
D. The son is entitled to the house.
E. There is no presumption of advancement as the son is an adult.

QUESTION 3

The testator's will contains the following clause: 'My residuary estate to be held on trust for my only daughter'. The daughter predeceased the testator. The testator did not alter his will before he died.

Which of the following best describes what happens to the residue?

A. The residue is held on presumed resulting trusts for the daughter's estate.
B. The residue is held on presumed resulting trust for the testator's estate.
C. The residue is held on automatic resulting trust for the daughter's estate.
D. The residue is held on automatic resulting trust for the testator's estate.
E. The residue should pass to the daughter's next of kin.

QUESTION 4

A man paid for a house which was conveyed to the man and his girlfriend jointly. After the relationship broke down, the man claims to be entitled absolutely and that his former girlfriend has no beneficial interest in the house.

Which of the following best describes the entitlement to the house?

A. The man cannot rely on presumed resulting trust to claim the house.
B. The girlfriend holds the house on automatic resulting trust for the man.

C. The girlfriend holds the house on presumed resulting trust for the man.
D. The girlfriend provided no consideration and has no entitlement to the house.
E. The girlfriend has no entitlement to the house as she and the man were not married.

QUESTION 5

A daughter contributed 30% towards a house that was conveyed to her father, who paid the remainder of the purchase price. The father died and left the house to his son.

Which of the following best describes the entitlement to the house?

A. The daughter has no entitlement to the house.
B. The daughter has a 30% beneficial interest in the house.
C. The son is absolutely entitled to the house.
D. The son and the daughter share the house equally.
E. The daughter is absolutely entitled to the house.

■ ANSWERS TO QUESTIONS

Answers to 'What do you know already?' questions at the start of the chapter

1) False. A resulting trust is a type of implied trust. The three certainties are only required in an express trust.
2) False. Just like in an express trust, the trustee of a resulting trust is liable for breaches of trust.
3) No, this is not a scenario giving rise to a presumed resulting trust. Where the legal title is in joint names, this may give rise to a different type of trust (like a family home constructive trust – see **Chapter 8**) but not a resulting trust.
4) The express trust failed to fully dispose of the beneficial interest in the residue. The testator did not leave instructions on the distribution of the residue in the event that the niece died childless. On the death of the niece, the trustees hold the residue on automatic resulting trust for the testator's estate.

5) No. The transfer of the flat without consideration would normally give rise to a presumed resulting trust. However, the relationship of father and son gives rise to a presumption of advancement which prevails over the presumption of resulting trust. The flat is a gift to the son.

Answers to end-of-chapter SQE1-style questions

Question 1:
   The correct answer was C. The woman paid the purchase price for a flat in the name of the boyfriend. This gave rise to a presumed resulting trust in her favour (therefore Option A is incorrect). In the absence of any evidence that it was meant as a gift to the boyfriend, he holds the whole proceeds of sale on resulting trust for her (therefore Options B, D and E are wrong).

Question 2:
   The correct answer was D. There are two presumptions at play here. When the father transferred the house to his son, there is a presumption of resulting trust in the father's favour. However, the relationship of father and son gives rise to a presumption of advancement (therefore Option E is wrong), which presumes a gift from father to son. The presumption of advancement prevails over the presumption of resulting trust (therefore Option C is wrong); the house belongs to the son (therefore Options A and B are incorrect).

Question 3:
   The answer was D. There was a failure of beneficial interest as the daughter predeceased the father, meaning that the daughter was never entitled to the residue (and thus her estate is not entitled – Options C and E are therefore incorrect). This is an event giving rise to an automatic resulting trust. Now that the testator has died, and his will was unaltered, the trustees hold the residue on automatic resulting trust for the testator's estate. This is not a presumed resulting trust-type situation, so Options A and B are incorrect.

Question 4:
   The answer was A. The house was conveyed to the man and his girlfriend jointly. This means they both hold the legal title. Their entitlement is determined by another type of trust (an implied trust of land – considered in *Revise SQE Land Law*) but resulting trust is not relevant (therefore all other options are incorrect).

Question 5:
   The correct answer was B. The daughter contributed towards the purchase price of the house that was in the father's name. This gave

rise to a presumed resulting trust in her favour (therefore Option A is wrong). The father held the house on trust for himself and the daughter proportionate to their contributions (therefore Option E is wrong). This meant that the father could only leave his share of the house (70%) to the son (therefore Options C and D are incorrect).

■ KEY CASES, RULES, STATUTES AND INSTRUMENTS

Please note that there is no need to remember the name of this case but you must remember the guidelines laid down by the Supreme Court on whether to take illegal purposes into consideration:
- *Patel v Mirza* [2016] UKSC 42.

8
Family home trusts

■ MAKE SURE YOU KNOW

This topic deals with disputes in the family home and explains how claimants can claim a share (beneficial interest) in the property. You must learn to identify the different methods of establishing beneficial interests in the family home and apply the relevant method to client-based situations in your SQE assessments.

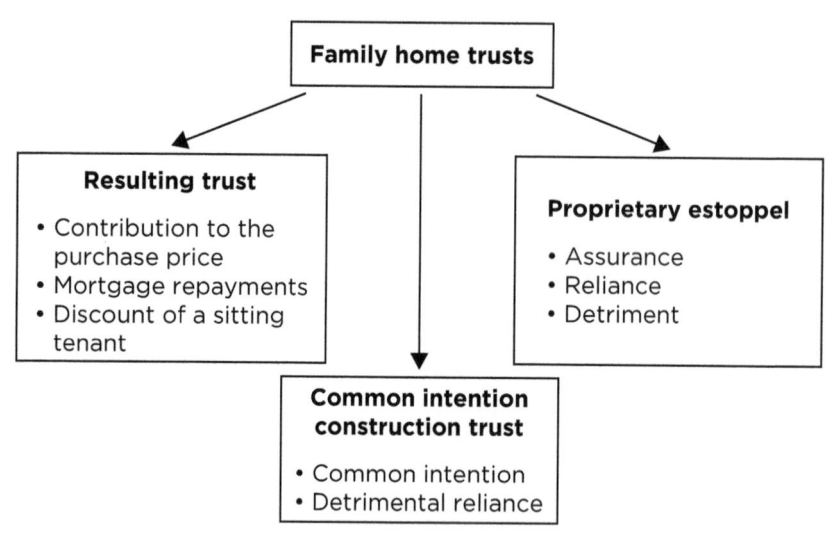

```
                    Family home trusts
                   /        |        \
```

Resulting trust
- Contribution to the purchase price
- Mortgage repayments
- Discount of a sitting tenant

Proprietary estoppel
- Assurance
- Reliance
- Detriment

Common intention construction trust
- Common intention
- Detrimental reliance

■ SQE ASSESSMENT ADVICE

As you work through this chapter, remember to pay particular attention in your revision to:
- Identifying whether a beneficial interest has arisen through a presumed resulting trust, a common intention constructive trust or proprietary estoppel.
- The evidence required to establish a share by way of a presumed resulting trust.

- The evidence required to establish a share by way of a common intention constructive trust.
- The two types of common intention constructive trusts and their differences.
- The requirements of proprietary estoppel.

■ WHAT DO YOU KNOW ALREADY?

Have a go at these questions before reading this chapter. If you find some difficult or cannot remember the answers, make a note to look more closely at that during your revision.

1) True or false: A cohabitee who is not a legal owner of the family home is automatically entitled to a share of the house.
   [Introduction to family home trusts, page 132]
2) A woman invited a man to move in with her. The woman owns the house outright. The man and the woman share their daily expenses and the man spent many hours improving the house. Can the man claim a share of the house?
   [Introduction to family home trusts, page 132]
3) True or false: To successfully claim an interest by way of proprietary estoppel, there must be written evidence of a promise by the legal owner.
   [Proprietary estoppel, page 140]
4) Does the following scenario give rise to a common intention constructive trust?
   A house was purchased as a family home for a man and a woman. The woman had left her husband and was about to divorce him. The house was purchased in the name of the man. He explained that he would not put the property in their joint names yet as it would be prejudicial towards the divorce proceedings between the woman and her husband. The man paid the deposit and mortgage instalments and the woman covered all other expenses thus allowing him to concentrate on the mortgage instalments.
   [Common intention constructive trust, page 134]
5) An elderly mother asked her son to move in with her and act as her caregiver. She promised him that she would leave the house to him in return for his care. The son had to give up his job in another city in order to comply with his mother's request. The mother died last month and her will left the house to the daughter. Who is entitled to the house?
   [Proprietary estoppel, page 140]

INTRODUCTION TO FAMILY HOME TRUSTS

In this chapter, we are dealing with disputes over the ownership of the family home; generally, but not always, between cohabiting couples. Where the couple is married or in a civil partnership, the court has statutory powers to deal with the distribution of assets in the event of divorce/dissolution. The statutory powers relating to couples who are married or in a civil partnership are inapplicable to unmarried couples, so the court must resort to trusts law to settle any claims in the family home.

> **Exam warning**
>
> Pay close attention to the couple's relationship in your SQE assessment, read the question carefully to ascertain whether the parties are married or are civil partners, or whether they are unmarried. This will have a significant bearing on how a claim in the family home is handled (see the **Introduction to family home trusts**).

Where the property (the family home) has been transferred to the parties jointly (**joint names**), they hold the property on an implied trust of land and the presumption is that they share the beneficial interest *equally* (this is covered in *Revise SQE Land Law*). This was established by the House of Lords in *Stack v Dowden* [2007] UKHL 17. This case also demonstrates that the presumption of equal shares can be rebutted by evidence to the contrary. Here, a man and a woman were joint owners of the family home. She was able to claim a 65% share of the house (instead of a half-share) by proving that she had contributed 65% of the purchase price, and that they never pooled their resources but instead kept their finances separate. According to the House of Lords, when quantifying each party's share, the court is entitled to 'undertake a survey of the whole course of dealings between the parties in assisting the court to arrive at a fair result'.

> **Key term: joint names**
>
> Where the legal title is in both parties' names. Both are the legal owners.

This chapter will focus on how a person can claim a share in the family home where the legal title is held in the **sole name** of their unmarried partner.

> **Key term: sole name**
>
> Where the legal title is in one person's name. There is only one legal owner.

Where the conveyance is in one party's name alone, the other party (the claimant) may be able to establish a share in the family home through one of the following methods:

- Resulting trust principles apply if the claimant contributed to the purchase price (fully or partly). Acceptable contributions giving rise to a presumed resulting trust include:
  - direct contributions to the purchase price.
  - making mortgage repayments.
  - the discount available to a **sitting tenant**.
- Common intention constructive trust principles apply if the claimant can show there was a common intention to share the property and they acted to their detriment in reliance of that common intention. This will be explained below.
- Proprietary estoppel principles apply if the claimant can show a promise (on the part of the legal owner) that they are to have a share in the family home which the claimant relied on to their detriment. This will be explained below.

Key term: sitting tenant
A sitting tenant is the tenant currently in possession of the leasehold and, depending on the type of tenancy, may be entitled to a discount when buying the freehold from the landlord.

We will now consider each method in turn:

RESULTING TRUST

When preparing for the SQE, remember that a claimant can establish a share in the family home by using presumed resulting trust principles. A presumed resulting trust can arise in family home claims where the claimant has contributed towards the purchase price of the family home but the title is in their partner's name. The legal owner holds the property on trust for themselves and the claimant in shares proportionate to their respective contributions.

The types of contribution giving rise to a presumed resulting trust are:
- Direct contribution towards the purchase price
- Paying the mortgage instalments
- The discount available to a sitting tenant.

For a fuller explanation on the principles of presumed resulting trust, please refer to **Chapter 7**.

Practice example 8.1 illustrates a claim by way of presumed resulting trust arising from a discount available to a sitting tenant.

> **Practice example 8.1**
>
> As a sitting tenant, a man is entitled to a 50% discount of the purchase price of a flat. The man and his girlfriend decided to buy the flat. The girlfriend paid the purchase price from her savings and the flat was conveyed into their joint names. The couple sold the flat a few years later and used the proceeds to buy a house that was conveyed into the sole name of the girlfriend. In the absence of any discussion to share the house, is the man entitled to a beneficial share of the house?
>
> Assuming the purchase price of the house was paid exclusively from the proceeds of sale of the flat, the man's entitlement to a 50% discount in the flat gave rise to a presumed resulting trust in the house proportionate to his contribution (50% share).

COMMON INTENTION CONSTRUCTIVE TRUST

The common intention constructive trust is a type of implied trust used in relation to family homes. The rationale is that if the property is meant to be a family home, even if the legal title is in one party's name alone, it is likely that the couple intended to share it. The court will try to give effect to the parties' intention by imposing a common intention constructive trust thus allowing them to award the claimant a share.

The requirements of a common intention constructive trust are:
- A **common intention** to share, and
- **Detrimental reliance**.

We will explore the requirements for each element below.

> **Key term: common intention**
>
> Where both parties are in agreement that the claimant should have a share of the family home.

> **Key term: detrimental reliance**
>
> The claimant must show that they acted to their detriment based on the agreement that they are to have a share in the family home.

It is generally accepted that there are two categories of common intention constructive trusts:
- The first is where the claimant has evidence of common intention. The common intention is evidenced by *express agreement* between the parties.
- The second is where the court must *infer* common intention from the *conduct* of the parties.

Both categories require the claimant to also prove detrimental reliance.

We will now consider the two types of common intention constructive trust in turn:

Common intention constructive trust where there is an express agreement

This category of constructive trust requires proof that the parties had discussed sharing the property at some point before purchase or very soon thereafter. The claimant must also show that they acted to their detriment in expectation of a share.

To successfully claim a beneficial interest, a claimant must prove both elements:
- Agreement to share (the common intention)
- Acts of detriment (detrimental reliance)

The following, complete with practice examples, explains the evidence required to establish both elements.

The common intention

The court requires evidence that the parties intended to share the property. Generally, an oral agreement by the parties prior to or concurrent with the purchase of the family home is acceptable. There is no need for the agreement to be in writing although a written agreement will facilitate the claim. The onus is on the claimant to prove an agreement (written or verbal) with the legal owner that they were to share the property.

> **Revision tip**
>
> Generally, an oral declaration of trust of land is unenforceable due to s 53(1)(b) Law of Property Act 1925. Such trusts must be evidenced in writing. However, the very act of detrimental reliance allows the court to treat the agreement as enforceable by imposing a

constructive trust. As you know, according s 53(2) LPA 1925, implied, resulting or constructive trusts are exempt from the usual formality requirements.

Where the parties did not discuss sharing the property but the legal owner provided an *excuse* for why the property was not conveyed to the two of them as joint legal owners, the court may treat the *excuse* as evidence of common intention, see **Practice example 8.2**.

Practice example 8.2

An unmarried couple lived together for four years and had two children together. After the relationship ended, there was a dispute concerning the ownership of the house. When the house was bought, the man told the woman that the title could not be in joint names as she was under 21. He later admitted that this was just an excuse. The woman made no financial contribution but the house was dilapidated when they moved in and she did a lot of heavy work on it. Is she entitled to a beneficial share of the house?

These are the facts of *Eves v Eves* [1975] 1 WLR 1338 where the court awarded the woman a quarter share of the house by way of a common intention constructive trust. She had been led to believe that she was to have a share in the house and the work she put into the house (to her detriment) was in reliance of the belief. The excuse given by the man was accepted as evidence of a common intention to share.

Note that the court will not accept every 'excuse' as evidence of common intention. Have a look at **Practice example 8.3**.

Practice example 8.3

The property was in the sole name of the man, who paid for it using a mixture of proceeds of sale from a previous property (belonging solely to him) and a mortgage. The woman did not contribute to the purchase. In answer to the woman's query on why the house was not in their joint names, the man gave the excuse that to do so would require two life insurance policies, thereby increasing the premiums. Is the excuse given by the man evidence of common intention?

The facts are from the case of *Curran v Collins* [2015] EWCA Civ 404, where the Court of Appeal held that no common intention could be inferred as the excuse was clearly designed to appease the woman. The court also distinguished the case of *Eve v Eves*, where the man had told the woman that the house was to be a home for both of them and their children at the time of purchase. He assured her that but for her age, it would have been in joint names. In the current case, Mr Collins made no such promise to Miss Curran. Additionally, Miss Curran was unable to show that she suffered any detriment.

Detrimental reliance

Merely proving that there was a common intention to share the family home is insufficient to establish a beneficial interest; the claimant must also prove that they acted to their detriment in reliance of the common intention. Acceptable acts of detrimental reliance include:

- Heavy work done on the house by the claimant, as in *Eves v Eves*.
- The claimant paying the deposit, purchase price or mortgage instalments.

What about acts such as looking after the home and children, paying the household expenses, etc? Let's have a look at **Practice example 8.4**.

Practice example 8.4

An unmarried couple lived together for 17 years. The woman made no direct financial contribution; she stayed home to look after the home and their two children, paid some household bills and redecorated the house. On their separation, the woman claimed a beneficial interest in the house by reason of her contributions to the household over the past 17 years.

These are the facts of *Burns v Burns* [1984] 1 All ER 244, where the Court of Appeal held that the claimant's contribution to the family by performing the domestic duties and bringing up the children were not factors that could be taken into account as acts of detrimental reliance. The claimant was also unable to prove that there was a common intention to share the house. Even if she could prove the necessary common intention, her claim would fail due to the lack of acceptable acts of detrimental reliance.

If you wondered why the court in *Eves v Eves* and *Burns v Burns* had to resort to trusts law instead of using their statutory powers derived from the various family law legislation, it was because the couples in these cases were not married. The women in both instances changed their names by deed poll.

Common intention constructive trust inferred from conduct

Where the claimant is unable to show an express agreement to share the property, the court must rely entirely on the conduct of the parties to infer the common intention. Generally, the same conduct is also used as evidence of an act in detriment.

The type of conduct from which the court can infer common intention is the claimant's contribution towards the purchase price (paying part of the purchase price, contribution to the initial deposit or the discount available to a tenant). The reasoning behind such an inference is that the parties must have intended to share the property, there being no other reason for the claimant's financial contribution. In fact, such contributions can be used to prove both elements of the common intention constructive trust as shown in **Practice example 8.5**.

> **Practice example 8.5**
>
> Mr and Mrs C got married and moved into a house which was in Mr C's sole name. The house was paid for using his savings, a mortgage and a joint wedding gift of £1,100 from Mr C's parents. The house was remortgaged to support Mr C's business but he failed to keep up with the repayments. The bank (mortgagee) sought possession of the house. Mrs C claimed a share of the house.
>
> These are the facts of *Midland Bank v Cooke* [1995] 4 All ER 562. The Court of Appeal awarded the wife a half-share based on common intention constructive trust. The initial contribution (from the wedding gift) to the purchase price is evidence from which the court can infer *common intention* as well as evidence of *detrimental reliance*. Note that the wife's share in the house was unaffected by the mortgage due to the issue of undue influence (which is dealt with in contract law).

Table 8.1 provides a summary of the requirements for the two types of common intention constructive trusts.

Table 8.1: Types of common intention constructive trusts

Requirements	Common intention constructive trust based on an agreement to share	Common intention constructive trust based on inferred conduct
Common intention	• An agreement (verbal/written) to share. • An *excuse* by the legal owner.	• Initial payment towards the purchase price by the claimant.
Acts of detrimental reliance by the claimant	• Initial payment towards the purchase price. • Paying mortgage instalments. • Heavy work done on the house.	• The same initial payment to the purchase price. • Paying mortgage instalments. • Heavy work done on the house.

Exam warning

As we can see from the summary above, the acceptable acts of detriment require some financial contribution towards the purchase price or some improvement to the property that increases its value. However, it has been suggested in obiter statements from various case law that *indirect* financial contributions may suffice where without the claimant's contributions towards the household expenses, the legal owner could not have made the mortgage repayments. It is important to remember this for the purposes of the SQE as you may encounter a scenario where the claimant may not have contributed towards the purchase price but made significant contribution to the household expenses thus enabling the legal owner to pay the mortgage instalments.

The relationship between resulting trust and common intention constructive trust

The court has clarified that once the claimant can prove an intention to share property, resulting trust principles are displaced. This means that the court is not bound to award beneficial interests proportionate to the claimant's contribution but is free to award a larger beneficial interest.

The final method of establishing a share in the family home is through proprietary estoppel.

PROPRIETARY ESTOPPEL

Proprietary estoppel is based on the equitable doctrine that it would be unconscionable for a landowner to go back on their promise if another has relied on that promise to their detriment.

Where a claimant can prove that the legal owner promised them a share of the family home and they relied on this promise and suffered detriment as a result, they will have succeeded in a claim of proprietary estoppel.

The important thing to remember in an estoppel claim is that the promise must come first. Mere detriment without an initial promise of a share by the legal owner is insufficient. The claimant must prove that any detriment they suffered was due to their reliance on the promise.

For an illustration of the doctrine in practice, have a look at **Practice example 8.6**.

Practice example 8.6

A man bought a house in his sole name and lived there with a woman (the claimant). He assured her that the house and its contents were hers. He later moved out but she stayed and spent money repairing and improving the house (plumbing, roof repairs, redecorations). The man is now seeking an order to evict her. Is the claimant entitled to the house?

The facts are from the case of *Pascoe v Turner* [1979] 1 WLR 431, where the Court of Appeal held that the requirements of proprietary estoppel were met and transferred the house to the woman.

Exam warning

When preparing for the SQE, remember that the remedy awarded by the court in a successful claim of proprietary estoppel is based on the promise made by the legal owner. In *Pascoe v Turner* above, the man promised the house and its contents to the woman. If the assurance had been a share in the house, the award would have reflected that.

Summary: proprietary estoppel

Promise/Assurance	The legal owner promised the claimant a share of the family home.
Reliance	The claimant relied on the promise.
Detriment	The claimant acted to their detriment on the strength of the promise.

Exam warning

The requirements of common intention constructive trust and proprietary estoppel may seem very similar so you must ensure that you can tell the difference between them as the SQE assessment may require you to decide whether a family home claim is based on one or the other. The best way to distinguish between the two is to consider whether the legal owner made a promise (estoppel) or whether there was a verbal discussion to share (constructive trust). Another distinguishing factor is the timing of the discussions/promise. Generally, the evidence supporting a claim for constructive trust stems from discussions held before or at the time of purchase. The promise in estoppel claims could be made at any time, so long as it precedes the acts of detriment.

■ KEY POINT CHECKLIST

This chapter has covered the following key knowledge points. You can use these to structure your revision around, making sure to recall the key details for each point, as covered in this chapter.

- The presumed resulting trust is normally the starting point in a claim for a share of the family home.
- The common intention constructive trust can be used to establish a share of the family home.
- The common intention constructive trust may arise in one of two ways.
- The first category of common intention constructive trust requires evidence of an agreement to share coupled with detrimental acts by the claimant.
- Where there was no agreement to share, the court may rely on the conduct of the parties to infer the trust.
- If the evidence supports a claim by way of common intention constructive trust, resulting trust principles are displaced and the

claimant is not restricted to a proportionate share of the property but may be awarded up to a half-share.
- Proprietary estoppel can be used to support a claim in a family home; the claimant must show a promise made by the legal owner which the claimant relied on to their detriment.

■ KEY TERMS AND CONCEPTS

- joint names (**page 132**)
- sole name (**page 132**)
- sitting tenant (**page 133**)
- common intention (**page 134**)
- detrimental reliance (**page 134**)

■ SQE1-STYLE QUESTIONS

QUESTION 1

A man and a woman started dating. The woman bought a house and the man moved in with her. The house was paid for using her savings plus a mortgage. The man made no contribution to either the purchase price or the mortgage instalments. There were no discussions about sharing the house. The man was unemployed and received 'pocket money' from the woman. The woman later received an improvement grant from the council and she agreed with the man that he should carry out the work covered by the grant in return for her keeping him. The man carried out work worth more than £15,000 and claimed an interest in the house.

Which of the following best describes the man's entitlement to the house?

A. The man can claim a proportionate share in the house by way of presumed resulting trust.

B. The man can claim a 50% share in the house by way of common intention constructive trust.

C. The man can claim a share in the house by way of proprietary estoppel.

D. The man cannot claim a share in the house as the woman made him no promises.

E. The man cannot claim a share in the house as he was already living rent free and receiving pocket money.

QUESTION 2

A married couple bought a house with the help of a mortgage. The couple had four children in quick succession. The husband died before the mortgage was paid off and his widow had to work several jobs to keep the family fed and make the mortgage repayments. Each child left school as soon as they could to find work in order to contribute towards the household expenses and mortgage instalments. The widow repeatedly said that the house belonged to each and every one of the children. The widow died recently and her will left the house to a lodger she had recently taken in to earn extra money.

Which of the following best describes the entitlement to the house?

A. The lodger and the children will share the house equally.
B. The children can claim the house using proprietary estoppel.
C. The lodger and the children share the house, the proportions to be calculated based on the principles of presumed resulting trust.
D. The children are entitled to equal shares of the house by way of common intention constructive trust.
E. The house belongs to the lodger.

QUESTION 3

An unmarried couple bought a house which was conveyed to the man's sole name. The woman paid the deposit, which was 20% of the purchase price. The man paid the rest of the purchase price using his savings plus a mortgage. The mortgage instalments were paid by the man. The couple separated after 10 years. The woman is claiming an equal share of the house.

Which of the following provides the best advice regarding the woman's claim?

A. The woman can claim a larger share in the house by way of common intention constructive trust.
B. The woman can claim a share in the house by way of proprietary estoppel.
C. The woman can only claim a 20% share in the house by way of presumed resulting trust.
D. The woman cannot claim a share in the house as there was no written evidence of a trust.

E. The woman cannot claim a share in the house as there was no oral agreement to share.

QUESTION 4

An unmarried couple decided to move in together. The pair bought the man's flat at a 25% discount as he was a sitting tenant. The woman paid the full purchase price. The flat was conveyed into their joint names. Two years later, they sold the flat and used the proceeds to buy a small cottage which was conveyed to the woman as sole legal owner. The couple have since separated, and the man is claiming a half share of the cottage.

Which of the following best reflects the man's entitlement to the cottage?

A. The man has no claim to the cottage as he paid no money towards the cottage.

B. The man has no claim to the cottage as there was no written agreement to share the cottage.

C. The man has no claim to the cottage as there was no common intention to share.

D. The man has a claim to the cottage by relying on proprietary estoppel.

E. The man has a claim to the cottage by way of a common intention constructive trust.

QUESTION 5

A mother decided to buy a flat using her savings so that she could rent it out. This was to be her sole income after her retirement. The mother was short of 10% of the purchase price and her daughter made up the deficit. The flat was conveyed to the mother as the sole owner and duly rented out. The daughter helped her mother with some of the tenancy paperwork. The mother and daughter have now fallen out and the daughter is claiming a half share in the flat.

Which of the following best describes the daughter's entitlement to the flat?

A. The daughter has a claim to the flat by way of common intention constructive trust.

B. The daughter has a claim to the flat by way of proprietary estoppel.
C. The daughter has a claim to the flat by way of resulting trust.
D. The daughter has no claim to the flat as it is not a family home.
E. The daughter has no claim to the flat as there was no agreement to share.

■ ANSWERS TO QUESTIONS

Answers to 'What do you know already?' questions at the start of the chapter

1) False. A cohabitee who is a non-legal owner may be able to establish a share in the home if they can show a presumed resulting trust, a common intention constructive trust or proprietary estoppel in their favour. They have no automatic right to a share of the house.
2) The man is unlikely to be awarded a share in the house unless he can prove that there is a common intention constructive trust or proprietary estoppel in his favour. It is unlikely that he can prove a presumed resulting trust as sharing the household expenses and carrying out home improvements are not acceptable contributions giving rise to a presumed resulting trust.
3) False. Proprietary estoppel requires the claimant to prove an assurance or promise by the legal owner which the claimant relied on and suffered a detriment as a result. There is no requirement that the promise should be in writing.
4) To succeed in a claim of common intention constructive trust, the woman must prove there was a common intention to share the family home and that she acted to her detriment on the faith of the common intention. The excuse given by the man may be accepted as evidence of common intention. Her contribution to the household expenses could be an act of detrimental reliance if she can prove that he would not have been able to make the mortgage repayments without her contribution.
5) The son can claim the house using proprietary estoppel. The mother made a promise to him (the house) which he relied upon to his detriment (giving up his job and caring for his mother). On successfully proving proprietary estoppel, the remedy is that which the legal owner promised. As the mother promised him the house, the court will award the house to the son.

Answers to end-of-chapter SQE1-style questions

Question 1:
The correct answer was D. There was no resulting trust in the man's favour as he did not contribute towards the purchase price or the mortgage instalments (therefore Option A is wrong). Option B is incorrect as there was no evidence of common intention to share giving rise to a common intention constructive trust. There was no promise giving rise to a claim of proprietary estoppel (therefore Option C is wrong). Option E is incorrect as his living arrangements are not relevant to his entitlement.

Question 2:
The correct answer was B. The assurance made by the mother was relied upon by the children who suffered detriment as a result (their contribution to the household expenses and the mortgage repayments). The remedy is based on the promise: equal shares in the house. Option D is wrong as the children cannot rely on common intention constructive trust as they cannot show common intention that they were to have a share when the house was bought (they were not yet born). The lodger has no entitlement to the house (therefore Options A, C and E are incorrect).

Question 3:
The correct answer was A. The fact that the woman paid the deposit is evidence from which the court could infer both common intention as well as the act of detrimental reliance. The common intention is inferred so there is no need to provide evidence of an agreement (so Option E is incorrect). Option D is incorrect as the trust is implied so there is no need for written evidence. Option B is wrong as the elements of proprietary estoppel are not present. Although the woman did contribute 20% of the purchase price giving rise to a presumed resulting trust, this trust is displaced once the court finds that there is a common intention to share so Option C is wrong.

Question 4:
The correct answer was E. The cottage was paid for from the proceeds of the sale of the flat, in which the man had a 25% beneficial interest (presumed resulting trust) by way of his discount. This means he contributed 25% of the purchase price of the cottage from which the court could infer both common intention and detrimental reliance and thus award him a share (up to 50%) of the property (so Options A–C are wrong). Option D is wrong because the requirements of proprietary estoppel are not present.

Question 5:
The correct answer was C. The daughter's 10% contribution gives her a proportionate share of the beneficial interest by way of a presumed resulting trust in the absence of any contrary intention (so Options D and E are incorrect). The court cannot infer a common intention constructive trust as the flat was not intended as a family home but was purchased for investment purposes (so Option A is wrong). Option B is wrong as the elements of proprietary estoppel are not present.

■ KEY CASES, RULES, STATUTES AND INSTRUMENTS

The cases cited in this chapter are merely for illustrative purposes. They demonstrate the approach taken by the courts in navigating disputes in the family home between unmarried parties. There is no need for you to remember the names of these cases but you may use them as a reference for further reading.

9

Liability of strangers and the fiduciary relationship

■ MAKE SURE YOU KNOW

This chapter covers two inter-related topics: the liability of strangers as constructive trustees and the possible imposition of a constructive trust where there is a fiduciary relationship. Do not worry if you are unfamiliar with some of the terms, they are explained later on in this chapter. In the SQE assessment, you may encounter questions on whether a stranger to the trust is liable as a constructive trustee, and you may be required to confirm whether a party is a fiduciary and is therefore subject to the restrictions and duties placed upon all fiduciaries.

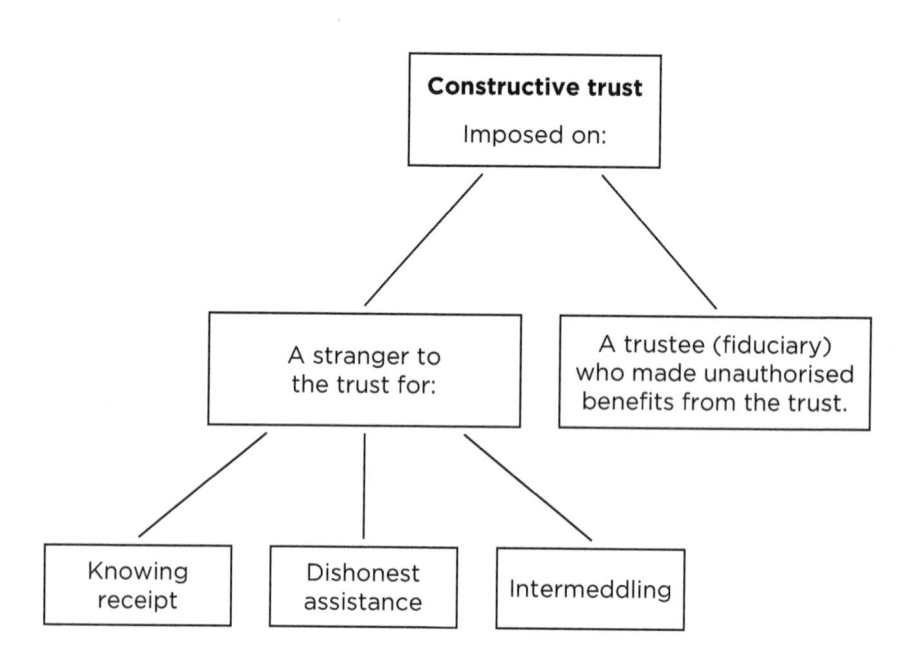

```
                    Constructive trust
                       Imposed on:
                    /              \
                   /                \
        A stranger to          A trustee (fiduciary)
        the trust for:         who made unauthorised
                               benefits from the trust.
         /     |    \
        /      |     \
   Knowing  Dishonest  Intermeddling
   receipt  assistance
```

■ SQE ASSESSMENT ADVICE

As you work through this chapter, remember to pay particular attention in your revision to:
- The actions by a stranger that could result in their liability as a constructive trustee.
- The requirements for establishing recipient liability.
- The requirements for establishing accessory liability.
- The fiduciary relationship.
- The duties and obligations of a fiduciary.

■ WHAT DO YOU KNOW ALREADY?

Have a go at these questions before reading this chapter. If you find some difficult or cannot remember the answers, make a note to look more closely at that during your revision.

1) True or false: Anyone who receives trust property from a trustee in breach of trust becomes a constructive trustee.
   [The liability of strangers, page 150]

2) A trustee sold trust property to May, who paid market value and did not know that it was trust property. The trustee used the purchase money for his own purposes. Does May hold the property on constructive trust for the beneficiaries?
   [The liability of strangers, page 150]

3) True or false: To prove accessory liability, the claimant must show that the stranger assisted in a breach of trust and that the trustee had acted dishonestly in the breach.
   [The liability of strangers, page 150]

4) Jules and Kerry are trustees. They each took £5,000 from the trust fund as payment for work they carried out on behalf of the trust. Jules and Kerry are not professional trustees. Are they allowed to keep the money?
   [The fiduciary relationship, page 156]

5) Ty and Tate are trustees. They decided to sell a cottage belonging to the trust and invest the money in shares. Ty bought the cottage at an open auction. Is the transaction valid?
   [The fiduciary relationship, page 156]

INTRODUCTION TO THE LIABILITY OF STRANGERS AND THE FIDUCIARY RELATIONSHIP

This chapter will focus on two separate but inter-connected issues: the liability of **strangers** and the **fiduciary** relationship. The first part of the chapter explains the liability of strangers as constructive trustees. The second part of the chapter deals with the obligations and duties of a fiduciary and the imposition of a constructive trust on any profits made by the fiduciary in breach of their duties.

In the SQE assessment, you may be called upon to decide on a non-trustee's liability as a constructive trustee, or to decide whether a trustee has breached their fiduciary duty. Familiarise yourself with the types of constructive trust and the restrictions placed on fiduciaries.

Key term: stranger
A stranger includes everyone who does not have a duty to the trust apart from the constructive trust. Once a person becomes a constructive trustee, the beneficiaries can take action against this person as if they had been appointed a trustee. The remedies available against the constructive trustee include recovering the property, tracing or a personal claim.

Key term: fiduciary
A fiduciary is someone who has undertaken to act for or on behalf of another in a particular matter in circumstances which give rise to a relationship of trust and confidence.

THE LIABILITY OF STRANGERS

Generally, if a beneficiary has suffered loss due to the actions of a trustee or fiduciary, the beneficiary has a personal claim against the trustee or fiduciary. However, if the trustee or fiduciary is insolvent or has no money (is impecunious), the beneficiary may have a personal claim against a stranger (non-trustee) who has the means to pay. In certain circumstances, a stranger to the trust can become liable as if they were a trustee if equity imposes a **constructive trust** on them.

Key term: constructive trust
A constructive trust is a trust imposed by equity to satisfy the demands of justice and good conscience without reference to any express or presumed intention of the parties.

Exam warning

Note that this type of constructive trust is different from the common intention constructive trust covered in the previous chapter. The type covered in the previous chapter only applies to family home disputes.

In understanding the imposition of the constructive trust, remember the following principles:
- It arises by operation of law independent of any express or implied intention of the parties.
- It is imposed by equity when justice and good conscience require the person in possession of property to hold it for another.
- It is exempt from the formality requirements of s 53(1) Law of Property Act 1925: s 53(2).
- It is a residual category used where the court feels a trust should be imposed when no other is appropriate.
- A constructive trust is not really a trust at all, but merely an equitable remedy to enable the claimant to obtain **restitution**.
- A constructive trustee, generally, has the single duty of transferring the property to the entitled beneficiary by means of:
  - tracing and recovering the property if the constructive trustee still has possession, or, tracing its equivalent if the property has been disposed of and there is something to show for it (see **Chapter 12**).
  - enabling a personal action to be brought against the constructive trustee even if they do not have the property.

Key term: restitution

Restitution is the remedy based upon the principle of unjust enrichment, which is an equitable principle that no person should be allowed to profit at another's expense without making restitution for the reasonable value of the property, services or other benefits that have been unfairly received.

Equity imposes a constructive trust on a stranger once one of the following has been established:
- Recipient liability
- Accessory liability
- Intermeddling

We will now examine each of these in turn.

Establishing recipient liability

Recipient liability, also known as *knowing receipt*, can be established in one of three ways:

Type 1 recipient liability

Where a stranger received property knowing it to be in breach of trust or in breach of a fiduciary duty, they are liable as a constructive trustee for knowing receipt. The liability of knowing receipt requires proof that the stranger had *knowledge* of the breach of trust or the breach of fiduciary duty. The various case law on this issue agree that the following types of knowledge are sufficient to impose recipient liability:
- **Actual knowledge.**
- **Constructive knowledge.**

> **Key term: actual knowledge**
>
> Actual knowledge, or actual notice, is where the stranger knew about the breach of trust.

> **Key term: constructive knowledge**
>
> Constructive knowledge, or constructive notice, is where the stranger had no actual knowledge of the breach but wilfully shut their eyes to the obvious, or wilfully and recklessly failed to make enquiries that an honest and reasonable person would have made.

Type 2 recipient liability

Where a stranger receives trust property without notice of the trust but afterwards becomes aware of the trust and deals with it in a manner inconsistent with the trust. By doing so, the stranger becomes a constructive trustee. **Practice example 9.1** provides an illustration.

> **Practice example 9.1**
>
> A trustee withdrew money from the trust account and gave the money to her friend, who is an investment banker, to invest. The trustee intended to make a personal profit from the investments and after a year, to pay the original sum back into the trust account. The friend later discovered that the money belongs to the trust but continued to pay the investment dividends to the trustee's personal account. The trustee was later declared a bankrupt. Do the beneficiaries have a claim against the investment banker?

> The investment banker is liable as a constructive trustee, with type 2 recipient liability. Once the truth about the origin of the money came to light, the investment banker should have paid the profits to the beneficiaries of the trust.

Type 3 recipient liability
Where a stranger receives trust property knowing it to be such but without breach of trust and subsequently deals with it in a manner inconsistent with the trust. By doing so, the stranger becomes a constructive trustee.

Establishing accessory liability

A stranger who never received trust property may yet be liable to the trust if they have *dishonestly assisted* the trustee in a breach of trust. Traditionally, a stranger with accessory liability is described as a constructive trustee but recent case law takes the view that it gave rise to a personal liability rather than a constructive trust. The stranger becomes liable to make good the loss to the trust. The claim against the stranger is a personal one, not proprietary as the stranger was never in receipt of trust property. In other words, tracing is not available against the stranger.

The requirements for dishonest assistance are:
- The existence of a trust. This includes not just a formal trust but also a trust implied by virtue of a fiduciary relationship.
- There was a breach of trust or a breach of fiduciary duty.
- The assistance by a stranger in that breach.
- The stranger's dishonesty in providing that assistance.

The test for dishonesty is an objective one, as determined by the court. This was confirmed by the Privy Council in *Barlow Clowes International v Eurotrust Intl* [2006] 1 All ER 333: '... acting dishonestly ... means simply not acting as an honest person would in the circumstances'.

An example of accessory liability can be found in **Practice example 9.2**.

Practice example 9.2

Joan, a trustee, took large sums of trust money for her own purposes. Her accountant, Amin, who manages her accounts for her, made sure that the money was transferred to offshore accounts out

154   Liability of strangers and the fiduciary relationship

of reach of the beneficiaries. He knew that the money was taken in breach of trust. Joan pays Amin very well for his services. What is Amin's liability?

Amin was aware of the breach of trust and yet helped her hide the money. There was clear dishonesty on his part. He is liable for dishonest assistance and is personally liable to the beneficiaries.

Intermeddling

A stranger who is not a trustee but takes it upon themself to intermeddle (to interfere) with trust matters or to act as a trustee will be considered a constructive trustee if their actions result in a loss to the trust. By their actions, the stranger is treated as if they had been appointed as a trustee and become personally liable to the trust. This person is known as a **trustee de son tort**.

Key term: trustee de son tort

A trustee in his own wrong. A person whose actions have caused loss to the trust thereby resulting in them having the liability of a trustee.

An example of a trustee de son tort is provided in **Practice example 9.3**.

Practice example 9.3

Anne, a trustee, was asked by the beneficiaries of the trust to have an antique belonging to the trust valued, with a view to selling it. Anne took the antique home, intending to show it to an expert the following day. Anne's brother Henry, who fancied himself an antiques expert, decided to help his sister and sold it for £5,000. The antique was actually worth double that. Is Henry liable to the trust?

Henry is liable as a constructive trustee as he intermeddled with trust matters without authority and his actions caused loss to the trust. He is personally liable for the loss.

Exam warning

Although the mechanism of constructive trust is traditionally imposed on a stranger with recipient liability, accessory liability or for intermeddling, the usual remedies of a constructive trust are not always available. Generally, the claimant has a personal claim against the stranger in all cases but a proprietary claim (tracing) is only available against the stranger if they have trust property (or its equivalent) in their possession. In the SQE, do not assume that tracing is automatically available against all constructive trustees. Check to see whether the defendant was ever in receipt of trust property.

Table 9.1 summarises each type of stranger liability and their requirements.

Table 9.1: Summary of stranger liability and their requirements

Summary	Requirement	Result	Remedies against the stranger
Recipient liability (knowing receipt)	Stranger receives trust property knowing it to be in breach of trust.	Stranger becomes liable as a constructive trustee.	• Personal claim. • Recovery of property. • Tracing.
Accessory liability (dishonest assistance)	Stranger dishonestly assisted the trustee in a breach of trust.		• Personal claim. NB: the stranger is not in possession of trust property so there is no property to recover or trace.
Intermeddling	Stranger took on the role of a trustee without authority thereby causing loss to the trust.		• Personal claim. • Recovery of property if in their possession. • Tracing if they no longer have the property but have its equivalent.

On a final note, remember that not everyone who receives or deals with the trust property is a constructive trustee. Below is a list of strangers and an examination of their liability (or not) to the trust.

Types of strangers
- Bona fide purchaser for value of the legal estate without notice
  - Such a person cannot be made a constructive trustee; they take the property free from all equitable rights. If the trustee has sold

trust property in breach of trust, the beneficiaries' remedy will be against the trustees for any loss on the proceeds of sale of the trust property.
- Innocent volunteer
  - Such a person has received the trust property without consideration and in good faith (not knowing that it was trust property). They cannot be made a constructive trustee but may have the remedy of tracing used against them. This means they must return the property (or its equivalent) to the trust (see **Chapter 12**).
- Purchasers and volunteers taking with notice of the breach of trust
  - Such persons are treated as constructive trustees for knowing receipt of the trust property. The beneficiaries have a personal action against them. Tracing is also available against them.

Having examined the situations where a constructive trust can be imposed on a stranger, we will now look at the situations where a constructive trust may be imposed on a fiduciary.

THE FIDUCIARY RELATIONSHIP

A fiduciary is someone who has undertaken to act for or on behalf of another in a particular matter in circumstances which give rise to a relationship of trust and confidence.

A trustee is a fiduciary and as such has an overriding duty to avoid conflict between their personal interests and their duty to the trust. As such, a trustee is not allowed to profit from their position through:
- Making unauthorised profits
- Retaining directors' fees
- Remuneration as a trustee
- The purchase of trust property
- Competition with the trust business.

You may encounter a question in the SQE on the trustee's liability for breaching their fiduciary duty. It is important that you understand the different aspects of the trustee's fiduciary duty towards the trust.

We will now consider each in turn.

Unauthorised profits

As noted above, a trustee must not profit from their role as a trustee: the trustee holds all unauthorised profits on constructive trust for the beneficiary. The remedy against the trustee is called an **account of profits**. Consider **Practice example 9.4**.

Practice example 9.4

The trustee held a lease on trust for a minor beneficiary. Before the lease expired, the trustee applied for its renewal on behalf of the trust. The landlord refused to grant a renewal on behalf of the trust but offered the lease to the trustee personally. The trustee renewed the lease for himself. Is he allowed to keep the lease for his own benefit?

The facts are from the case of *Keech v Sandford* [1726] 25 ER 223, where the court held that the trustee must hold the lease for the benefit of the trust.

Key term: account of profits

An equitable remedy commonly used in cases of breach of fiduciary duty that enables the claimant to recover (from the defendant) the profits taken as a result of the breach.

Even though *Keech v Sandford* deals specifically with the trustee's liability, remember that the rule on unauthorised profits applies to all fiduciaries, not just to trustees. However, if there is no fiduciary relationship, there is no need to account for profits. Have a look at **Practice example 9.5**.

Practice example 9.5

A testator ran a business from leasehold premises. On his death, his widow (the administrator of his estate) and their children continued to run the business from the premises. The widow applied to renew the lease on behalf of the estate but the landlord instead granted the lease to one of the adult children (a son) personally. The widow claimed that the son held the lease on behalf of the estate and that he must account for any rent and profits received.

The facts are from the case of *Re Biss* [1903] 2 Ch 40, where the Court of Appeal held that the son may keep the lease for his own benefit as he was not in a fiduciary position.

> **Exam warning**
>
> The outcome of *Re Biss* would have been different if the son was a personal representative (executor or administrator) of his father's estate. A personal representative is a fiduciary and must account for any incidental profits. Be aware of this in the SQE assessment. Before concluding that a constructive trust should be imposed, you must first ensure that the defendant is a fiduciary.

Directors' fees

The rule that a fiduciary must not profit from a trust extends to directors' fees. A trust holding a substantial shareholding in a company may result in the trustee being appointed as a director of the same company. The trustee must account for any director's fees they received because even if the remuneration is for services as the director of the company, the *opportunity* to obtain that remuneration came from their position as the trustee. This means that the trustee holds the fees on constructive trust for the beneficiaries.

A trustee may retain the fees if they can prove one of the following:
- The directorship predated the trusteeship.
- They were appointed as director independently of the votes of the trust.
- The trust instrument expressly authorised the trustee to retain the fees.

Remuneration of trustees

The general rule that trustees must not profit from the trust extends to remuneration. Professional trustees have a statutory right to remuneration under Part V of the Trustee Act 2000. However, non-professional trustees (or lay trustees) are still subject to the general no-profit rule and are not automatically entitled to be paid for their services. Such trustees are only allowed remuneration if:
- Authorised by the trust instrument: There must be an express clause in the trust instrument authorising remuneration.
- Authorised by the courts: The courts have an inherent jurisdiction to grant or increase remuneration if it is in the interests of the beneficiaries.
- Authorised by the beneficiaries: The beneficiaries must be sui juris in order to be able to authorise remuneration for the trustees.

> **Revision tip**
>
> You must distinguish between remuneration and reimbursement. According to s 31 of the Trustee Act 2000, trustees are entitled to be reimbursed from the trust fund for their out-of-pocket expenses.

Purchase of trust property by trustees

When considering the purchase of trust property by trustees there are two rules to consider: the self-dealing rule and the fair-dealing rule. Each will be explained in turn.

Where a trustee purchases trust property, this is called self-dealing. There is a clear conflict with the trustee acting as both vendor and purchaser. Consequently, such a transaction is voidable at the instance of any interested beneficiary no matter how fair, open or honest the transaction. This means that the beneficiary is entitled to set aside the transaction and the trustee must return the property. Of course, the beneficiary is also free to approve the transaction if they have no objection to it.

The trustee cannot evade the self-dealing rule by first retiring before making the purchase. Nor can they evade the rule by using a nominee to make the purchase. Have a look at the **Practice example 9.6** for an illustration of the consequences of using nominee.

> **Practice example 9.6**
>
> Tara and Trent are trustees and they decided to sell an antique clock belonging to the trust and invest the proceeds of sale in shares. Tara asked her sister Dina to buy the clock for her. Dina paid a fair price for the item. Is Tara allowed to keep the clock?
>
> **Dina was acting as Tara's nominee and the transaction is caught by the self-dealing rule. The beneficiaries can choose to approve the transaction or to set it aside. If approved, Tara can keep the clock. If not, she must return the clock (she gets her money back).**

The self-dealing rule does not apply to the following:
- If authorised by the trust instrument.
- If all the beneficiaries, being sui juris, authorised it.
- If the purchase is pursuant to an option or contract prior to the trusteeship.

160 Liability of strangers and the fiduciary relationship

- If the court uses its discretion to approve the purchase in advance or retrospectively.

Self-dealing must be distinguished from fair-dealing. The fair-dealing rule applies where the trustee purchases a beneficiary's beneficial interest (the seller is the beneficiary and the purchaser is the trustee). According to this rule, the transaction is only voidable if the trustee acted unfairly. The transaction stands if the trustee can show that:
- They had not taken advantage of their position.
- They made full disclosure to the beneficiary.
- The transaction was fair and honest.

Figure 9.1 provides a summary of the self-dealing and fair-dealing rules.

```
                    Trustee purchases trust property
                         /                    \
         Purchase from the trust         Purchase from the beneficiary
              Self-dealing                      Fair-dealing
                    |                                |
         Can the beneficiary set aside   Can the beneficiary set aside
              the transaction?                the transaction?
                    |                                |
                   YES                   The trustee did not take
         No need to consider if the      advantage of their position.
         transaction was fair, open      The trustee made full
              and honest.                disclosure to the beneficiary.
                                         The transaction was fair and
                                         honest.
                                              /              \
                                           TRUE              FALSE
                                     The transaction    The transaction
                                        stands.         can be set aside.
```

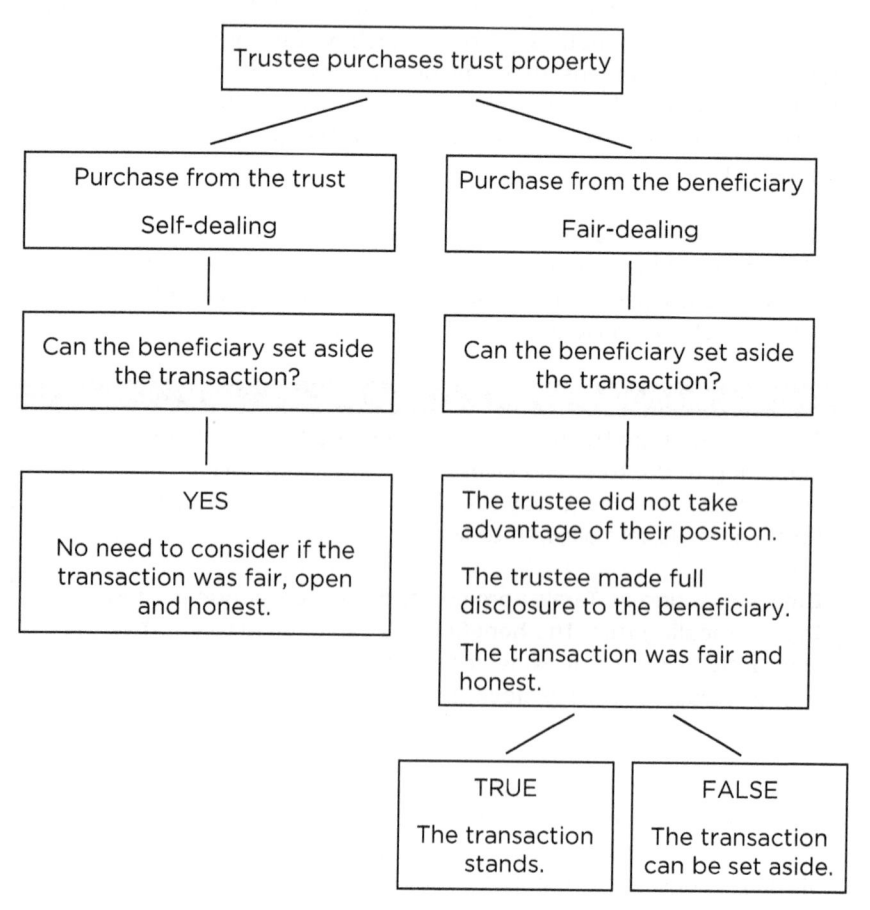

Figure 9.1: Summary of the self-dealing and fair-dealing rules

Trustees must not compete with the trust

As a fiduciary, the trustee must not put themself in a position where their interest and duty conflict. **Practice example 9.7** illustrates this point.

Practice example 9.7

The testator, a yacht broker, died and by his will appointed the defendant as his executor and trustee and directed the defendant to carry on the yacht brokerage business after his death for the benefit of his daughter (the claimant). A few months later, the defendant attempted to set up a similar business in competition with the testator's business. Is the defendant entitled to continue with his business?

The facts are based on the case of *Re Thomson* [1930] 1 Ch 203, where the judge confirmed that the defendant could not continue his business as it was in direct competition with the testator's. The defendant's action was a breach of his fiduciary duty towards the beneficiary (the claimant).

Revision tip

The practice examples above were limited to the constraints placed on the trustee as a fiduciary but remember that all fiduciaries are subject to the same rules and must ensure that their duty as a fiduciary does not conflict with their personal interests.

Below are case examples of fiduciaries who are not trustees.

Fiduciaries other than trustees

In the case of *Boardman v Phipps* [1967] 2 AC 46, Boardman was a solicitor to the trust of which Phipps was a beneficiary. The trust owned 8,000 out of 30,000 shares in a company. Boardman attended an AGM of the company and was unhappy with the running of the company. He bought shares in the company and used his personal shareholding plus the trust's shareholding to take a controlling interest in the company and made it more profitable. Both Boardman and the trust profited from his actions. In an action brought by a beneficiary against Boardman, the court held that Boardman must account for his profits to the trust. As a solicitor to the trust, he was in a fiduciary position and any insider knowledge of the company was gained from his position as a fiduciary.

We know from the subtopic on remuneration above that the courts have an inherent jurisdiction to award remuneration. This was utilised in *Boardman v Phipps*. The court concluded that Boardman had acted honestly and openly throughout and allowed him to retain a generous part of the profits by way of remuneration.

Finally, consider **Practice example 9.8** which deals with unauthorised profits by fiduciaries who are not trustees.

> **Practice example 9.8**
>
> T and H were business partners (fiduciaries). They dissolved the partnership but left a common leasehold in a farm. H died and his executors purchased the reversion for £7,500 without involving T. T was later declared bankrupt and his trustee sought a declaration that the reversion was held on trust for T and the estate of H jointly. H's executors sold the farm for £93,000. Does the profit belong solely to H's estate or must it be shared with T?
>
> The facts came from the case of *Thompson's Trustee in Bankruptcy v Heaton* [1974] 1 All ER 1239, where the court held that Heaton's executors were accountable for half of the profits as constructive trustees for Thompson.

In summary, the overriding principle to bear in mind is that a fiduciary must not profit from their position by allowing their duty as a fiduciary to conflict with their personal interests. If they do, they must account for any profits accrued from the breach of fiduciary duty. **Figure 9.2** provides a summary.

A fiduciary must not allow their duty as a fiduciary to conflict with their personal interests.

A trustee is a fiduciary and cannot:

⬇

- Keep unauthorised profits
- Keep director's fees
- Claim remuneration
- Purchase trust property
- Compete with the trust

⬇

Note that there are exceptions to each of the above.

Figure 9.2: Summary of fiduciary duties

■ KEY POINT CHECKLIST

This chapter has covered the following key knowledge points. You can use these to structure your revision around, making sure to recall the key details for each point, as covered in this chapter.
- A stranger to the trust can become liable for recipient liability.
- A stranger to the trust can become liable for accessory liability.
- A stranger to the trust can become liable for intermeddling with trust affairs.
- A fiduciary has an overriding duty to ensure that their personal interests do not conflict with their duty to their client.
- A trustee is a fiduciary and must not profit from their position as trustee.
- The no-profit rule includes unauthorised profits, directors' fees, remuneration, purchase of trust property and competing with the trust business.

■ KEY TERMS AND CONCEPTS
- stranger (**page 150**)
- fiduciary (**page 150**)
- constructive trust (**page 150**)
- restitution (**page 151**)
- actual knowledge (**page 152**)
- constructive knowledge (**page 152**)
- trustee de son tort (**page 154**)
- account of profits (**page 157**)

■ SQE1-STYLE QUESTIONS

QUESTION 1

The trustee of a trust fund used some of the money to pay off his brother's personal debt. The brother knew where the money came from and promised the trustee that he would pay the money back to the trust once he finds employment. The trustee is now bankrupt and the beneficiaries of the trust are seeking to recover the funds from the brother.

Which of the following statements best describes the brother's liability?

A. The brother is not liable as he did not personally misappropriate the money.

B. The brother is not liable as he was not an appointed trustee.

C. The brother is not liable as he is not a fiduciary.

D. The brother is liable for knowing receipt.
E. The brother is liable as a fiduciary.

QUESTION 2

A trustee used trust money for her own personal investments. Her friend, an investment banker, manages her investment portfolio and ensures that all profits are transferred to accounts out of reach of the beneficiaries of the trust. The friend is aware that the money was taken in breach of trust.

Which of the following statements best describes the friend's liability?

A. The friend is liable as a fiduciary.
B. The friend is liable for his dishonest assistance.
C. The friend is not liable as he was not an appointed trustee.
D. The friend is not liable as he never received any trust money.
E. The friend is not liable as he was not the one who misappropriated the money.

QUESTION 3

A trust has a substantial shareholding in a private company. A man, the trust's solicitor, inspected the company accounts and found that the company was not being run efficiently. The man bought shares in the company and took control of it using both his and the trust's shareholding. The man worked hard and within a year managed to maximise the company's productivity. The shares are now worth more. The beneficiaries of the trust seek advice on whether the man should account for the profit he made on the shares.

Which of the following provides the best advice?

A. The man must account for the profit as he is a fiduciary.
B. The man must account for the profit as he has recipient liability.
C. The man need not account for the profit as he used his own money to buy the shares.
D. The man need not account for the profit as it was the result of his hard work and expertise.
E. The man need not account for the profit as the trust also made a profit.

QUESTION 4

The trustees of a trust hold a portfolio of trust investments which included a cottage. At their last meeting, the trustees unanimously decided to sell the cottage. One of the trustees bought the cottage, paying full market value for it. The trustee also ensured that the minutes of the meeting recorded her intention to buy the cottage. The beneficiaries are unhappy with the transaction and are insisting that transaction be set aside.

Which of the following statements provides the best advice regarding the cottage?

A. The transaction stands as the trustee made no attempt to hide it from the beneficiaries.

B. The transaction stands as the trustee paid the full market value.

C. The transaction stands as the sale was approved by all the trustees.

D. The transaction must be set aside due to conflict of interest.

E. The transaction must be set aside as the cottage was not bought at an open auction.

QUESTION 5

A trustee of a trust is also a director of a company in which the trust has a substantial shareholding. The trustee is paid a generous director's fee by the company. The beneficiaries of the trust are unhappy that the trustee is profiting from the trust and are demanding an account of the fees paid to the trustee.

Which of the following statements best describes what the trustee should do?

A. The trustee must account for the fees regardless of whether the directorship preceded the trusteeship.

B. The trustee must account for the fees even if he can prove that his appointment as director was secured independently of the votes from the trust's shareholding.

C. The trustee must account for his fees if his appointment as director depended on votes from the trust's shareholding.

D. The trustee need not account for the fees as they are paid by the company, and not from trust funds.

E. The trustee need not account for the fees as they are considered reimbursement for out-of-pocket expenses.

■ ANSWERS TO QUESTIONS

Answers to 'What do you know already?' questions at the start of the chapter

1) False. The recipient of trust property can only be labelled a constructive trustee if they received the property knowing it to be in breach of trust. In the absence of such knowledge, they are considered to be an innocent volunteer.
2) May provided consideration and had no knowledge of the trust. She is a bona fide purchaser for value and is not a constructive trustee.
3) False. To establish accessory liability, it must be shown that the stranger had been dishonest. There is no need to show dishonesty on the part of the trustee.
4) Only professional trustees have a statutory right to remuneration. Lay trustees are subject to the general rule that fiduciaries must not profit from the trust and therefore are not automatically entitled to remuneration. They can only keep the money if they can show entitlement to it (if authorised by the trust instrument, authorised by the beneficiaries who are sui juris or authorised by the court).
5) There is a conflict of interest with the trustee acting as both the vendor and the purchaser. The transaction can be set aside by the beneficiary regardless of how fair, open or honest it had been. However, the beneficiary can also approve the transaction if they have no objection to it.

Answers to end-of-chapter SQE1-style questions

Question 1:
The correct answer was D. The trustee has breached the trust by misappropriating trust property. The brother is a constructive trustee as he has received the money knowing that it came from a breach of trust. Option A is incorrect as the brother need not personally misappropriate the trust property; receipt of the money knowing of its source is sufficient to attach liability. Options B and C are incorrect as the brother need not be a trustee or a fiduciary to be liable. Option E is wrong as the brother is not in a fiduciary position.

Question 2:
   The correct answer was B. The friend dishonestly assisted the trustee in a breach of trust making him liable as an accessory (therefore Options C-E are wrong). The friend was not in a fiduciary position to the trust so Option A is wrong.

Question 3:
   The correct answer was A. As a solicitor to the trust, the man owes a fiduciary duty to the trust and must ensure that his duty does not conflict with his own personal interest. He would not have been in a position to profit but for his fiduciary relationship with the trust. It therefore follows that all profits made belong to the trust (Options C-E are therefore wrong). Option B is incorrect as the man is not a knowing recipient of misappropriated funds.

Question 4:
   The correct answer was D. By purchasing the cottage, the trustee was acting as both the vendor and purchaser. According to the self-dealing rule, the transaction can be set aside at the insistence of the beneficiaries. Options A and B are wrong as the self-dealing rule operates even where the transaction is not hidden and where the trustee pays full market value. Option C is wrong because it is beneficiary consent required to avoid a breach of the self-dealing rule and not the trustees. Option E is wrong as it places too much emphasis on the lack of an open auction; the self-dealing rule would still apply at an open auction.

Question 5:
   The correct answer was C. If the trustee's directorship came as a direct result of his fiduciary position, he is not allowed to profit from it and must account for the profits. Option A is incorrect as the trustee is not liable to hold the profits on account if they were appointed a director prior to becoming a trustee. Option B is wrong as there must be a causal link between the use of the trust shareholding and the appointment as director. Option D is wrong as the focus is on whether the trustee gained their position as a director by virtue of the trust; it is irrelevant where the money comes from to pay the fees. Option E is wrong for similar reasoning to Option D.

■ KEY CASES, RULES, STATUTES AND INSTRUMENTS

The cases cited in this chapter are for illustrative purposes. There is no need to remember the names. You only need to remember the principles outlined in the various cases.

10

Trustees

■ MAKE SURE YOU KNOW

All trusts must have trustees who are responsible for the administration of the trust. This chapter will explain who can be appointed as a trustee and outline circumstances where a trustee can be removed. It will also explain the trustee's duties and powers within a trust and the standard of care expected of a trustee when carrying out their duties. You can expect questions in this area in the SQE assessment which require understanding of these subtopics as applied to client-based scenarios.

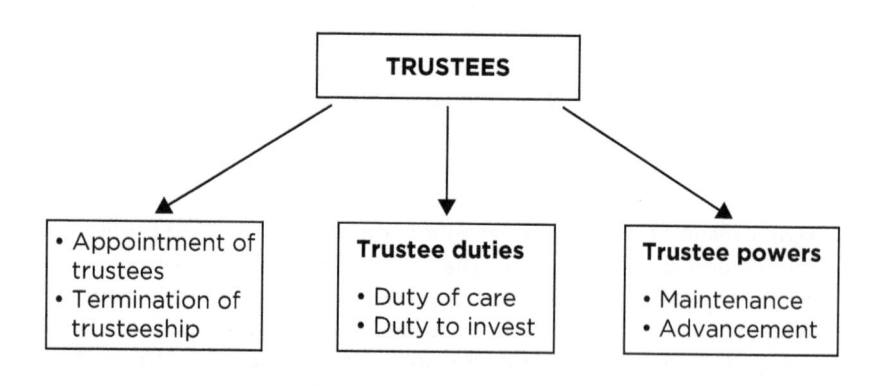

```
                    ┌─────────────┐
                    │  TRUSTEES   │
                    └─────────────┘
                   /      │      \
                  /       │       \
                 ▼        ▼        ▼
┌──────────────────┐ ┌──────────────┐ ┌──────────────────┐
│ • Appointment of │ │Trustee duties│ │ Trustee powers   │
│   trustees       │ │              │ │                  │
│ • Termination of │ │• Duty of care│ │ • Maintenance    │
│   trusteeship    │ │• Duty to     │ │ • Advancement    │
│                  │ │  invest      │ │                  │
└──────────────────┘ └──────────────┘ └──────────────────┘
```

■ SQE ASSESSMENT ADVICE

As you work through this chapter, remember to pay particular attention in your revision to:
- Who can be a trustee.
- How a trustee is appointed.
- The various ways to remove a trustee.
- How a trustee can retire.
- The trustees' duty of care.
- The duty to invest and the general principles governing investment.
- The power of maintenance.
- The power of advancement.

■ WHAT DO YOU KNOW ALREADY?

Have a go at these questions before reading this chapter. If you find some difficult or cannot remember the answers, make a note to look more closely at that during your revision.

1) True or false: only the settlor has the right to appoint new or replacement trustees.
   [Appointment of trustees, page 170]
2) What rights do the beneficiaries in a trust of land have to appoint or remove trustees?
   [Appointment by the beneficiaries in a trust of land, page 172]
3) True or false: The same standard of care is expected of all trustees.
   [The duty of care, page 176]
4) What powers do trustees have to invest?
   [Duty to invest, page 177]
5) Are trustees duty bound to use trust funds for the benefit of beneficiaries who are under 18?
   [Trustees' powers, page 180]

APPOINTMENT OF TRUSTEES

In a trust, the trustees hold the legal title to the trust property. The following rules on the appointment of trustees apply to *expressly created* trusts. A settlor creating a trust would do so by executing a trust deed and appointing the first trustees. These trustees are usually parties to the deed.

Who can be appointed a trustee?

Before we consider the rules on the appointment of trustees, when preparing for the SQE assessment, it is worth examining who can be appointed as a trustee.

The general rule is that any *adult* person can be a trustee. However, there are a few exceptions. A person is considered unfit to act as a trustee if:
- They are an undischarged bankrupt (that is someone who is legally bankrupt and still has debts to pay).
- They have been convicted of offences involving dishonesty or deception.
- They lack capacity to act due to mental disorder, ill health or other disability.

How many trustees?

The number of trustees depends on the type of trust property. If the trust property is pure **personalty**, then there should be at least one trustee at a minimum. There is no maximum number of trustees.

If the trust property consists of land, the minimum number of trustees is two (to enable overreaching) and the maximum is four. Overreaching allows a purchaser of land to take it free of any beneficiaries' rights. (This is covered in Land Law.)

> **Key term: personalty**
> Movable assets; any property other than realty.

Who can appoint new trustees?

The first trustees are usually appointed by the settlor or testator. The first trustees would have the trust property vested in them (thereby constituting the trust) and hold jointly until they retire, die or are removed and the trust property will always vest in the survivor or survivors of them through the **right of survivorship**.

> **Key term: right of survivorship**
>
> When property is held by two or more persons as joint tenants, on the death of a joint tenant, the property will automatically pass to the survivors. This process continues until there is one sole owner.

What about appointment of replacement or additional trustees?

The persons who can appoint new trustees are (in order):
- The person or persons nominated for the purpose of appointing new trustees by the instrument creating the trust, or, if no such person or persons exist,
- The surviving or continuing trustees or trustee for the time being, or the personal representatives of the last surviving or continuing trustee.
- The court which has the power to appoint as a last resort: s 41 Trustee Act 1925.

As you can see from the list above, the persons given the power of appointment by the trust instrument have priority over the continuing or surviving trustees. However, the words used in the trust instrument are construed strictly as we can see from **Practice example 10.1**.

> **Practice example 10.1**
>
> The settlor in a marriage settlement expressly empowered the husband and wife of the settlement with the authority to appoint new trustees in the event that a trustee 'dies, desires to be discharged, refuses to act or becomes incapable of acting'. One of the trustees was declared a bankrupt. Do the husband and wife have the power to appoint a replacement trustee?
>
> **The bankrupt trustee is considered 'unfit to act'. The husband and wife had been nominated by the trust instrument to appoint a replacement trustee for specified reasons, which did not include a trustee becoming unfit to act. This means the appointment must be made by the next group of persons entitled to do so: the continuing trustees.**

As equity will not allow a trust to fail for want of a trustee, we will now consider the law governing the appointment or replacement of additional trustees.

Appointment of replacement trustees

Replacement trustees can be appointed using s 36(1) Trustee Act 1925. This provision can be expressly excluded by the trust instrument but if not excluded, a new trustee may be appointed (in writing) in the place of a trustee who:
- is dead
- remains out of the UK for more than 12 months
- desires to be discharged
- refuses to act in the trusts
- is unfit to act in the trusts
- is incapable of acting in the trusts
- is an infant
- has been removed under a power contained in the instrument creating the trust.

Exam warning

If you encounter a question in the SQE assessment on s 36(1), remember the difference between 'unfit to act', which includes bankrupts and persons convicted of offences involving dishonesty or deception, and 'incapable of acting', which includes persons who lack capacity due to health reasons, mental disorder, disability, etc.

Appointment of additional trustees

Additional trustees can be appointed using s 36(6) Trustee Act 1925 where there are no more than three trustees, so long as the number of trustees is not increased beyond four.

Appointment by the beneficiaries in a *trust of land*

The Trusts of Land and Appointment of Trustees Act 1996 (as amended by the Mental Capacity Act 2005), thereafter TOLATA 1996 gives certain beneficiaries the right to appoint or replace their trustees. These beneficiaries must be adults, be mentally capable and (together) are absolutely entitled to the trust property. In order to exercise this right, the beneficiaries must all be in agreement.

s 19 TOLATA 1996

They can give directions regarding the appointment or retirement of trustees. Where there is no one nominated for the purpose of appointing new trustees by the trust instrument, the beneficiaries may:
- Give a written direction to a trustee to retire from the trust.

- Give a written direction to the trustee/s for the time being to appoint a specified person/s to be a trustee/s.

A trustee who has been given a direction to retire must ensure that after their retirement there will be either a **trust corporation** or at least two trustees remaining, and the replacement trustee or continuing trustees must consent to the retirement by deed.

> **Key term: trust corporation**
>
> A trust corporation is a business or individual professional who undertakes the administration of trusts and estates as a professional trustee.

s 20 TOLATA 1996
They have the right to appoint a substitute for a trustee who lacks capacity where:
- There is no one entitled and willing and able to appoint a replacement trustee under s 36(1) of the Trustee Act 1925.
- By giving a written direction to appoint a specified person/s to be a trustee/s.

Appointment by the court

According to s 41(1) of the Trustee Act 1925 whenever it is expedient to appoint a new trustee or new trustees, and it is inexpedient, difficult or impractical so to do without the court's assistance, the court may make an order appointing a new trustee/s either *in substitution* for or *in addition* to any existing trustee/s, or although there is no existing trustee.

The provision allows the court to *appoint* or *remove* trustees. In exercising the power to appoint, the court must take the following factors into account:
- The court will have regard to the wishes of the settlor.
- The court will not appoint a trustee who would not be even-handed towards all the beneficiaries.
- The court will have regard to whether an appointment will promote or impede the execution of the trust.

If there is no one willing to act as a trustee, the court can appoint:
- **The Public Trustee**, or
- A **judicial trustee**.

Key term: the Public Trustee

The Public Trustee is a trust corporation. The office of Public Trustee was established by the Public Trustee Act 1906. Its role is to administer trusts for whom no trustee can be found, such as when a person dies intestate (without a valid will).

Key term: judicial trustee

A judicial trustee is appointed by the High Court where the ordinary trustees have failed in their administration of the trust.

A trust must be completely constituted, which means that the legal title to the trust property must be vested in (transferred to) the trustees. This is true not only for the original trustees but applies to all newly appointed trustees.

Vesting of trust property

According to s 40(1) Trustee Act 1925, the vesting of most types of property is automatic if the appointment was made by deed. If the appointment was in writing, the continuing trustees must execute a deed of vesting after the appointment. There are certain exceptions, property such as stocks and shares do not automatically vest. Instead, the continuing trustees must execute the necessary transfer forms.

Before we move on to the subtopic on the termination of trusteeship, spend a moment looking at **Figure 10.1** which summarises the appointment of trustees. You may find it useful when revising for the SQE1 assessment.

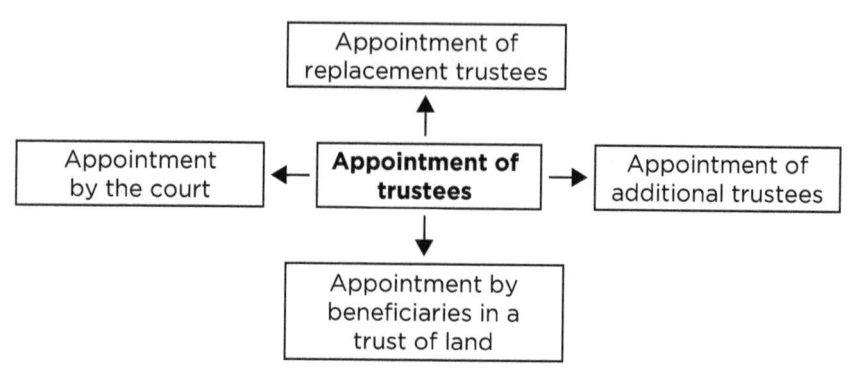

```
                    ┌─────────────────────┐
                    │   Appointment of    │
                    │ replacement trustees│
                    └──────────▲──────────┘
                               │
┌──────────────┐    ┌──────────┴──────────┐    ┌──────────────────┐
│ Appointment  │◄───│   Appointment of    │───►│  Appointment of  │
│ by the court │    │      trustees       │    │additional trustees│
└──────────────┘    └──────────┬──────────┘    └──────────────────┘
                               ▼
                    ┌─────────────────────┐
                    │   Appointment by    │
                    │  beneficiaries in a │
                    │    trust of land    │
                    └─────────────────────┘
```

Figure 10.1: Summary of the appointment of trustees

TERMINATION OF TRUSTEESHIP

Now that we know how a trustee is appointed or replaced, we need to consider how a trusteeship can end. A trusteeship can be terminated through one of several ways:

Disclaimer

A person who has been appointed as a trustee can disclaim (refuse the role) at any time before acceptance but can no longer disclaim once they have accepted. Disclaimer can be by deed, oral or inferred from conduct or length of time.

Death

On the death of a trustee, their trusteeship automatically terminates and the trust property vests in the surviving trustees through survivorship. On the death of a sole trustee, the trusteeship devolves onto their personal representatives who may then appoint new trustees.

Retirement

A trustee may expressly retire by complying with s 39(1) of the Trustee Act 1925. The requirements are:
- There must be a deed declaring the trustee's desire to be discharged.
- The remaining trustees must consent to the retirement in the same deed.
- After their retirement, there will be either a trust corporation or at least two trustees remaining.

Removal

A trustee may be removed in one of the following ways:
- Following one of the grounds listed in s 36(1) Trustee Act 1925.
- By the court under s 41 Trustee Act 1925.
- By beneficiaries in a trust of land under the Trust of Land and Appointment of Trustees Act 1996.

Figure 10.2 summarises the different ways to terminate a trusteeship.

176 Trustees

```
                    ┌──────────────────────┐
                    │ Disclaimer by the    │
                    │ trustee              │
                    └──────────────────────┘
                              ▲
┌────────────────────────┐    │    ┌──────────────────────┐    ┌──────────────────────┐
│ Removal:               │    │    │                      │    │                      │
│ • By replacement       │◄───┼────│ Termination of       │───►│ Death of the         │
│ • By the court         │         │ trusteeship          │    │ trustee              │
│ • By the beneficiaries │         │                      │    │                      │
│   in a trust of land   │         └──────────────────────┘    └──────────────────────┘
└────────────────────────┘              │
                                        ▼
                              ┌──────────────────────┐
                              │ Retirement           │
                              └──────────────────────┘
```

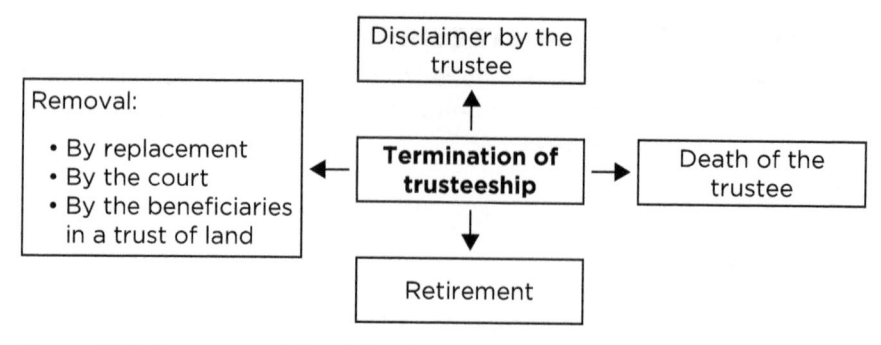

Figure 10.2: Summary of the different ways to terminate a trusteeship

THE DUTY OF CARE

In preparing for the SQE assessment it is important for you to understand that in acting for the trust, trustees owe a duty of care to the beneficiaries and they must act with such care and skill as is reasonable in the circumstances. Failing to do so may lead to a breach of trust.

On appointment, a trustee must:
- Ascertain the terms of the trust and the identity of the beneficiaries.
- Examine the trust instrument and other relevant documents and proceed against any trustee who may be in breach of trust.
- Find out what the trust property is and ensure that it is vested in their name.

A trustee's continuing duties include:
- Exercising their powers unanimously (with the other trustees).
- Keeping accounts and records.
- Acting impartially between the beneficiaries.
- Investing.
- Ensuring that their personal interests do not conflict with their duty towards the trust (explained in **Chapter 9**).

In exercising their duties, the trustees must conform to the standard of care set out in s 1 of the Trustee Act 2000, which sets differing standards of care depending on the trustee's expertise:
- Lay trustees must exercise such care and skill as is reasonable in the circumstances.
- A higher standard is expected of a trustee with relevant knowledge or experience. For example, in relation to an investment in stocks and

shares, a trustee who is an investment banker will be held to a higher standard than one who is not.
* Finally, professional trustees are rightly held to a higher standard compared to lay trustees.

Trustees have certain duties when administering the trust and, as required by the SQE, we will focus on the trustee's duty to invest.

Duty to invest

Trustees have a duty to invest the trust property and when preparing for the SQE assessment, you will need to consider the following:
* The trustees must be even-handed
* The meaning of investment
* The modern portfolio theory
* The power to invest.

Trustees must be even-handed

This means that the trustees must treat all the beneficiaries fairly when selecting investments. This requirement is especially important if the trust has different classes of beneficiaries. For example, beneficiaries with a life interest are entitled to the income produced by the trust assets but beneficiaries with a remainder interest are entitled to the capital on the death of the life beneficiaries. This means the trustees must select investments that produce income whilst also protecting the capital.

The meaning of 'investment'

The Trustee Act 2000 expanded the meaning of investment to include the purchase of property for income yield as well as investments of pure capital growth. Clearly, the trustees must choose investments suitable to the trust and the beneficiaries.

The modern portfolio theory

Since the Trustee Act 2000, the trustees' standard of care is measured in light of the modern portfolio theory which emphasises the risk level of the entire portfolio rather than the risk attached to each investment taken in isolation. This means the trustees will be judged on whether all the investments taken together have made a profit where before they would have been liable for separate failed investments even if the trust fund as a whole has made a profit.

> **Revision tip**
> The modern portfolio theory is mentioned in the explanatory notes of the Trustee Act 2000 and is now considered part of general law.

The power to invest

As we know, trustees are under a duty to invest the trust assets but their power to do so could derive from the trust instrument or from statute. The settlor is free to specify the trustees' powers of investment and even exclude the statutory power.

Assuming it has not been expressly excluded by the trust instrument, the trustees are given a general power of investment by the Trustee Act 2000. According to s 3, the trustee may make any kind of investment as if they were absolutely entitled to the trust assets and s 8 allows investment in land.

When investing, the trustee must have regard to the standard investment criteria, which means that:
- The trustee must review the investments from time to time and consider whether they should be varied, based on
  - the suitability of the investment to the trust, and
  - the need for diversification.

Before investing, the trustee must obtain and consider proper advice from a person who is reasonably believed by the trustee to be qualified to give it by their ability in and practical experience of financial and other matters relating to the proposed investment.

One final issue to consider in trustee investments is whether trustees are free to take non-financial considerations into account when investing.

Ethical investments

You will recall that trustees have a duty to act in the best interest of the beneficiaries, and this generally means their best *financial* interest. Failure to do so may result in a breach of trust. Therefore, trustees may only take non-financial considerations into account when investing provided:
- They were given express authority to do so by the trust instrument.
- The beneficiaries are all sui juris (of full age and under no disability) and have given their consent to the trustees.
- When following an ethical investment policy, the trustees can show that the selected investments are as financially sound as those which were rejected.

Consider **Practice example 10.2** in light of this.

Practice example 10.2

Trustees of a pension fund for coal mine workers rejected an investment plan submitted by a panel of experts on the basis that it went against union policy. The plan included investing in energy companies in competition with coal. By rejecting the proposal, had the trustees acted in breach of trust?

The facts are from *Cowan v Scargill* [1985] Ch 270, where the court held that the trustees would be in breach if they refused to adopt the plan. Their duty is to exercise their powers in the best interest of the beneficiaries, ie financial interest, putting aside their own social or political views.

Exam warning

Check the wording of any questions carefully. In the case of charitable trusts, there are rare instances where the trustees could take non-financial considerations into account, such as where a particular investment would directly conflict with the objects of the charity or may alienate potential donors or recipients.

Summary	Duty to invest
General principles	• Even-handedness towards all beneficiaries. • Investment includes income yield and capital growth. • Standard of care based on looking at the risk level of the entire portfolio.

The power to invest	Sources:
	• The trust instrument, or
	• Trustee Act 2000:
	  – trustee to invest as if absolutely entitled but must
	  – review at regular intervals and vary the investments based on suitability and the need for diversification.
	  – trustee must obtain proper advice before investing.

Ethical considerations	• If trustees can prove that the ethical investment policy is just as financially sound. • If the beneficiaries consented to it. • If authorised by the trust instrument.

TRUSTEES' POWERS

When preparing for the SQE assessment, remember that, in addition to the duties outlined above, trustees also have powers to act within the trust. Unlike duties, which are obligatory, trustees' powers are discretionary. The powers could be expressed in the trust instrument but if the instrument is silent, the trustees can rely on their statutory powers. Similarly, these powers could be expressly excluded by the trust instrument. We will consider the trustees' powers of maintenance and advancement as provided by statute.

Power of maintenance

The trust instrument may give the trustees the power to apply income for the maintenance or education of the beneficiaries but, even without express authorisation, the trustees have a statutory power to do so. The maintenance of a beneficiary would include any payments towards the benefit of the beneficiary.

According to s 31 of the Trustee Act 1925 (as amended by the Inheritance and Trustees' Powers Act 2014), trustees holding on trust for a minor beneficiary may, at their sole discretion, apply the whole or part of the income of the trust property towards the maintenance, education or benefit of the beneficiary. The trustees can exercise this power even if there is another fund available for that purpose or if there is someone else bound by law to provide for the child's maintenance or education.

> **Exam warning**
>
> Bear in mind that the trustees' power to maintain is subject to any prior interests. If property is held on trust for A for life, remainder to B (the minor), the trustees have no power to use the income to maintain B since A is absolutely entitled to the income. In the SQE, you must ascertain that there is no prior life interest preventing the trustee from using the power to maintain.

The power to maintain is also not available in a discretionary trust because the beneficiaries of a discretionary trust have no automatic right to payment, only the right to be considered by the trustees in the exercise of their discretion.

The power of maintenance applies to all minors with the following interests:
- vested interest
- contingent interests provided the **trust carries the intermediate income**.

Note: for an explanation of vested and contingent interests, please refer to **Chapter 5**.

> **Key term: trusts that carry the intermediate income**
> These are trusts where the beneficiary is entitled to the income earned by the gift from the date of the gift until the gift is actually transferred to them. Generally all vested and contingent testamentary gifts (gifts of property in a will) apart from pecuniary legacies (gifts of cash in a will) carry the intermediate income. Do not worry too much if you find this difficult; it is likely that you will be told in the SQE assessment whether a particular gift carries the intermediate income. Your focus should be on the power of maintenance.

Power of advancement

According to s 32 of the Trustee Act 1925 (as amended by the Inheritance and Trustees' Powers Act 2014), trustees may pay or apply, in their absolute discretion, any trust capital in a trust for the advancement or benefit of any beneficiary entitled. As you will see in the practice examples below, the court adopts a wide meaning on the *advancement* of a beneficiary.

The trustees' exercise of the power of advancement is subject to the following:
- The advancement must not exceed the beneficiary's share of the trust assets.
- Once the beneficiary becomes absolutely entitled to their share, the sum advanced must be taken into account. This means that any money advanced must be deducted from their share when they are eventually paid. Have a look at **Practice example 10.3** by way of illustration.
- If there is someone with a prior life interest in the trust fund, this person must be an adult and they must give consent in writing to the advancement.

For example, where a settlor left £60,000 on trust for his three children, each child's presumptive share is £20,000. The trustees can advance a maximum of £20,000 to each child. Any advancement must be taken into account when the beneficiary becomes absolutely entitled to their share, as shown in **Practice example 10.3**.

> **Practice example 10.3**
>
> Betty settled money on trust for her two children equally, with a direction that they become absolutely entitled on reaching the age of 23. Betty has two children, Vic and Lily. A few years ago, the trustees advanced £20,000 to Vic to pay for his college fees. Vic has just turned 23. The trust fund is valued at £120,000. How much is Vic entitled to?
>
> **To calculate Vic's share, the trustees must add the sum advanced to Vic to the trust's present value (£20k + £120k = £140k). Vic is entitled to half, so £70,000. However, the earlier advancement of £20,000 must be taken into account, so Vic is to receive £50,000 (£70k – £20k).**

> **Exam warning**
>
> Note that for trusts taking effect *before* 1 October 2014, the maximum amount that the trustees can advance is half the beneficiary's presumptive share.

In considering the meaning of 'advancement', the court accepts that it includes any use of the money which will improve the material situation of the beneficiary. This includes an advancement of the capital to the beneficiary with a remainder interest to avoid having to pay inheritance tax on the death of the life beneficiary. See **Practice example 10.4** by way of illustration.

> **Practice example 10.4**
>
> The testator's will left £2m on trust for her husband for life, remainder to her two children. One of the children has just turned 18 and would like the trustees to advance his share so as to reduce the amount paid by way of inheritance tax when the life tenant (the husband) dies.
>
> **The savings made in avoiding inheritance tax will improve the material situation of the beneficiary and is an acceptable reason to advance the money.**

What about a payment which may involve a financial loss to the beneficiary? Could it be considered an 'advancement'? **Practice example 10.5** explores this scenario.

> **Practice example 10.5**
>
> The trustees held on trust for the son and daughter of the settlor with directions to accumulate the income for the beneficiaries until they turn 18, and thereafter to pay the income to the beneficiaries until they reach the age of 30 when their interests will vest. When the son turned 18, he asked for one-seventh of his share to be paid to a named charity. Do the trustees have the power to advance the money for that purpose under s 32?
>
> These are the facts of *Re Clore's Settlement Trusts* [1966] 1 WLR 955, where the court approved the advancement. The reasoning being that a wealthy person (the son) who felt a moral obligation to donate to charity was *materially benefited* by having the obligation discharged out of the trust fund instead of directly from his own pocket.

As we can see from the practice example, the advancement must improve the material, if not financial, situation of the beneficiary. If a beneficiary seeks an advancement of a sum that exceeds their own resources to be gifted to charity, the court is likely to refuse the advancement on the basis that it would not improve the beneficiary's material situation.

Once the advancement has been made, if the trustees became aware that the beneficiary had misapplied the money, they should not make further advances without ensuring that the money is being properly applied.

Summary	
Power of maintenance	• To pay the income. • For the maintenance, education or benefit of the beneficiary.
Power of advancement	• To pay the capital (not exceeding the beneficiary's share). • For the advancement or benefit of the beneficiary.

■ KEY POINT CHECKLIST

This chapter has covered the following key knowledge points. You can use these to structure your revision around, making sure to recall the key details for each point, as covered in this chapter.

- If the trust instrument is silent on appointment of additional or replacement trustees, the relevant statutory provisions are applicable.
- The court can appoint or remove trustees as a last resort.
- There are several ways to terminate a trusteeship, including retirement. Remember the requirements that a retiring trustee must meet.
- In considering the trustees' duty of care, remember the differing standards of care according to the expertise of the trustee and the difference between a lay trustee and a professional trustee.
- Trustees are under a duty to invest. Remember the general principles and what the trustees must do to ensure that they comply with the duty of care when investing.
- Trustees have the power to use trust income to maintain minor beneficiaries provided there is no one with a prior entitlement to the income.
- Trustees can advance trust capital to beneficiaries for their benefit.

■ KEY TERMS AND CONCEPTS

- personalty (**page 170**)
- right of survivorship (**page 171**)
- trust corporation (**page 173**)
- the public trustee (**page 174**)
- judicial trustee (**page 174**)
- trusts that carry the intermediate income (**page 181**)

■ SQE1-STYLE QUESTIONS

QUESTION 1

A man died and his will left his estate to three trustees to hold on trust for his three children until they attain the age of 21. Two of the children have reached the age of 21 and have received their share of the trust fund. One of the children is still under the age of 21. The trust fund comprises a portfolio of shares. One of the trustees has just died.

Which of the following best describes whether it is necessary to appoint a replacement trustee?

A. There is no requirement to appoint a replacement trustee as there are two surviving trustees.
B. There is no requirement to appoint a replacement trustee because there is no land in the trust investments.
C. A replacement trustee must be appointed because one of the trustees has died.
D. A replacement trustee must be appointed because one of the beneficiaries is still under the age of 21.
E. A replacement trustee must be appointed because the original appointment consisted of three trustees.

QUESTION 2

The testator's will appointed two trustees to hold property on trust for her five grandchildren until they attain the age of 20. The will also provided that the testator's son has the right to appoint replacement trustees. All the beneficiaries are still under the age of 20. The testator's son predeceased her. One of the trustees has just died.

Which of the following has the best right to appoint the replacement trustee?

A. The son's personal representative.
B. The surviving trustee.
C. The personal representative of the trustee who died.
D. The testator's personal representative.
E. The court.

QUESTION 3

The trustees of a large fund commissioned an investment advisor to draw up an investment plan but rejected the plan as they had strict views on investing in sustainable companies. The beneficiaries of the trust are all under 18. The trust instrument is silent on the issue of investment.

Which of the following provides the best advice regarding this issue?

A. The trustees are in breach of their duty of care.

B. The trustees are not in breach of their duty of care as they have the power to invest as if they were absolutely entitled to the trust property.
C. The beneficiaries can consent to a more ethical investment plan.
D. The trustees must prove that any investment they choose is just as financially sound as the plan they rejected.
E. The trustees must accept the original investment plan.

QUESTION 4

A woman died last month leaving an estate of £90,000 to be divided equally between her three children when they attain the age of 25. All of her children are under 25. Her eldest son, who is 22, has requested an advance of capital to set up his online fitness business. The woman's will makes no mention of the trustees' power of advancement.

What is the maximum amount the trustees can apply in accordance with the request?

A. £0.
B. £15,000.
C. £30,000.
D. £45,000.
E. £60,000.

QUESTION 5

A man died last week leaving his estate on trust to his wife for life, remainder to his four children. All the children are under 18. The eldest child, who is aged 16, wants to attend catering college and would like the trustees to use some of the trust income to pay her college fees.

Which of the following best describes the trustees right to pay towards the maintenance of the eldest child?

A. The trustees are under a duty to maintain the beneficiary and must pay the college fees.
B. The trustees can use no more than 1/4 of the income to pay the college fees.
C. The wife must give consent before the trustees can use the trust income to pay the college fees.

D. The trustees cannot use their power of maintenance unless expressly authorised by the trust instrument.
E. The trustees have no right to use the trust income for the college fees.

■ ANSWERS TO QUESTIONS

Answers to 'What do you know already?' questions at the start of the chapter

1) False. The settlor generally appoints the first trustees but according to statute, the persons with the right to appoint subsequent trustees are:
   - The persons nominated in the trust instrument; if there are no such persons, then
   - The surviving or continuing trustees, or the personal representative of the last surviving trustee.
   - As a last resort, the court can make the appointment.
2) The beneficiaries of a trust of land have statutory powers under the Trust of Land and Appointment of Trustees Act 1996 to appoint new or substitute trustees and to remove trustees.
3) False. According to s 1 of the Trustee Act 2000, lay trustees must exercise such care and skill as is reasonable in the circumstances but a higher standard is imposed on trustees with relevant expertise and on professional trustees.
4) The trustees' power to invest could be expressed in the trust instrument and if not, they can rely on the statutory power under which they may make any investment as if they were absolutely entitled to the trust assets.
5) Trustees are given statutory powers of maintenance and advancement but these powers are discretionary. Unless expressly provided by the trust instrument, the trustees have no obligation to pay towards the maintenance or advancement of minor beneficiaries.

Answers to end-of-chapter SQE1-style questions

Question 1:
   The correct answer was A. There is no need to appoint a replacement trustee (therefore Options C–E are wrong). The same is true even if the trust consists of land (therefore Option B is wrong). Two trustees

are sufficient to give good receipt for the sale of land and ensure overreaching.

Question 2:

The correct answer was B. The persons with the right to appoint (in order) are:

- The person nominated in the instrument to make appointments. The son was nominated but he has died.
- The surviving or continuing trustees.
- If all the trustees are dead, then the personal representative of the last surviving trustee.

From the facts, there is one surviving trustee who has the right to appoint the replacement trustee. All other options are therefore incorrect.

Question 3:

The correct answer was D. The trustees are not in breach if they can prove that their investment plan was just as profitable as the rejected investments (therefore Options A and E are wrong). Option B is incorrect because the power to invest is always subject to their duty of care. The trustees' primary duty in investing is to seek the best financial return. Option C is incorrect as minor beneficiaries cannot give valid consent.

Question 4:

The correct answer was C. The trustees have the power to advance to a beneficiary the full presumptive share of that beneficiary. As her eldest son is entitled to 1/3 of the trust funds (£30,000), the trustees can advance up to that full amount. If the trust had been created prior to 1 October 2014, the eldest son would have only been entitled to up to half of his presumptive share (ie £15,000). All other options are therefore incorrect.

Question 5:

The correct answer was E. The trustees' power to maintain is subject to a prior life interest. The wife has a life interest in the trust property and is entitled to the trust income. This means the income cannot be used to maintain any person with an interest vested in remainder, including the children. All other options are therefore incorrect.

■ KEY CASES, RULES, STATUTES AND INSTRUMENTS

Although the chapter cited several statutory provisions and cases, there is no need to remember any of them. It is more important to understand the relevant law in each subtopic.

11

Trustees' liability

■ MAKE SURE YOU KNOW

In acting on behalf of the trust, we know that the trustees have a duty of care towards the beneficiaries and that their actions are measured to a reasonable standard of care. A failure of their duty of care leading to a loss to the trust assets could be considered a breach of trust. In this topic, you will learn what amounts to a breach of trust and the defences available to the trustees. You may encounter questions in the SQE requiring your assessment on whether there has been a breach of trust and the types of defences the trustee can raise. The remedies available to the beneficiaries are covered in **Chapter 12**.

Trustees' liability

Breach of trust
- Includes action or omission.
- Must prove loss resulting from the breach.
- Trustee only liable for own breaches.
- Trustee's liability is joint and several.
- Trustee can claim indemnity in certain circumstances.
- The measure of damages is compensation – trustee to restore the fund to its original position before the breach.

Protection of trustees
- An exemption clause may excuse the trustee or limit liability.
- The court has the discretion to excuse a trustee for breach.
- Defences available to a trustee due to beneficiary involvement.
- Six-year limitation period: action against the trustee may be time-barred. Note the exceptions.

Trustees' liability

■ SQE ASSESSMENT ADVICE

As you work through this chapter, remember to pay particular attention in your revision to:
- What actions or omissions may amount to a breach of trust.
- The requirement that the breach must lead to a loss to the trust fund.
- The trustee's liability for breach and their entitlement to indemnity from a fellow trustee or from a beneficiary.
- The measure of damages.
- The means of protection and defences available to a trustee who is being sued for breach of trust.

■ WHAT DO YOU KNOW ALREADY?

Have a go at these questions before reading this chapter. If you find some difficult or cannot remember the answers, make a note to look more closely at that during your revision

1) A trust settlement contains a clause limiting the trustees' power of investment to stocks and shares. The trustees invested in land and made a profit. Are they liable to the trust for breach?
   [Breach of trust, page 191]

2) True or false: A trustee is only liable for a breach of trust resulting from their action, not their inaction.
   [Breach of trust, page 191]

3) Is a breach of fiduciary duty the same as a breach of trust?
   [Breach of trust, page 191]

4) A trustee holding on trust for an adult beneficiary took the beneficiary's investment advice which resulted in a loss. Must the trustee compensate the trust for the loss?
   [Protection of trustees, page 196]

5) True or false: In an action for breach of trust, the court has a discretion to refuse the grant of an injunction even if the action lies within the limitation period.
   [Protection of trustees, page 196]

BREACH OF TRUST

A trustee is said to be in breach of trust where they have failed to discharge their duties in relation to the trust property or to the beneficiaries. You are likely to encounter a question in the SQE on this topic. The general principles governing breach of trust will be considered first.

General principles

Before considering the trustees' liability, you must first understand the principles governing a breach of trust in general:
- There is no doctrine of mens rea; the intention of the trustee is not relevant to their liability for breach.
- A breach of trust can occur by action or omission. This means a breach can occur either:
  - when the trustee acted outside their scope of powers; or
  - when the trustee failed to take adequate action to protect the trust assets.
- Whether a trustee is in breach would depend on whether their actions have fallen below the statutory standard of care (see **Chapter 10**).
- Actions against a trustee in breach may be personal or proprietary. An explanation of the trustee's personal liability can be found in the subtopic Trustee liability in this chapter. Proprietary action against the trustee requires the process of tracing, which will be dealt with in **Chapter 12**.
- A breach does not automatically lead to liability. A trustee is only liable if the breach led to a loss to the trust or to an unauthorised gain by the trustee – see **Practice example 11.1** for an illustration of this.

Practice example 11.1

A testator died 70 years ago. He left a portfolio of investments (worth about £50,000) on trust for his wife for life, remainder to his two sons; he appointed a bank as his sole executor and trustee. The will contained a power to invest in 'any investments of a similar nature' to those belonging to the testator at the time of his death or in the 'stocks and shares of any other railway or other company'. The bank took no legal advice and regarded that clause as limiting its power to invest in ordinary shares generally. The bank also failed to conduct regular reviews of the investments. The beneficiaries brought an action for breach of trust, claiming that had the bank exercised its duty to invest properly, the fund would have been worth £1m today instead of merely £250,000. Is the bank liable for breach of trust?

> The bank is not liable for breach of trust because the beneficiaries cannot prove that they had suffered loss as a result of the bank's breaches of duty. The facts originated from the case of *Nestle v NatWest Bank* [1994] 1 All ER 118, where the Court of Appeal agreed that the bank was in breach of its duty towards the trust by misunderstanding the scope of its investment powers under the will, failing to obtain legal advice to clarify the misunderstanding, and for failing to review the investments regularly. However, the onus is on the beneficiaries to prove that they suffered loss as a result of the bank's breaches, which they had failed to do.

Exam warning

Remember that for a successful claim for compensation against a trustee, the beneficiary must prove that the trustee had breached the trust *and* the trust suffered a loss due to the breach. There must be some causal connection between the breach of trust and the loss to the trust fund.

Moving on from the general principles governing a breach of trust, we now need to consider the liability of the trustee.

Trustee liability

Where there is more than one trustee, does it automatically follow that all the trustees are equally liable for every breach of trust? The following principles apply when considering a trustee's liability:

- A trustee is liable for their own breaches and not vicariously liable for those of their co-trustees. However, even if the trustee has not actively committed a breach, they may nevertheless have committed a breach by omission for neglecting their duties. In other words, they are liable if they should have known what their co-trustees were up to. After all, trustees are required to act unanimously.
- A trustee is not liable for breaches committed before they were appointed. However, we must bear in mind the trustee's duty on being appointed, which is to ensure proper administration of the trust by inspecting the trust documents and accounts. If a breach is discovered, the trustee must take action. Failing to do so amounts to a breach of omission by that trustee.
- A trustee is not liable for breaches committed after their retirement unless they retired in order to facilitate a breach (see **Practice example 11.2**). Similarly, a trustee cannot escape liability for a breach by retiring. They remain liable for breaches committed whilst in office.

- A trustee's liability is joint and several. This means that the beneficiaries can sue all or some or anyone of those liable and claim the whole sum against any one trustee. This is useful where there are several trustees, all of whom have breached the trust and all but one are impecunious (have no money). The beneficiaries can choose to sue the one trustee who has money.
- Under the Civil Liability (Contribution) Act 1978, the court has a discretion to determine the contributions each defendant trustee must make according to what the court finds to be just and equitable having regard to the extent of that person's responsibility for the damage in question.

Practice example 11.2

In a marriage settlement, the trustees held property on trust for the husband and wife for life, remainder to their children. The trustees were allowed to pay up to half the presumptive share of any child for the benefit of that child. On the death of the husband, the wife experienced financial difficulties, and at her request the trustees made several payments to her and her children. After they reached the limit of payments they were allowed to make, the trustees refused the wife's requests for more money. However, they decided to retire and be replaced by trustees (who are friends of the family) who were willing to make further payments. The new trustees made further advances in breach of trust resulting in a loss to one of the child beneficiaries. Are the retired trustees equally liable for the loss to the trust?

These are the facts of *Head v Gould* [1898] 2 Ch 250, where the court held that the retired trustees remained liable, together with the current trustees, for the breach as it was clear that they retired in order to facilitate the breach.

Indemnity

A trustee found to be in breach of trust must compensate the trust for any loss suffered out of their personal funds. This trustee can claim **indemnity** from a fellow trustee or even from a beneficiary in the following circumstances:
- Where that co-trustee was fraudulent, the trustee can claim indemnity from the fraudulent trustee.
- Where the co-trustee is a solicitor–trustee who exercised a controlling influence over the other, indemnity is available from the controlling trustee.

- Where a beneficiary who is also a trustee has exclusively benefitted from a breach of trust, the beneficiary-trustee must indemnify the co-trustee to the extent of their beneficial interest.
- Where a beneficiary has instigated the breach, or consented to the breach in writing, the court may **impound a beneficiary's interest** by way of indemnity to the trustee. The court can impound up to the full value of this beneficiary's beneficial interest: s 62 Trustee Act 1925.

> **Key term: indemnity**
> A sum of money paid by way of compensation.

> **Key term: impound a beneficiary's interest**
> To seize or take control of a beneficiary's entitlement under the trust; in this instance, so that it can be used to indemnify the trustee. This beneficiary is also barred from suing the trustee for the breach.

Once the breach of trust has been established and the ensuing loss is proven, the court must calculate the measure of damages due to the beneficiaries.

Measure of damages

In an action for breach of trust, the beneficiaries must prove that the breach resulted in a loss to the trust fund. The remedy is **compensation**. The trustee is personally liable for any loss and must restore the fund to the position it was in before the breach. The trustee is liable to compensate the trust using their own personal funds. The beneficiaries need not prove that the trustees have any trust property in their possession.

In an action for breach of fiduciary duty where the trustee has made an unauthorised profit, the remedy is restitution. This means that the trustee must account for any profits made (see **Chapter 9**).

> **Key term: compensation**
> A sum of money awarded to make up for a loss.

> **Revision tip**
> Remember that the trustee's liability is both personal and proprietary. If the trustee is still in possession of trust property (or its equivalent), the beneficiaries can exercise their proprietary right to trace against the trustee. (The process of tracing is covered in **Chapter 12**.)

Interest on damages awarded

The court has a discretion to award interest on any sum awarded. Generally, **simple interest** is awarded; the rate of interest is at the court's discretion. **Compound interest** may be awarded where the trustee has been fraudulent or where the trustee has made unauthorised profits.

> **Key term: simple interest**
> The interest payable based on the principal sum awarded.

> **Key term: compound interest**
> Compound interest is calculated based on the principal sum plus the interest accumulated on it.

Before we move on from breach of trust, there is one final point to bear in mind:

Distinguishing a breach of trust from a breach of fiduciary duty

In **Chapter 9**, we learnt that a trustee is a fiduciary and must act in the best interest of the beneficiaries and not allow their personal interest to conflict with their duty. A breach of their fiduciary duty is not necessarily a breach of trust.

An example of a breach of trust is where a trustee makes investments which are expressly forbidden by the trust instrument. If this action resulted in a loss to the trust fund, the trustee must compensate the trust for the loss out of their personal funds.

An example of a breach of fiduciary duty that is not a breach of trust is where the trustee used their position to make unauthorised profits. The trustee may be subject to an injunction to restrain the breach and, as they have been unjustly enriched by the breach, they must account for the profits.

Summary: breach of trust	
General principles	Breach can be by action or omission.
	Must prove loss resulting from the breach.
Trustee liability	Trustee is only liable for their own breaches.
	Liability is joint and several.

| Indemnity | Available from:
• A fraudulent trustee.
• A solicitor-trustee who exercised a controlling influence.
• A beneficiary-trustee who benefitted from the breach.
• A beneficiary who instigated or consented to the breach. |
|---|---|
| Measure of damages | Compensation for the loss. |

Based on what we have covered so far, you are probably of the opinion that the role of a trustee is both onerous and subject to far too many pitfalls. Whilst that is true, the trustee is entitled to a certain level of protection and you may be examined on these in the SQE. Let's consider this issue next.

PROTECTION OF TRUSTEES

There are several means of protection and defences available to a trustee who is being sued for breach of trust. The first of these is exemption clauses. Second, the trustee may be able to convince the court to release them from liability. Third, if a beneficiary played a role in the breach, the trustee can raise this fact as a defence. Finally, the trustees may be able to claim that an action is time-barred due to the Limitation Act 1980. We will consider each in turn.

Exemption clauses

The trust instrument may contain a clause that exempts or limits the trustee's liability for breach of trust (see **Practice example 11.3**). Generally, the court must construe such clauses fairly without preference for either party. However, any ambiguity in the clause is construed against the trustee seeking to rely on it.

> **Practice example 11.3**
>
> A trust settlement contained a clause exempting the trustee from liability for loss or damage to the trust fund or its income 'unless such loss or damage shall be caused by the trustee's own actual fraud'. The trustee knowingly and deliberately breached the trust by acting beyond his powers. Does the clause exempt the trustee from liability?

The facts are derived from the case of *Armitage v Nurse* [1997] 3 WLR 1046, where the Court of Appeal held that the exemption clause absolved the trustee from liability. Although the trustee had deliberately committed a breach of trust, their conduct was not fraudulent if they did so in good faith and in the honest belief that they were acting in the interest of the beneficiaries. According to the clause, the trustee is only liable for breaches resulting from fraud, which requires proof of dishonesty on the part of the trustee.

Exam warning

If you come across an exemption clause in the SQE assessment excluding the trustee from all liability, including fraud, be aware that the Court of Appeal in *Armitage v Nurse* clarified that a fraudulent trustee cannot rely on such an exemption clause because the 'irreducible core' of a trust is the trustee's obligation to act honestly in the best interest of the beneficiaries. A trust without this obligation is not a trust.

The court may relieve the trustee of liability

According to s 61 of the Trustee Act 1925, the court has a discretion to excuse a trustee for a breach if it appears to the court that they acted honestly and reasonably and ought fairly to be excused. The court can choose to relieve the trustee wholly or partly of personal liability.

Both lay trustees and professional trustees may claim the protection of this provision but the court is less likely to excuse a breach by a professional trustee bearing in mind the higher standard imposed on them by s 1 of the Trustee Act 2000.

The defence of beneficiary involvement

In an action for breach of trust, the trustee has a valid defence if they can show that the breach happened due to beneficiary involvement or that the beneficiary has excused the breach.

Consent or instigation by a beneficiary

This defence is available if the trustee can prove that the breach was at the instigation of a beneficiary, or where the trustee had the consent of the beneficiary before committing the breach. The beneficiary must be sui juris (of full age and under no disability) in circumstances where they can make their own decisions. They need not be aware that the actions amounted to a breach of trust so long as they fully understand the actions. There is also no need to show that the beneficiary benefitted from the breach. The trustee can only raise this defence against the beneficiary who instigated or consented to the breach. It is not available against the other beneficiaries.

> **Revision tip**
>
> Remember the court's power to impound a beneficiary's interest (by way of damages to the other beneficiaries or by way of indemnity to the trustee) if they consented to or instigated a breach of trust.

Release or acquiescence by a beneficiary
Another defence available to the trustee is where they can show that having discovered the breach, the beneficiary decided to excuse it. This is known as **acquiescence**. By doing so, the beneficiary is in fact waiving their right to sue thus releasing the trustee from liability. The beneficiary must be sui juris and have full knowledge of the facts.

> **Key term: acquiescence**
>
> A beneficiary is said to have acquiesced in the breach where the beneficiary knows about the breach but decides to take no action against the trustee. Delay in taking action may be evidence of acquiescence. This is a question of fact to be determined by the court.

The limitation period

An action against a trustee for breach of trust may be time-barred due to the Limitation Act 1980. This means that the action was taken after the limitation period has passed. The limitation period for breach of trust actions is six years.

Six-year limitation period
According to s 21, any action for breach of trust must be brought within six years of the date on which the right to take action accrued. The countdown only begins once a beneficiary's interest comes into possession. So, in a trust where there is a life interest followed by a remainder interest, the limitation period for the remainderman starts on the death of the life tenant.

Similarly, a life tenant who is out of time cannot take advantage of the fact that a remainderman can still sue (see **Practice example 11.4**).

> **Practice example 11.4**
>
> A and B are beneficiaries in a settlement where trustees are holding on trust for A for life, remainder to B. A and B are both adults. The settlement included a clause forbidding the trustees from investing in land. Seven years ago, the trustees invested in land in breach of trust. The value of the land fell very soon after the purchase. Can A and B sue the trustees for breach of trust?
>
> Provided A was aware of the breach at the time and assuming A did not consent to it, the limitation period has passed and A is barred from suing. On A's death, the clock starts running against B, who has six years in which to pursue the trustees for breach.

Exceptions

There are exceptions to the six-year time period, such as:

- There is no limitation period in actions against a trustee who was party to a fraud.
- There is no limitation period in actions to recover trust property or its proceeds from a trustee.
- Where a beneficiary was under a disability when the breach occurred, the limitation period only starts running when the disability has ended. Persons under a disability include infants and persons of unsound mind. Once the infant beneficiary turns 18, time starts running. As for beneficiaries with an unsound mind, their disability ends on death so that their estate can take action.
- In an action for fraud, concealment or mistake, time only starts running from the point when the beneficiary discovers the fraud, **concealment** or **mistake**, or could with reasonable diligence have discovered it.

> **Key term: concealment**
>
> Where the defendant deliberately conceals the breach, the limitation period does not begin to run until the claimant discovers the concealment; or could with reasonable diligence discover it.

> **Key term: mistake**
>
> Where the breach of trust was the result of a mistake, such as the trust money being paid to the wrong person, the limitation period does not begin to run until the claimant discovers the mistake; or could with reasonable diligence discover it.

Doctrine of laches and acquiescence

The **doctrine of laches** is an equitable defence raised by a defendant. The defendant must show that the claimant's undue delay in asserting their rights meant that the claimant is no longer entitled to the equitable remedy as it would be unjust to the defendant.

> **Key term: doctrine of laches**
>
> This is a defence available against an equitable claim and is based on the fact that the claimant delayed taking action to such an extent that it has become inequitable to enforce their rights against the defendant.

According to the Act, the limitation period does not apply to claims for equitable remedies such as specific performance and injunctions. (For an explanation of these remedies, see **Chapter 12**.)

This means that in an action for breach of trust where the claimant is seeking specific performance or an injunction (equitable remedies), the court is not bound by the six-year limitation period. The court can refuse to grant the equitable remedy even if the application was brought within the six-year period.

A defence related to this doctrine is acquiescence. A claimant can acquiesce in one of two ways: by confirming their intention not to sue, or by delaying taking action to the point that the doctrine of laches applies. Whether the delay amounts to acquiescence is a question of fact for the court to determine.

Summary: protection of trustees	
Exemption clause	Any ambiguity is interpreted against the trustee (not in their favour).
	Cannot exempt the trustee from dishonest or fraudulent acts.
The court's discretion	The court can excuse a trustee who acted honestly and reasonably.
Beneficiary involvement	It is a defence where the beneficiary: • Instigated the breach or consented to the breach before the trustee committed it. • Acquiesced to the breach (after discovering it) thus releasing the trustee by waiving their right to sue.

| Limitation Act 1980 | Generally, a claim expires after six years except:
• Where the trustee was party to a fraud.
• In an action to recover trust property (or its proceeds) from a trustee.
• Where the beneficiary was under a disability.
• Where there was fraud, concealment or mistake. |
|---|---|

■ KEY POINT CHECKLIST

This chapter has covered the following key knowledge points. You can use these to structure your revision around, making sure to recall the key details for each point, as covered in this chapter.

- The meaning of breach of trust and the fact that it includes both action as well as omission.
- The breach must result in a loss to the trust.
- The trustee is only liable for their own breaches and where there is more than one trustee in breach, their liability is joint and several.
- The trustee in breach who has had to compensate the trust can claim indemnity in certain instances.
- The effect of an exemption clause in protecting the trustee from liability.
- The court's discretion to excuse an honest trustee for breach.
- The defence of beneficiary involvement, both before and after the breach.
- The six-year limitation period and the exceptions.

■ KEY TERMS AND CONCEPTS

- indemnity (**page 194**)
- impound a beneficiary's interest (**page 194**)
- compensation (**page 194**)
- simple interest (**page 195**)
- compound interest (**page 195**)
- acquiescence (**page 198**)
- concealment (**page 199**)
- mistake (**page 199**)
- doctrine of laches (**page 200**)

■ SQE1-STYLE QUESTIONS

QUESTION 1

Trustees are holding property on trust for a man for life, remainder to his son absolutely. Twelve years ago, the trustees invested in shares in breach of their investment powers. The father decided not to sue the trustees for the breach. He died five years ago. His son, who is now aged 24, wishes to take action for breach of trust.

Which of the following statements best explains the son's entitlement to sue?

A. The son is barred from suing as the father had consented to the breach.

B. The son is barred from suing as the breach occurred more than six years ago.

C. The son is barred from suing as there was no fraud involved.

D. The son can sue as he was only a child when the breach occurred.

E. The son can sue as his interest accrued less than six years ago.

QUESTION 2

Trustees are holding property on trust for a woman for life, remainder to her son absolutely. Fifteen years ago, the trustees invested in land in breach of their investment powers. The woman decided not to sue the trustees. She died ten years ago. Her son, who is now aged 22, wishes to take action for breach of trust.

Which of the following statements best explains the son's entitlement to sue?

A. The son is barred from suing as the breach occurred 15 years ago.

B. The son is barred from suing as the mother died ten years ago.

C. The son is barred from suing as there was no fraud involved.

D. The son can sue as his interest accrued less than six years ago.

E. The son can sue as the mother did not instigate the breach.

QUESTION 3

Three trustees hold a portfolio of investments on trust for the testator's infant children. The settlement expressly prohibits the trustees from investing in land. The first and second trustee decided to use part of the trust assets to buy a piece of land which they were convinced would increase in value within a year of the purchase. They did not discuss their plan with the third trustee. The third trustee signed all the documents relating to the purchase whenever asked to do so by the other trustees. The land has significantly decreased in value.

Which of the following best explains the liability of the third trustee?

A. The third trustee is liable as she is required to actively participate in the management of the trust.
B. The third trustee is vicariously liable for breaches committed by the other trustees.
C. The third trustee is not liable because she was not informed of the other trustees' decision to invest in land.
D. The third trustee is not liable because she never agreed to invest in land.
E. The third trustee is not liable because she is only liable for her own breaches.

QUESTION 4

Two trustees are holding assets on trust for the children of the settlor until they turn 30. The trust assets comprise a portfolio of stocks and shares. The trust instrument prohibits investments in land. The trustees used 1/4 of the trust fund to buy a large plot of land five years ago. The land has now tripled in value. The beneficiaries are all adults under the age of 30 and they wish to take action against the trustees for breach of trust.

Which of the following provides the best advice regarding the trustees' liability?

A. The trustees are not liable as the trust suffered no loss.
B. The trustees are not liable as they can raise the defence of acquiescence since the beneficiaries are all adults.
C. The trustees are not liable as they acted honestly and reasonably, and the court must excuse the breach.
D. The trustees are liable as the beneficiaries did not consent to the breach.
E. The trustees are liable as they invested outside their powers.

QUESTION 5

A settlor set up a trust for the benefit of his children just before he died. The trust instrument contained a clause exempting the trustee from liability for loss or damage to the trust fund 'even if such loss or damage shall be caused by the trustee's own actual fraud'. The trustee is the testator's brother and he is a professional musician. He used trust money to pay off his gambling debts. He had planned to pay the money back to the trust as soon as he received his next pay cheque but he was out of work for more than a year and his actions were discovered before he could cover his tracks. On being sued for breach of trust, the trustee claimed the protection of the exemption clause.

Which of the following best explains the trustee's liability for breach of trust?

A. The trustee is not liable for breach of trust as he intended to pay back the trust money.
B. The trustee is not liable for breach of trust as his actions are absolved by the exemption clause.
C. The trustee is not liable for breach of trust as he is a close family member.
D. The trustee is liable for breach of trust because there is no limitation period to recover trust property.
E. The trustee is liable for breach of trust because his actions cannot be absolved by the exemption clause.

■ ANSWERS TO QUESTIONS

Answers to 'What do you know already?' questions at the start of the chapter

1) A breach of trust does not automatically lead to liability. The beneficiaries must prove that the breach led to the trust fund suffering a loss, which was not the case here.
2) False. A breach of trust can be by action or omission. An example of a breach of trust by omission is where a trustee, knowing that their fellow trustees are in breach, failed to take action to stop the breach.
3) Not all breaches of fiduciary duty are breaches of trust. A trustee is said to have breached their fiduciary duty if they allow their personal

interest to conflict with their duty to the trust. Examples include using their position as a fiduciary to make unauthorised profit or using knowledge gained from their fiduciary position to go into competition with the trust business. The remedy for a breach of fiduciary duty, apart from an injunction to restrain the trustee's actions, is an account for profits made. A breach of trust occurs where the trustee had failed to comply with the requisite standard of care when performing their trustee duties. If the breach caused the trust to lose money, the trustee must compensate the trust for the loss out of their personal funds.

4) From the facts, it is unclear whether the trustee was in breach of trust but even assuming there was a breach of trust, the trustee can raise the defence that the beneficiary had instigated and consented to the breach.

5) True. The grant of an equitable remedy is at the sole discretion of the court. The court is not bound by the limitation period but rather by the doctrine of laches. The court can refuse to grant the remedy if the claimant's unreasonable delay in taking action is seen as prejudicial to the defendant.

Answers to end-of-chapter SQE1-style questions

Question 1:
The correct answer was E. The limitation period for breach of trust is six years. Time started running for the son when his interest came into possession on his father's death five years ago (by this time, the son had reached the age of majority) and not when the breach occurred (so Option B is wrong). This means he has one year remaining to take action. Option A is incorrect as if the father did consent to the breach, that would not impact on the son's position. Option C is wrong as fraud is irrelevant to this case; the situation focuses on when the interest of the beneficiary accrues. Option D is wrong because it is irrelevant whether the beneficiary was an adult or a child when the breach occurred.

Question 2:
The correct answer was D. The son was a minor when his mother died and was therefore under a disability. His disability ended, and time started running, when he turned 18. This means he has two years remaining to take action. Option A is incorrect as time begins to run from the point the child attains the age of majority, and not when the breach occurred. Option B is wrong as the child was still a minor when his mother died and since attaining the age of majority, the six-year period has not yet expired. Option C is wrong as fraud is

irrelevant to this case; the situation focuses on when the beneficiary attains majority. Option E is wrong as it is irrelevant whether the mother instigated the breach or not.

Question 3:
The correct answer was A. The third trustee may not have actively committed the breach but her neglect of her duties led to the breach. She breached the trust by failing to take adequate action to stop the other trustees from committing the breach (therefore Options C and D are wrong). A trustee is only liable for their own acts or omissions (so Option B is incorrect). Option E is wrong because she has breached the trust through her omission.

Question 4:
The correct answer was A. Although the trustees had technically breached the trust by investing outside their powers, their actions had not caused loss to the trust fund. Breach of trust is only actionable if the beneficiaries can prove that they suffered loss as a result of the breach (Option D and E are therefore incorrect). Option B is wrong because there is no evidence of acquiescence. Option C is wrong as it supposes that the court *must* excuse the breach; such excusal is discretionary.

Question 5:
The correct answer was E. Despite the exemption clause's wording, it is clear from *Armitage v Nurse* that a trustee cannot rely on an exemption clause excluding liability for fraud or wilful wrongdoing as the core of a trust is the trustee's obligation to act honestly in the best interest of the beneficiaries (Option B is therefore incorrect). Option A is irrelevant; an intention to pay back money will not rid the trustee of liability. Option C is wrong as being a family member is irrelevant. Option D is incorrect because the issue of the limitation period is irrelevant if the trustee could rely on the exemption clause.

■ KEY CASES, RULES, STATUTES AND INSTRUMENTS

The SQE1 Assessment Specification has not specified that you need to memorise the statutory provisions or the names of any of the cases mentioned in this chapter. You may, however, find it useful to be familiar with the following:
- s 61 Trustee Act 1925.
- s 62 Trustee Act 1925.
- Limitation Act 1980.
- *Armitage v Nurse* [1997] 3 WLR 1046.

12

Equitable tracing and equitable remedies

■ MAKE SURE YOU KNOW

The topic of tracing in equity completes the journey on the law of trusts. We know that in the event of a breach of trust, the trustee is personally liable for any loss. However, the right to take personal action against the trustee may be futile if the trustee cannot be found; or is bankrupt. The right to trace the trust property is, therefore, a useful tool available to the beneficiary. You may encounter questions in the SQE requiring an understanding of the requirements and the rules of tracing.

This chapter will also explain the nature of equitable remedies using two examples, specific performance and injunction.

Tracing in equity

Requirements
- Fiduciary relationship.
- Claimant has equitable proprietary interest in the property.
- Property is traceable.
- Not inequitable to trace.
- No unreasonable delay.

Rules
- Unmixed funds
- Mixed funds:
  - Between trustee and trust
  - Between two trusts
  - Between trust and innocent volunteer
- Bank accounts:
  - Between trustee and trust
  - Between two trusts
  - Between trust and innocent volunteer

Defences
- Change of position.
- Property has been dissipated.
- Bona fide purchaser
- Doctrine of laches.

Equitable tracing and equitable remedies

■ SQE ASSESSMENT ADVICE

As you work through this chapter, remember to pay particular attention in your revision to:
- The persons who may be subject to a tracing action.
- The requirements of tracing.
- The rules governing tracing into mixed funds.
- The rules governing tracing into bank accounts.
- The defences against tracing.
- The nature of equitable remedies.

■ WHAT DO YOU KNOW ALREADY?

Have a go at these questions before reading this chapter. If you find some difficult or cannot remember the answers, make a note to look more closely at that during your revision.

1) True or false: Tracing is only available to the legal owner.
   [Requirements of tracing, page 210]
2) Carl is a trustee. He withdrew £10,000 from the trust account and used the money to buy a car for his father, who was unaware that the money came from the trust. What are the remedies available to the beneficiaries?
   [Tracing in equity: introduction, page 209]
3) A trustee withdrew £10,000 from the trust account and used it, together with £10,000 of her own money, to buy a sculpture. The sculpture has doubled in value. What are the remedies available to the beneficiaries?
   [Tracing in equity: introduction, page 209]
4) True or false: As with all actions for breach of trust, the right to trace is subject to the six-year limitation period.
   [Requirements of tracing, page 210]
5) True or false: Tracing is not available against someone who has paid for the trust property.
   [Defences against tracing, page 218]

INTRODUCTION

This chapter's focus is on equitable tracing. Tracing is the process whereby beneficiaries who have lost trust assets due to fraud, misappropriation or mistake by a trustee can recover their property, or identify substitute property purchased using trust funds, and claim it. A tracing claim is available against a trustee, a constructive trustee or an innocent volunteer. Tracing can take place at common law or in equity but, for the purposes of the SQE, we only need to consider tracing in equity.

To complete the chapter, there is a brief explanation at the end on the nature of equitable remedies using specific performance and injunctions as examples. These remedies are available in general; and are not confined to actions for breach of trust.

TRACING IN EQUITY: INTRODUCTION

Tracing is the process whereby the claimant can follow the property to the defendant from whom they can recover either the property or its equivalent. If the trust property has been sold and the proceeds used to buy something else, tracing is available so long as the substitute is identifiable. For example, if a trustee used trust money to buy herself a car (the substitute), the beneficiaries can trace and claim the car.

The claimant may choose to trace where:
- **The trustee is bankrupt:** A personal claim against the trustee is pointless as the claimant (the beneficiary) must join the queue with the other creditors. A tracing action gives the claimant priority over the other creditors by claiming the property as their own.
- **The trustee cannot be found:** The trust property may be in the possession of another who is not personally liable to the beneficiaries but who is subject to a tracing action, like an innocent volunteer.
- **The defendant is an innocent volunteer:** If the trust property is in the hands of an innocent volunteer, the claimant has no personal claim against them but tracing is available.
- **Tracing is more profitable:** Where the claimant has a choice of suing the defendant for compensation (personal claim) or tracing, the claimant may choose to trace if the property (or its equivalent) has increased in value.

Tracing allows the claimant to identify the asset and, having done so, the claimant may:
- **Have a charge over the asset:** This entitles the claimant to sell the property and claim what they are owed from the proceeds.

- **Claim a constructive trust over the asset:** This entitles the claimant to an equitable proprietary interest in the asset and take advantage of any increase in value.

It is for the claimant to choose the most advantageous remedy.

Before considering the requirements of tracing, let's refresh our memory on who can be subject to a tracing action:
- The trustee who has taken trust property.
- The constructive trustee who has received trust property knowing it to be in breach of trust.
- The innocent volunteer who is in possession of trust property.

(To refresh your memory on the liability of constructive trustees, please refer to **Chapter 9**.)

Exam warning
If there is a question in the SQE on tracing, remember that the right to trace is lost if the property no longer exists. An example is when a trustee used trust property to pay for dental treatment. However, the trustee is still personally liable to the beneficiaries. In a personal action, the trustee must compensate the trust from their own personal funds.

REQUIREMENTS OF TRACING

To successfully trace in equity, the following requirements must be met:
- There must be a fiduciary relationship.
- The claimant must have an **equitable proprietary interest** in the property.
- The property must be traceable.
- Tracing must not produce an inequitable result.
- There must be no unreasonable delay.

We will consider each of the requirements in turn.

Key term: equitable proprietary interest
A proprietary interest refers to the property owner's legally enforceable right to the property. This right is enforceable against third parties. The beneficiary of a trust has an equitable proprietary interest in the trust property.

The fiduciary relationship

A fiduciary relationship (ie one between a trustee and a beneficiary) must exist before tracing in equity is possible. The fiduciary relationship need not be between the beneficiary who is tracing and the person against whom they are tracing so long as there was an *initial* fiduciary relationship. In a tracing action by a beneficiary of a trust, this requirement is easily met due to the fiduciary relationship between trustee and beneficiary.

The claimant must have an equitable proprietary interest

The right to trace is not available to just anyone. The claimant must show that they have an equitable proprietary interest in the property being traced. Clearly, the beneficiary of a trust has such an interest.

The property must be traceable

Tracing is only available if the property is traceable: this means that the property must be identifiable.

Substituted property

Tracing is possible even where the property has been substituted, as illustrated by **Practice example 12.1**.

Practice example 12.1

A trustee sold a valuable piece of artwork belonging to the trust and used the proceeds to buy herself a holiday cottage. What are the remedies available to the beneficiaries of the trust?

The beneficiaries can choose to do one of two things: they can sue the trustee and claim compensation for the loss of the painting, or they can trace and claim the holiday cottage. Their choice may depend on which course of action is more profitable. If you were wondering whether the beneficiaries can trace and claim the piece of art from the purchaser, the answer is no if the purchase was made in good faith.

Mixed property

Tracing is possible even where the property has been mixed, as illustrated in **Practice example 12.2**.

> **Practice example 12.2**
>
> M, a property developer, used clients' money (around £20,000) to pay part of the premium on a life insurance policy worth £1m. The first three instalments were paid using his own money but the final two instalments were paid using clients' money. The beneficiaries of the policy were his three children. M later committed suicide. In a tracing action, the clients claim to be entitled to the proceeds of the policy. Are the clients entitled only to a refund of their money plus interest, or are they entitled to trace and claim the proceeds proportionate to the premiums paid?
>
> This was what happened in *Foskett v McKeown* [2000] 3 All ER 97, where the House of Lord held that, as this was a tracing action, the clients' had a proprietary right to receive 40% of the policy fund.

As we can see, an advantage of tracing is that it enables the claimant to benefit from an increase in the value of the property. In *Foskett v McKeown*, 40% of the premiums came from money belonging to the claimants which in turn meant that they were entitled to 40% of the policy pay out.

By the same token, however, if the property (purchased with trust money) has decreased in value, the claimants will have to accept the loss. In practice, tracing is useful where the trustee is bankrupt as it gives the claimant first charge over the property. This gives them priority over the other creditor's claims on the bankrupt trustee's assets. Tracing is also useful if the property has increased in value and the claimant wishes to take advantage of the increase.

> **Revision tip**
>
> Remember that the beneficiaries can take personal action against the defendant (the trustee or constructive trustee) where the defendant's actions resulted in a loss to the trust. In a personal action against the defendant, there is no need to prove that they are in possession of trust property (or its equivalent). Compensation is paid from the defendant's personal funds.

Tracing must not have an inequitable result

As with all equitable remedies, the claimant will not be allowed to trace if it results in unfairness to the defendant. This requirement is relevant if the defendant is an innocent volunteer (as opposed to a trustee or constructive trustee).

For example, let's say a trustee withdrew trust money and gave the money to his mother, telling her that he won it on the lottery. The mother then used the money to renovate her house. The mother is an innocent volunteer as she had no knowledge of the breach of trust. However, she has been unjustly enriched and may be subject to a tracing action. Would she be forced to sell the house to repay the money? Are the beneficiaries entitled to a proportionate share in the proceeds of sale of the house?

The general consensus is that tracing is not allowed into a mixed fund where the innocent volunteer has mixed trust money with their own money as the mother has done. To do so would be inequitable (she would have to sell her house). The mother can raise the defence of change of position to stop the tracing action. Change of position will be explained in the subtopic defences against tracing.

No unreasonable delay

As tracing is an equitable remedy, it is not subject to limitation periods. Instead, the doctrine of laches (where there has been an undue delay in the claimant asserting their rights) applies and can be used as a defence against tracing. (See **Chapter 11** for more detail.)

Having considered the requirements of tracing, we must now learn the rules of tracing.

THE RULES OF TRACING

Tracing rules differ depending on whether the trust money has been mixed. There are also special rules for tracing into a bank account.

Tracing into unmixed funds

Tracing into unmixed funds is relatively straightforward:
- If the trust asset is separate and not mixed, the asset can be reclaimed. In fact, the exercise of locating the asset is called following, rather than tracing.
- If the asset has been sold, there are three possible outcomes:
  – First, the proceeds of sale can be claimed if there was no mixing.

- Second, if the proceeds were used to buy property, the claimant can trace and claim it.
- Third, the claimants can follow the asset itself and claim it if the purchaser is a constructive trustee. For example, if the purchaser purchased the asset knowing of the trustee's fraudulent behaviour.

Tracing into mixed funds

Tracing can be more difficult if the funds have been mixed, and the rules differ depending on whether the mix happened in a bank account or elsewhere.

Tracing against the trustee

Where the trustee used trust money and their own money in a purchase, the beneficiaries have first claim over any property purchased. The onus is on the trustee to prove that part of the mixed fund belongs to them. If the trustee is able to distinguish the separate assets, the assets will be divided between the trustee and beneficiaries on a **pro rata** basis. See the case of *Foskett v McKeown* as explained in **Practice example 12.2** above.

> **Key term: pro rata**
>
> This means the assets are divided proportionally.

Tracing against another trust or against a third party

Where the trustee has mixed the funds of two trusts; or transferred trust money to an innocent volunteer who mixed it with his own, the two funds have a pro rata claim in the mixed funds or on any property purchased with it. This means that the two claimants share the profits or loss proportionally.

For example, a trustee used £2,000 from Trust A and £4,000 from Trust B to buy herself a car which is now worth £3,000. The beneficiaries of Trust A and Trust B in a tracing action can claim the car and sell it. The proceeds are shared proportionately: £1,000 to Trust A; £2,000 to Trust B.

Tracing into funds mixed in bank accounts

If the trust money has been mixed in a bank account, special tracing rules apply and are considered below.

Funds belonging to trustee and beneficiary

Assuming the trustee has placed trust money into their personal account thereby mixing their own money with the trust's money, there are several principles to bear in mind when attempting to trace:

- According to *Re Hallett's Estate* [1880] 13 Ch D 696, the trustee is presumed to spend their own money first – see **Practice example 12.3**.

> **Practice example 12.3**
>
> A trustee deposited £5,000 of trust money into his account, which had a starting balance of £3,000. He then withdrew £5,000 to pay for a holiday. The trustee has now died and the beneficiaries in a tracing action are claiming the balance in the account. However, the trustee's next of kin claim to be entitled to the money. To whom does the money belong?
>
> Where the mixed funds in a bank account belong to the trustee and the trust, the presumption when tracing is that the trustee has withdrawn his own money first. The beneficiaries have first claim over the balance.

- The rule that the trustee is presumed to spend their own money first is subject to the primary rule that the beneficiaries have a right to claim any property purchased using a mixed fund – see **Practice example 12.4**.

> **Practice example 12.4**
>
> A trustee paid £3,000 of trust money into his personal account which had a starting balance of £2,000. The trustee later withdrew £2,000, to invest in shares. The balance of the account was later dissipated (squandered). Are the beneficiaries entitled to trace and claim the shares?
>
> Where the trustee purchased property using mixed funds, the rule in *Re Hallett* (that the trustee is presumed to spend his own money first) does not apply. Instead, the relevant rule is that the beneficiaries have first charge over any property bought using mixed funds (the shares).

- The principle of lowest intermediate balance means that the trust's claim is limited to the account's lowest balance after the trust money has been paid in. This means that there can be no tracing into an overdrawn account if the overdraft exceeds the amount paid in. For

example, a trustee paid £3,000 of trust money into his personal account which had an overdraft of £1,000. The trust will only be able to trace and claim £2,000, even if the account balance was higher at the time of tracing. There is an exception to this rule (see later).
- No backwards tracing. Tracing from asset to asset must follow a chronological order. For example, if a trustee takes out a loan to buy property, then used trust money to discharge the loan, the beneficiaries' right to trace is lost. They cannot claim the property because the property was not directly bought using trust money. There is an exception to this rule (see below).

The Privy Council recently confirmed an exception to the two rules of *lowest intermediate balance* and *no backwards tracing*. This exception is called the *coordinated scheme exception*. In other words, the two rules will not apply in cases where the court is satisfied that the various steps taken by the defendant are part of a coordinated scheme to defeat tracing. If so, the two rules will not prevent the beneficiaries from tracing and claiming what is due to them. It remains to be seen whether this new exception will make it easier for beneficiaries in a tracing action.

To understand the application of this exception, have a look at **Practice example 12.5**.

Practice example 12.5

The mayor of a city took US$10.5m in bribes in connection with a road-building contract. The money was paid into an account held by the mayor's son. At some point the account balance went down to $7.7m. The defendant tried to rely on the rule of lowest intermediate balance to limit the amount traced to $7.7m. The account balance at the time of tracing was $13.5m.

The facts came from *Federal Republic of Brazil v Durant International* [2016] AC 297, where the Privy Council allowed the claimant to trace and claim the full $10.5m because the facts show that there was a coordinated scheme by the defendant to defeat a tracing action.

Funds belonging to two trusts; or to a trust and an innocent volunteer

Where the mixed fund in a bank account came from two different trusts, or from a trust and an innocent volunteer, the first in, first out rule applies – see **Practice example 12.6**.

The rules of tracing 217

Practice example 12.6

T is a trustee of two trusts, the Jones Trust and the Smith Trust. T paid £1,000 taken from the Jones Trust into a newly opened personal account. He later paid £2,000 taken from the Smith Trust into the same account. He then withdrew £500 from the account to pay for a holiday. The balance is £2,500. How much is the Jones Trust entitled to claim in a tracing action?

Using the rule in *Clayton's Case* [1816] 35 ER 767, the first sum of money paid into the account came from the Jones Trust. It follows that the £500 withdrawn from the account is presumed to have come from the Jones Trust. The Jones Trust is entitled to claim £500. The balance belongs to the Smith Trust.

Later case law has confirmed that whilst the first in, first out rule is still the primary rule for mixed bank accounts, it would not be applied if the court considers it to be impractical or unjust and there's a preferable alternative method available. For example, in the case of *Barlow Clowes International Ltd v Vaughan* [1992] 4 All ER 22, the court decided that the money in the account was to be shared by the claimants rateably (proportionally). It would be up to the court to decide which rule to apply.

Summary: tracing rules

Unmixed funds	Asset is still available.	Claim the asset.
	Asset has been sold.	Claim the proceeds.
	Proceeds used to buy property.	Claim the property.
Mixed funds	Property bought with trust money and trustee's money.	Beneficiaries have first claim over property.
	Property bought with money from two different trusts.	Both trusts share the property rateably.
	Property bought with trust money and innocent volunteer's money.	The trust and the innocent volunteer share the property rateably.

Bank accounts	Trustee's money mixed with trust money.	Trustee is presumed to spend own money first.
	Money from two different trusts.	First in, first out rule.
	Money from trust fund and innocent volunteer.	First in, first out rule.

DEFENCES AGAINST TRACING

A defendant of a tracing action can raise certain defences which you may encounter in the SQE. Most of the defences have already been explained in detail earlier in this chapter, or in previous chapters. This list is merely recapping the information.

Change of position

This defence is open to innocent volunteers who have received trust property and on the faith of the receipt of that property, suffered a change to their personal circumstances making it unfair to trace against them. An example is included in the earlier section explaining that tracing must not have an inequitable result.

Exam warning

Bear in mind that change of position is only available as a defence to an innocent volunteer, not to a trustee or constructive trustee.

Property has been dissipated

The right to trace is lost if the money has been **dissipated**. For example, where the trustee has used trust money to pay for a cruise, or towards cosmetic surgery, the right to trace is lost as the property is no longer traceable. The beneficiaries' only recourse would be a personal action against the trustee to compensate the loss.

Key term: dissipated

This means that the money has been spent or squandered and there is nothing to show for it. An example is where the trustee used trust money to pay for a holiday.

Bona fide purchaser for value without notice

Tracing is not available if the property is in the hands of a person who bought (paid consideration for) the property in good faith and who had no knowledge that the property belongs to the trust.

Doctrine of laches

Tracing actions are not subject to limitation periods but the right to trace may be lost if the claimant delayed taking action to such an extent that it has become inequitable to trace against the defendant.

Having considered the law on equitable tracing, we will now look at the nature of equitable remedies.

THE NATURE OF EQUITABLE REMEDIES

Once a claimant succeeds in proving their claim in court, they are generally entitled to an award of damages (money) as of right. Damages is a common law remedy. All other remedies are equitable. The following general principles apply to the grant of equitable remedies:

- Equitable remedies are discretionary (not as of right).
- Principles of equity apply, such as the **clean hands maxim**.
- The court will not grant an equitable remedy unless they can ensure that the remedy can be carried out. For example, in a contract for the sale of land between the claimant and the defendant, where the defendant has sold the land to a bona fide purchaser, the court will not grant specific performance as it would be futile.
- An equitable remedy is granted where an award of damages is inadequate or inappropriate.
- According to s 50 of the Senior Courts Act 1981, the court has the power to award damages as well as, or in substitution for, an injunction or specific performance.

> **Key term: clean hands maxim**
>
> The equitable maxim 'he who comes to equity must come with clean hands' means that anyone applying for an equitable remedy must have conducted themselves equitably. Otherwise, the court will refuse to grant the remedy.

EQUITABLE REMEDIES

We will briefly consider the equitable remedies of specific performance and injunction. Remember that these remedies are not confined to actions for breach of trust but are available in all civil actions.

Specific performance

Specific performance is an order for the defendant to perform his contractual duties. The claimant must have provided consideration before they can apply for an order of specific performance. It is only ordered where damages are considered inadequate. For example, where the subject matter of the contract are unique, such as a rare antique, an award of damages may be inadequate. **Practice example 12.7** provides further illustration.

> **Practice example 12.7**
>
> Ali is an avid collector of rare books. Ali found out that Piers (a book seller) has an extremely rare first edition book and they entered into a contract for Ali to buy it. She placed a down payment for the book and they agreed that the balance will be paid on delivery. Meanwhile, Piers received a better offer for the book from Dee, so he informed Ali that he could no longer sell it to her. He offered to return the deposit. Ali is devastated as she has been looking for this particular book for years. How can she get Piers to sell her the book?
>
> There is a contract between Ali and Piers, Ali having provided consideration for it (the down payment). The subject matter of the contract is unique and even if Piers paid damages to Ali for breaching the contract, it would be inadequate as she cannot buy a similar item elsewhere. It is likely that the court will grant her an order of specific performance against Piers. The effect of the order is that Piers must perform what he promised (to sell her the book).
>
> Of course, if Piers has already sold the book to Dee and Dee bought the book in good faith (not knowing that it had been promised to Ali), the order of specific performance will no longer be available.

> **Revision tip**
>
> In your Land Law studies, you will be aware that in English law, all land is regarded as unique and thus specific performance is available to enforce contracts of land.

As a general rule, according to s 236 of the Trade Union and Labour Relations (Consolidation) Act 1992, the court should not grant an order of specific performance or an injunction compelling an employee to work. To force someone to work where they do not wish to would be inequitable.

Injunction

An injunction is an order for the defendant to stop (prohibitory), to act (mandatory) or to prevent the defendant from committing a wrong. An injunction is granted at the court's discretion and anyone who breaches an injunction is in contempt of court and may be subject to either a fine or imprisonment, or both. An injunction may be granted at any stage of the court proceedings. The interim injunction is granted before final determination of the case whereas the final injunction is granted once the case has been heard. A good example of the use of an interim injunction in a tracing action is for the claimant to obtain an injunction preventing the defendant from dissipating the property.

The following general principles apply to all injunctions:
- Claimant must give **undertaking as to damages**, especially when applying for an interim injunction. It is an agreement to compensate the other party if it turns out that the injunction should not have been granted.
- The court can award damages in lieu of an injunction.
- An injunction is granted where damages is inappropriate.

Key term: undertaking as to damages
A promise by the claimant to compensate the defendant if it transpired that the injunction should not have been granted. An example is where a beneficiary of a trust obtained an injunction stopping the trustee's business because the beneficiary felt that it was in competition with the trust business. If the court later decides that the trustee had not been in competition, the injunction was wrongly granted. The beneficiary must compensate the trustee for the loss of earnings resulting from the injunction.

In summary, the most important thing to bear in mind with regard to equitable remedies is that they are never granted as of right, but at the court's discretion. They are granted where damages is considered to be inadequate or inappropriate.

■ KEY POINT CHECKLIST

This chapter has covered the following key knowledge points. You can use these to structure your revision around, making sure to recall the key details for each point, as covered in this chapter.
- Equitable tracing is available to allow beneficiaries to claim back trust assets. Remember the requirements for tracing in equity.

- Tracing is available against the trustee, the constructive trustee or an innocent volunteer.
- Remember the rules of tracing into an unmixed fund.
- Tracing is available where the funds have been mixed but remember that different rules apply depending on who the mixed funds belong to.
- There are special rules for tracing into money mixed in a bank account.
- Equitable remedies are granted at the court's discretion.

■ KEY TERMS AND CONCEPTS

- equitable proprietary interest (**page 210**)
- pro rata (**page 214**)
- dissipated (**page 218**)
- clean hands maxim (**page 219**)
- undertaking as to damages (**page 221**)

■ SQE1-STYLE QUESTIONS

QUESTION 1

A trustee for two trusts took £15,000 from the first trust and £5,000 from the second trust to buy a car. The trustee recently filed for bankruptcy. The car is currently valued at £10,000.

Which of the following best explains the outcome of a tracing action?

A. The first trust can claim the car.

B. Both trusts share the proceeds of sale of the car equally.

C. The second trust can claim the car.

D. The second trust can claim £2,500 from the proceeds of sale of the car.

E. The trustee in bankruptcy can claim the car.

QUESTION 2

The beneficiaries of a trust fund recently discovered that their sole trustee withdrew £60,000 from the trust account and deposited it into his personal account, which had a balance of £20,000. He then withdrew £20,000 from his account to pay for a piece of artwork. Finally, he withdrew the rest of the money to pay for a luxury holiday. The artwork has doubled in value. The trustee recently filed for bankruptcy and remains in possession of the artwork.

Which of the following best explains the outcome of a tracing action?

A. The beneficiaries are not entitled to claim the artwork as the trustee is presumed to spend his own money first.
B. The beneficiaries are entitled to trace against the holiday company.
C. The beneficiaries have lost their right to trace as the money has been dissipated.
D. The beneficiaries are entitled to a first charge over the artwork.
E. The beneficiaries and the trustee share the proceeds of the artwork equally.

QUESTION 3

A trustee used trust money to buy a painting by a local artist which he gave to his sister for her birthday. The trustee told her that he won the money used to buy the painting on the lottery. She believed him as he spent a considerable amount of money on lottery tickets each week. Soon after, knowing that the beneficiaries would find out about the money he took, he left the country without telling anyone where he was going.

Which of the following best explains the beneficiaries' remedies against the sister?

A. The sister has recipient liability and is personally liable to replace the money.
B. The beneficiaries can trace and claim the painting from her.
C. The sister is entitled to keep the painting as she had no knowledge of the breach of trust.
D. The sister is entitled to raise the defence of change of position and keep the painting.
E. The beneficiaries and the sister share the proceeds of the painting equally.

QUESTION 4

The beneficiaries of a trust discovered that their trustee withdrew £20,000 from the trust account and deposited it into his personal account in a different bank, which was overdrawn by £10,000. He later withdrew £10,000 from the account to pay for a hair transplant procedure.

Which of the following best explains the beneficiaries right to trace?

A. The beneficiaries are entitled to trace and claim £10,000 as the trustee only dissipated £10,000.
B. The beneficiaries are entitled to trace and claim the full £20,000.
C. The beneficiaries' right to trace is lost.
D. The beneficiaries are entitled to trace against the hair transplant clinic.
E. The beneficiaries are entitled to trace against the bank.

QUESTION 5

A trustee used trust money to pay for repairs to the roof of her father's flat. She told her father that the money came from the sale of her car which she no longer needed since she started working from home. The father obtains welfare benefits and has been trying for years to save enough to pay for the repairs. The trustee recently lost her job and has filed for bankruptcy.

Which of the following is the best advice regarding the remedies available to the beneficiaries?

A. Tracing is available against the father as he has recipient liability.
B. The father is personally liable to compensate the trust from his savings.
C. The flat must be sold and the beneficiaries are entitled to a proportionate share of the proceeds.
D. There can be no tracing against the father.
E. The beneficiaries can trace and claim the money from the trustee.

■ ANSWERS TO QUESTIONS

Answers to 'What do you know already?' questions at the start of the chapter

1) False. One of the requirements of tracing in equity is that the claimant has an equitable (as opposed to legal) proprietary interest in the property.

2) The beneficiaries can sue Carl for breach of trust and require him to compensate the trust for the loss. Alternatively, if Carl has no money and as the father is an innocent volunteer, they can trace against him and claim the car.
3) The beneficiaries have a personal claim against the trustee for breach of trust and the trustee must compensate the trust for the loss. Alternatively, they can choose to trace and claim the sculpture as this is the more profitable option.
4) False. Tracing is an equitable remedy and is not subject to the usual limitation period. Instead, the doctrine of laches applies.
5) The answer depends on the purchaser's knowledge. If they knew that the property was sold in breach of trust, they have recipient liability and are liable as a constructive trustee. Tracing is available against them. However, if they purchased the property in good faith having no knowledge of the breach, they are considered a bona fide purchaser and are not subject to tracing.

Answers to end-of-chapter SQE1-style questions

Question 1:
The correct answer was D. The car was bought from the mixed funds of both trusts so the rule is that they share the loss rateably/proportionately (the first trust can claim £7,500 and the second trust can claim £2,500). Therefore, Options A–C are incorrect. Option E is wrong because the car belongs to the two trusts, and cannot be claimed by the trustee in bankruptcy.

Question 2:
The correct answer was D. The rule that the trustee is presumed to spend his own money first is subject to the rule that beneficiaries have first charge over any property bought using mixed funds (therefore Option A is incorrect). The holiday company is a bona fide purchaser and is not liable to a tracing action (therefore Option B is wrong). Option C is wrong because whilst the money spent on the holiday has been dissipated, the money spent on the artwork has been realised into a new form and can be traced. Option E is incorrect as the trustee should not profit from his wrongdoing.

Question 3:
The correct answer was B. The sister clearly had no knowledge of the breach of trust, which makes her an innocent volunteer. She is not personally liable to the trust (therefore Option A is wrong) but tracing is available against her as she was unjustly enriched (therefore Option C is incorrect). The defence of change of position

is not applicable here as tracing will not lead to an inequitable outcome (therefore Option D is wrong). As the sister has no claim to the artwork, Option E is wrong.

Question 4:
The correct answer was C. The principle of lowest intermediate balance meant that £10,000 had been dissipated as soon as the money was deposited into the overdrawn account. The remaining £10,000 was used to pay for the procedure and is no longer identifiable (therefore Options A and B are wrong). The hair transplant clinic is a bona fide purchaser and is not subject to a tracing action (therefore Option D is wrong). The bank is only liable if there is proof of recipient liability, which is unlikely on the facts (therefore Option E is wrong).

Question 5:
The correct answer was D. The father is an innocent volunteer and is prima facie subject to a tracing action. The father is not a knowing recipient nor is he personally liable to the trust (therefore Options A and B are wrong). However, it is clear that he can raise the defence of change of position as the tracing action would lead to an unfair outcome (therefore Option C is wrong). Option E is incorrect as the trustee's liability towards the trust is a personal one but tracing is unavailable as she no longer has the trust money in her possession.

■ KEY CASES, RULES, STATUTES AND INSTRUMENTS
- *Re Hallett's Estate* [1880] 13 Ch D 696.
- *Clayton's Case* [1816] 35 ER 767.

Both cases introduced rules to tracing but there is no need to remember their names. Instead, make sure you remember the relevant tracing rules.

Index

absolute gifts 4-5, 6-7, 48, 124
absolute rights 31-2, 33, 44, 89, 94, 172-3, 179, 181-2, *see also* legal title
accessory (dishonest assistance) liability of strangers 148-50, 151, 153-4, 155, 163-4, 166, 167
account of profits remedy 157, 161, 163, 164-6, 167, 205
accounts/records duties of trustees 176, 192-3
acquiescence trustee defence/ protection 198, 200-1
actual knowledge 152-3, 163
additional appointments of trustees 172-3, 174
administrative unworkability issues 15, 17, 20
administrators 15, 17, 20, 65-7, 74, 157-8
admissible evidence 121-2, 125, 128
advancement powers of trustees 168, 181-4, 186-8
advancement presumption, presumed resulting trusts 120-1, 122, 128
after-acquired property 53-5, 56, 58-60
animals, purpose trusts 98, 101-2, 103, 105-6, 109-10, 111-12
appointment of trustees 46-51, 168-76, 184-8, 192-3; on appointment duties 176, 184, 192-3

assigning to a third party method, equitable interest transfers (dispositions) 29-31
Attorney-General 98, 108
automatic resulting trusts 114-16, 117, 122-5, 126-9, 131; summary 124; trusts against public policy 123, 125, *see also* resulting trusts

backwards tracing rule 216
bank accounts 7, 26, 69, 70, 207-9, 213-18, 222-6
bankruptcy 9, 56-7, 152, 162-3, 170-2, 207, 209, 212, 222-5
bare trusts 31-3, 37, 40, 41-2, 80-1, 88, 91, 94; definition 31-2, 88, 94
beneficial entitlement xiv, 10-11, 19, 52-6, 80-96; definition 80-91, *see also* beneficial interest; beneficial rights
beneficial interest 1, 10-13, 23-37, 46-8, 63-4, 80-96, 114-47, 177, 194-206, 207-26; definition 10-11, 13, 23, 46-8, 80-7; impound a beneficiary's interest concept 194, 198, 201; summary 87; terminology 82; transfers (dispositions) 24-5, 26, 28-37, 38-42, 50-1, 63-4; types 80-7, 91, 177, 181, *see also* beneficial entitlement; contingent; equitable interest; vested

beneficial rights 45–6, 52–4, 80–2, 87–96, 155–6, 170–5; bare trusts 80–1, 88, 91, 94; definition 80–2, 87–91, 170–4; discretionary trusts 80, 87–8, 89–90, 91, 95, 181; fixed trusts 80, 87–91; Saunders v Vautier case 80–1, 88–91, 94–6; summary 88; termination rights 80–1, 88–91, 92–5; types 80–2, 87–91, 170–5; volunteer beneficiaries 45–6, 52–4, see also beneficial entitlement; remedies

beneficiaries, administrative unworkability issues 15, 17, 20; advancement powers of trustees 168, 181–4, 186–8; appointments/removals of trustees by beneficiaries 172–3, 174, 175–6; class of beneficiaries 13–15, 16–17, 19, 22; conceptual uncertainty issues 15–16, 20, 22; consideration xiv, 29, 33–5, 44–5, 52–4, 55–6, 57, 59–60; definition 4, 10–11, 13–19, 46–8, 80–91, 98; discretionary trusts 1, 6, 13–14, 19, 22, 80, 87–8, 89–90, 91, 95; equitable interest transfers (dispositions) 24–5, 26, 28–37, 50–1, 63–4; equitable title of the trust assets 4, 29, 32–3, 80–2; evidential uncertainty issues 15–16; fixed trusts 1, 13–14, 19, 22, 80, 87–91; maintenance power of trustees 168, 180–1, 183–4, 186–7, 188; marriage consideration 52–4, 55–6, 57, 59–60, 132–47; non-charitable private purpose trusts 97–104; one-person gift test 15, 17; purpose trusts 97–9; sui juris beneficiaries 88–91, 94, 158–9, 197–8; summary 15, 18; volunteer beneficiaries xiv, 44–6, 49, 52–3, 55–60, 61–79, 156, see also beneficial; donees; objects

beneficiary-involvement defence/protection, trustees' liabilities 189, 197–8, 200–1, 205

binding aspects, settlors 43–6

breaches of contract 220

breaches of fiduciary relationship 149–50, 152, 156–67, 176, 190, 194–6, 204–5, 210

breaches of trust 115, 127, 149–67, 176, 188, 189–206, 207–26; concealment 199, 201; damages 189–93, 194–6, 207–9; defences/protection means 189–90, 196–206, 207–9, 213, 218–19, 224–6; definition 189–92, 200–1, 204–6; fiduciary duty breaches 194, 195–6, 204–5; fraud 193–4, 195–6, 199, 201, 204, 206, 209, 214–15, 223; general principles 191–2, 195; indemnity claims 189–90, 193–4, 196, 198, 201; joint and several liabilities 189, 193, 195–6, 201; losses to the fund resulting from breaches 189–96, 201, 203–6, 207, 212; mens rea irrelevance 191; mistakes 199, 201, 209; omissions/actions 189–91, 192–3, 201, 204, 206; personal claims 150–5, 191–3, 194–206, 207–10, 211–12, 218, 225; proprietary actions 150, 191, 194, 207–19; retirement of trustees 192–3; summary 195–6, 200–1; types 189–92, 200–1, 204–6; vicarious liabilities 189, 193, see also remedies; trustees' duties; trustees' liabilities

'bulk' term 10, 21, 23

capital-growth investments 177, 179
case law see separate Table of cases

Index 229

certainty requirements 1-23, 24-8, 37, 43-6, 97-101, 116; flowchart 18, 97, see also intention; objects; subject matter
change of position defence/protection, equitable tracing 207, 213, 218, 223, 225-6
charitable trusts 97-9, 101, 104-8, 108-13; Attorney-General 98, 108; benefits 107-8; cy-près doctrine 107-8, 108; failures 107-8; masses in church 101; political considerations 106-7; public benefit requirements 104, 105-6, 108, 109, 111, 112; taxes 107; tombs/monuments 100-1; types 104-5
charities 3, 57, 64, 68, 74, 97-9, 101, 104-8, 109-13, 183
Charity Commission 108
chattels 50-1, 56, 58-60, 69-71, see also tangible assets
cheques 8, 49, 50-1, 66-7, 70, 76, 78
choses in action 50, 51-2, 56
civil partnerships 132, see also marriage
class of beneficiaries 13-15, 16-17, 19, 22
clean hands maxim, equitable remedies 219, 222
climate change perspectives, charitable purpose trusts 107
common intention constructive trusts 130-3, 134-43, 145-7, 151; constructive trust contrasts 151; detrimental reliance 130, 134-6, 137-40, 142, 143, 145, 146; excuses 136-7, 139; express agreements to share 135-8, 139, 141-2, 151; indirect financial contributions 139; inference from conduct 135, 138-40, 141-2,
147, 151; resulting trust relationship 139-40, 141-2, 147; summary 138-9, see also constructive trusts; family home trusts
common law remedy 54-5, , , 209, 219, see also damages
compensation 189-92, 194-6, 201, 205, 209, 211-12, 225, see also damages; remedies
competition with trust business duty 156, 161-3, 205, 221
compound interest awards, damages 195, 201
concealment, breaches of trust 199, 201
conceptual uncertainty issues, objects 15-16, 20, 22, 112
conflicts of interest 156-67, 176, 195, 205, see also fiduciary relationship; trustees' duties
consent issues 181, 189, 196, 197-9, 200-1, 205
consideration xiv, 29, 33-5, 44-6, 52-3, 55-60, 78, 114-29, 155-6, 219-20; definition 44-5, 52-3, 55-6, 220; marriage consideration 52-4, 55-6, 57, 59-60; volunteer beneficiaries 44-6, 52-3, 55-60, 156
constitution of trusts xiv, 2, 41, 43-60, 61-79; definition 43-56, 61-3; vesting 43-6, 50-2, 55-6, 59-60, 62, 66-7, 69-78; volunteer beneficiaries 44-6, 49, 52-3, 55-60, see also creation; incomplete; legal title; trustees
constructive knowledge 152-3
constructive trusts 37, 87, 127, 130-42, 145-67, 209-10, 213, 222, 225; common intention constructive trust contrasts 151; flowchart 148;

innocent volunteers 156, 166, 209–10, 213, 216–17, 222; remedies 150–67, 209–10, 213, 222, 225; summary 155, see also common intention; equitable remedies; fiduciary relationship; liability of strangers
contingent beneficial interest 80–1, 83–7, 91–2, 93–6, 181; lives in being; perpetuity period 85–7; perpetuity period requirement 84–7, 91; vested interest contrasts 84, see also beneficial interest
contract law 29, 33–5, 71, 118–19, 220
coordinated scheme exception, equitable tracing 216
couples 132–47, see also family home trusts; marriage
courts, appointments/removals of trustees 173–4, 175–6, 184, 187; discretionary excuse trustee defence/protection 189, 196, 197, 200–1, 206; impound a beneficiary's interest concept 194, 198, 201
covenants to settle 44, 52–6, 58–60, 66–7; action by the trustees 55–6; after-acquired property 53–5, 56, 58–60; beneficiary parties to the covenant 54–5, 56; common law damages 54–5; marriage consideration 52–4, 55–6, 57, 59–60
creation of trusts xiv, 2–23, 24–42, 43–60, 114–29, 130–47, 170–4, 189, 196–7; exemption clauses 189, 196–7, 200–1, 204–6; flowcharts 18, 43; informal words and actions 7–9, 19, 22; precatory words 5–7, 9, 19, 22–3; 'trust' word effects 6–7, 9, 22; words/conduct 3, 4–9, 16, 19, 22–3, 25, 26–8, 32, 34–5, 38–42,

135–42, 151, see also constitution; formalities; intention; objects; subject matter
cy-près doctrine 107–8, 108

damages 54–5, 57–8, 60, 189–93, 194–6, 198–9, 201, 205, 209, 219–22, 225; breaches of trust 189–93, 194–6, 207–9; compensation 189–92, 194–6, 201, 205, 209, 211–12, 225; definition 54, 55, 60, 189, 219–22; impound a beneficiary's interest concept 194, 198, 201; interest awards 195, 201; measures 194–6; undertaking as to damages concept 221, 222, see also remedies
death, donatio mortis causa (DMC) 61–3, 67–71, 74, 77; perpetuity period requirement 85–7, 91; termination of trusteeship 170–1, 175, 176
death duty (inheritance tax) 34–5, 37, 63, 182
debtors 50–2, 56, 65
defences/protection means, equitable tracing 207–9, 213; trustees' liabilities 189–90, 196–206, 207–9
'dependants' term, conceptual uncertainty issues 16, 20
detrimental reliance 130, 134–6, 137–42, 143, 145, 146
directors' fees duty, fiduciary relationship 156, 158, 162–3, 165–6, 167
disabilities, limitation period exception 199, 201, 205–6, see also mental illness; minors
disclaimed equitable interest 36, 39, 41
disclaimer termination of trusteeship 175, 176

Index 231

discounts, sitting tenants 133–4, 138, 144, 146
discretionary trusts 1, 6, 13–15, 19, 22, 80, 87–8, 89–91, 95, 181; beneficial rights 80, 87–8, 89–90, 91, 95, 181; certainty requirements 1, 13–15, 19; individual ascertainability test 14–15, 19, 22; objects 1, 13–15, 19, 22; termination rights 89–90, 95, see also beneficiaries
dishonesty 148–50, 151, 153–4, 155, 163–4, 166, 167, 170
dissipated property trustee defence/protection 207, 210–12, 215, 218, 221, 222–6, see also tracing
doctrine of laches 200–1, 205, 207, 213, 219, 225
donatio mortis causa (DMC) 61–3, 67–71, 74, 77
donees, definition 48–9, 56, see also beneficiaries
donors, definition 48–9, 56, see also settlors
duties of trustees see trustees' duties

educational purpose trusts 98, 105–6, 109, see also charitable trusts
employees, specific performance orders 220
endorsement transfer formalities, cheques 50
equitable interest 4, 10–11, 13, 23, 24–5, 26, 28–37, 46–8, 63–4, 80–96, 114–29; definition 10–11, 13, 23, 46–8, 80–7, 91; subsisting equitable interest 29–33, 37, 41–2; summary 87; terminology 82; types 80–7, 91, see also beneficial; contingent; vested

equitable interest transfers (dispositions) 24–5, 26, 28–37, 38–42, 50–1, 63–4; assigning to a third party method 29–31; contract for valuable consideration assignment method 29, 33–5; declaring oneself a trustee method 29, 35–6, 38, 41; definition 28–9, 50–1; directing the trustees to hold the property method 29, 31–3; disclaimed equitable interest 36, 39, 41; evidenced in writing 29–30, 40, 41–2; fraud 30–1; Grey case 32–3; insurance policy nominations 37; legal title of the trust assets 29–33, 37, 63–4; methods 29–37, 38–42, 50, 63–4; pension fund nominations 37; Vandervell case 31–3, see also separate Tables; subsisting equitable interest
equitable proprietary interest requirement, equitable tracing 207, 210–12, 222, 224
equitable remedies 55, 148–67, 189–93, 194–5, 200–1, 205, 207–9, 219–22, 225–6; clean hands maxim 219, 222; definition 55, 207–9, 219–22, 225–6; injunctions 55, 200, 205, 207, 219, 221–2; nature 219; restitution concepts 151, 163, 194–5, 201, 225; specific performance orders 45, 54–5, 57–60, 200, 207, 219–22; summary 221; undertaking as to damages concept 221, 222, see also constructive trusts; equitable tracing; remedies
equitable rights see beneficial rights
equitable title of the trust assets, definition 4, 29, 32–3, 80–2, see also equitable interest

232 Index

equitable tracing 87, 150, 151, 155, 191, 194, 207-19, 221-6; no backwards tracing rule 216; bank accounts tracing rule 207-9, 213-18, 222-6; bankruptcy 207, 209, 212, 222-5; change of position defence/protection 207, 213, 218, 223, 225-6; coordinated scheme exception 216; defences/protection means 207-9, 213, 218-19, 224-6; definition 155, 194, 207-19, 221-2, 224-6; dissipated property defence/protection 207, 210-12, 215, 218, 221, 222-6; doctrine of laches defence/protection 207, 213, 219, 225; equitable proprietary interest requirement 207, 210-12, 222, 224; first in, first out rule 216-18; inequitable-result factors 207, 210-11, 212-13, 218, 226; innocent volunteers 209-10, 213, 216-17, 222, 224-6; limitation period exception 199-201, 204, 213, 219, 225; lowest intermediate balance rule 215-16, 226; mixed funds tracing rule 207-17, 222, 225; purchases in good faith (bona fide) 155-6, 166, 207, 208, 211, 219-20, 225-6; no unreasonable delay requirement 207, 210-11; remedy choices 209-10, 225; requirements 207-9, 210-13, 221-2; rules 207-9, 213-18, 222; substituted property 209, 211-12, 217; summary 217-18; traceable-property requirement 207, 210-12, 218; unmixed funds tracing rule 207-9, 213-17, 222; unreasonable-delay factors 207, 210-11, 213; uses 207-12, *see also* equitable remedies; proprietary actions; remedies

equity deems as done that which ought to be done maxim 45-6
equity looks to the substance rather than the form maxim 4, 8
equity will not assist a volunteer maxim xiv, 45, 49, 52, 61-79, *see also* exceptions; incomplete constitution
equity will not perfect an imperfect gift maxim 45, 48-9, 61-79, *see also* incomplete constitution
estoppel 61-3, 71-4, 76-8, 130-3, 140-2, 145
ethical investments 178-80, 185-6, 188
even-handed trustee duty to invest 177, 179
evidenced in writing 3, 25, 27-30, 32, 39, 40-2, 50-1, 63-4, 69-74, 77-8, 135-6
evidential uncertainty issues, objects 15-16
exceptions to the maxim that equity will not assist a volunteer xiv, 45, 61-79; donatio mortis causa (DMC) 61-3, 67-71, 74, 77; estoppel 61-3, 71-4, 77-8; Re Rose rule 61-5, 73-4, 77, 79; Strong v Bird rule xiv, 61-3, 65-7, 74, 77-9; summary 65, 67, 71, 73, *see also* imperfect inter vivos gifts; *separate Table of cases*
excuses, common intention constructive trusts 136-7, 139
executors 65-7, 74-5, 78, 99-104, 109-12, 158, 191-2
exemption clause trustee defence/protection 189, 196-7, 200-1, 204-6
express agreements to share 135-8, 139, 141-2, 151

Index   233

express private trusts 1-23, 24-42, 43-60, 98-101, 122-4, 170-88; certainty requirements 1-23, 24-8, 37, 43-7, 97-101; definition 3-4, 22-3, 170; intention 1-3, 4-9, 18-19, 22-3, 26-8, 48-9, 51, 116-17; objects 1-4, 10-11, 13-19, 20, 22-3, 26-8, 82; subject matter 1-4, 10-13, 18-19, 22-3, 26-8, see also creation; individual topics; private trusts
extrinsic evidence 16, 19

fair-dealing purchases from the beneficiary 159-60, 166
family home trusts 62, 71, 127, 130-47, 151; definition 130-42, 145-7, 151; flowchart 130; household expenses 131, 137-9, 145; joint names 127, 131, 132, 134, 136-7, 142, 144, 171; purchase price contributions 130, 132-4, 137-9, 146; sitting tenants 130, 133-4, 138, 142, 144, 146, see also common intention; proprietary estoppel; resulting trusts
'family' term, conceptual uncertainty issues 16, 17
fiduciary relationship 37, 148-50, 156-63, 176-80, 190, 194-6, 204-5, 207-19; account of profits remedy 157, 161, 163, 164-6, 167, 205; breaches 149-50, 152, 156-67, 190, 194-6, 204-5, 210; breaches of trust contrasts 194, 195-6, 204-5; competition with trust business duty 156, 161-3, 205, 221; conflicts of interest 156-67, 176, 195, 205; determination of relationship 157-8, 207, 210-11; directors' fees duty 156, 158, 162-3, 165-6, 167; fair-dealing purchases from the beneficiary 159-60, 166; non-trustee fiduciary types 161-2, 164, 167; purchases of trust property duty 156, 159-60, 162-3, 164-5, 167; reimbursed expenses 159, 166; remuneration of fiduciary duty 156, 158-9, 161-3, 166; self-dealing purchases from the trust 159-60, 165, 166-7; summary 160, 162-3; unauthorised profits duty 156-8, 161, 162-3, 167, 194-5, 205, see also constructive trusts; liability of strangers; trustees; trustees' duties
first in, first out mixed funds tracing rule 216-18
fixed trusts 1, 13-15, 19, 22, 80, 87-91; beneficial rights 80, 87-91; certainty requirements 1, 13-15, 19; objects 1, 13-15, 19, 22; termination rights 88-9, 90-1, see also beneficiaries
formalities for the creation of trusts xiv, 2-9, 24-42, 43-7, 50-1, 56, 63-9, 135-6, 170-4; definition 24-37, 40-2; equitable interest transfers (dispositions) 24-5, 26, 28-37, 50-1; inter vivos trusts 24-8, 37, 60; personalty trusts 24-5, 26-8, 37, 38-42; realty trusts 24-5, 26-8, 37, 39, 40-1, 43, 63-9, 135-6, 170-3; testamentary trusts (wills) 24-6, 28, 39, 41, 65-9, 174, see also creation
fraud 30-1, 37, 148-50, 193-4, 195-6, 199, 201, 204, 206, 209, 214-15, 223
freehold land 50, 133
'friends' term, conceptual uncertainty issues 16, 17, 22, 112

gift over in default of appointment 5-6, 19

234 Index

gifts 4-7, 10, 15, 17, 20-3, 45, 48-9, 56-60, 61-79, 119-20, 124-9; definition 48-9, 119-20, see also imperfect inter vivos gifts

household expenses, family home trusts 131, 137-9, 145

impartiality duties of trustees 176-7
imperfect inter vivos gifts 45, 48-9, 52, 55-6, 60, 61-79; donatio mortis causa (DMC) 61-3, 67-71, 74, 77; estoppel 61-3, 71-4, 76-7; Re Rose rule 61-5, 73-4, 79; Strong v Bird rule xiv, 61-3, 65-7, 74, 77-9; summary 65, 67, 71, 73, see also gifts; incomplete constitution; inter vivos trusts; separate Table of cases
implied trusts 37, 116, 127-8, 132, 134-5, 151, 153, see also common intention; resulting trusts
impound a beneficiary's interest concept, definition 194, 198, 201
inalienable property, definition 85, 91
incapable appointment factors, trustees 171-2
income-yield investments 177, 179
incomplete constitution of trusts 43-4, 45-6, 49-60, 61-79; covenants to settle 52-6, 66-7; definition 45, 56, 61-3, 77; donatio mortis causa (DMC) 61-3, 67-71, 74, 77; equity will not assist a volunteer maxim xiv, 45, 49, 52, 61-79; equity will not perfect an imperfect gift maxim 45, 48-9, 61-79; estoppel 61-3, 71-4, 76-8; Re Rose rule 61-5, 73-4, 77, 79; Strong v Bird rule xiv, 61-3, 65-7, 74, 77-9,

see also constitution; imperfect inter vivos gifts; void trusts
indemnity claims, breaches of trust 189-90, 193-4, 196, 198, 201
indirect financial contributions, common intention constructive trusts 139
individual ascertainability test, discretionary trusts 14-15, 19, 22
inequitable-result factors, equitable tracing 207, 210-11, 212-13, 218, 226
inference from conduct, common intention constructive trusts 135, 138-40, 141-2, 147, 151
informal words and actions 7-9, 19, 22
inheritance tax (death duty) 34-5, 37, 63, 182
injunctions 55, 200, 205, 207, 219, 221-2
innocent volunteers 156, 166, 209-10, 213, 216-17, 222, 224-6
insurance policy nominations 37
intangible assets 11-13, 19, 22-3, 69-71, 118-19, 170-1, see also property; shares
intention (settlor) certainty requirement 1-3, 4-9, 18-19, 22-3, 26-8, 48-9, 51, 78, 116-17; definition 4-9, 18-19, see also creation of trusts; settlors
inter vivos trusts 3, 19, 24-8, 37, 60, 61-79; definition 3, 24, 26-8; personalty trusts 24-5, 26-8, 37, 38-42; realty trusts 24-5, 26-8, 37, 39, 40-1
interest awards, damages 195, 201
interim injunctions 221-2
intermeddling (interference) liability of strangers 148, 151, 154-6, 163
intestate situations 174

Index   235

investments duty of trustees 81, 88, 152-3, 168-70, 176-80, 184, 185-8, 190-2, 202, 205; definition 176-80, 184, 187-8; ethical investments 178-80, 185-6, 188; even-handed duties 177, 179; income-yield/capital-growth investments 177, 179; modern portfolio theory 177-8, 179; summary 179-80, see also shares

joint names 127, 131, 132, 134, 136-7, 142, 144, 171, see also family home trusts
joint and several liabilities, breaches of trust 189, 193, 195-6, 201
judicial notice 102, 109
judicial trustees, court appointments of trustees 173-4, 184

land 24-5, 26-8, 39-41, 49, 50-1, 63-78, 117-47, 170-5, 178, 199-206, 220; evidenced in writing 25, 27-8, 39, 40-1, 50, 63-4, 69-74, 77-8, 135-6; formalities for the creation of trusts 24-5, 26-8, 39, 40-1, 50-1; transfer formalities 50-1, 56, 60, 63-4, 69-78, 117-20, 126-8; unregistered land 69-70, see also property; realty trusts
land law 128, 132, 170, 220
Land Registry 70
leasehold land 50-1, 133, 157, 162
legal proprietary interest 224
legal title of the trust assets 29-33, 37, 43-79, 80-2, 88-91, 114-47, 155-6, 170-4, 210-11; equitable interest transfers (dispositions) 29-33, 37, 63-4; subsisting equitable interest 29-33, 37; trustees 3, 29-33, 43-60, 62-79, 80-2, 88-91, 114-29,

170-1, 174, see also absolute rights; constitution; vesting
liabilities of trustees see trustees' liabilities
liability of strangers 37, 148-56, 163-7, 176, 210, 225-6; accessory (dishonest assistance) liability 148-50, 151, 153-4, 155, 163-4, 166, 167; actual knowledge 152-3, 163; constructive knowledge 152-3; definition 148-56, 166, 210; intermeddling (interference) liability 148, 151, 154-6, 163; recipient (knowing receipt) liability 148-50, 151, 152-3, 155-6, 163, 166, 225-6; remedies 148-56, 210, 225-6; summary 155; types of strangers 155-6, 226; wilful blindness 152, see also constructive trusts; fiduciary relationship
life interest 14, 34-5, 37, 81-3, 89-90, 91-5, 177, 180-2, 186-8, 193, 198-206; definition 34-5, 82-3, 177, see also remainder interest; vested in possession
limitation periods 189, 190, 196, 198-202, 204, 205-6, 208, 213, 219, 225; exceptions 199-201, 204, 213, 219, 225
lives in being 85-7, 100-2
loco parentis 120, 125
losses to the fund resulting from breaches of trust 189-96, 201, 203-6, 207, 212
lowest intermediate balance rule 215-16, 226

maintenance of beneficiaries power of trustees 168, 180-1, 183-4, 186-7, 188

236 Index

marriage 52-4, 55-6, 57, 58-60, 132-7, 138-47, 171-2, 193; consideration 52-3, 55-6, 57, 59-60; settlements 53-4, 55-6, 58-60, 171-2, 193, *see also* covenants to settle; family home trusts
masses in church, purpose trusts 101, 103
mens rea irrelevance, breaches of trust 191
mental illness 170, 172, 199, 201
minors, maintenance power of trustees 168, 180-1, 183-4, 186-7, 188; remainder interest 180-2, 186, 202, 205-6, *see also* disabilities
mistakes, breaches of trust 199, 201, 209
mixed funds tracing rule 207-17, 222, 225
modern portfolio theory 177-8, 179
money 69-70, *see also* donatio mortis causa
mortgage instalments/repayments 76-8, 130-4, 137-8, 143, 146, *see also* land; purchase price contributions

nominees, trustee self-dealing purchases from the trust 159-60
non-charitable (private) purpose trusts 97-104, 105, 107-8, 109-13; beneficiary principle exception 98, 99-100, 107, 112, 113; benefits 107-8; failures 108; judicial notice 102, 109; masses in church 101, 103; perpetuity period requirement 100-3, 107-13; pets 98, 101-2, 103, 105, 109, 111; Re Denley case 103, 113; Re Endacott case 99-103, 109, 113; summary 103, 107-8; tombs/monuments 100-1, 103, 111-13, 122-3, *see also* private trusts; purpose trusts
non-trustee fiduciary types 161-2, 164, 167
number of trustees 170-1, 172-3, 184-5, 187-8

objects (beneficiaries) certainty requirement 1-4, 10-11, 13-19, 20, 22-3, 26-8, 82, 97-9, 112; administrative unworkability issues 15, 17, 20; conceptual uncertainty issues 15-16, 20, 22, 112; definition 13-19, 22-3, 97-9; evidential uncertainty issues 15-16; issues to be considered 15-18; one-person gift test 15, 17; summary 15, 18, *see also* beneficiaries; discretionary trusts; fixed trusts
omissions/actions, breaches of trust 189-91, 192-3, 201, 204, 206
one-person gift test, objects 15, 17
overdrafts 215-16, 223, 226

patents 11
pension fund nominations 37
perpetuity period requirements 84-7, 91, 100-3, 107-13
personal claims 150-5, 191-3, 194-206, 207-10, 211-12, 218, 225, *see also* damages; remedies
personal representatives 67, 74, 158, *see also* administrators; executors
personalty trusts 24-5, 26-8, 37, 38-42, 118-19, 170-1, 184; definition 24-5, 26-8, 170, 184; formalities for the creation of trusts 24-5, 26-8, 37, 38-42; presumed resulting trusts 118-19
pets, purpose trusts 98, 101-2, 103, 105, 109, 110

political considerations, charitable purpose trusts 106-7
powers of trustees *see* trustees' powers
precatory words 5-7, 9, 19, 22-3, *see also* words/conduct
presumed resulting trusts 114-22, 124-9, 130-47; admissible evidence 121-2, 125, 128; advancement presumption 120-1, 122, 128; gifts 119-20; illegal purposes 118-19, 125, 129; Patel v Mirza case 118-19, 129; personalty 118-19; purchase in the name of another scenario 117, 119-22, 124-5, 130-4, 137-9, 146; realty 117-19; rebutting the presumption 119-21, 122, 125, 128, 132; scenarios 116-22, 124-5; summary 121-2; voluntary transfer of property to another scenario 117-19, 122, 124-5, *see also* family home trusts; resulting trusts
private trusts 1-23, 24-42, 43-60, 98-9, 170-88; certainty requirements 1-23, 24-8, 37, 43-7, 97-101; definition 3-4, 98-9, 170, *see also* creation; express; *individual topics*; non-charitable
pro rata 214, 222
professional/lay trustees 158-9, 166, 173, 177, 184, 187, 197, *see also* trustees
profits 156-8, 161, 162-3, 167, 194-5, 205
promisees 72-4, 133, 136-7, 140-2
promisors 71-4, 78, 133, 142, 145-6
promissory estoppel 71
property 1-5, 10-13, 18-19, 22-3, 24-42, 43-60, 117-29, 132-47, 207-26; definition 10-13, 18-19, 69-71; gift over in default of appointment

5-6, 19; objective assessments by courts 11; recovery remedy 118-19, 150, 155-6, 159, 163, 199, 201, 204, 209; residuary estate 10-11, 19, 21, 39, 41, 115, 126; specific performance orders 45, 54-5, 57-60, 200, 207, 219-22; summary 13, 18; tangible/intangible asset definitions 11-13, 19, 22-3, 26-8, 50-1, 69-71, 117-19, 170-1, 174; tracing 87, 150, 151, 155, 191, 194, 207-19; types 11-13, 22-3, 24-6, 50-1, 69-71, 117-19, 170-1, 174; vesting 43-6, 50-2, 55-6, 59-60, 62, 66-7, 69-78, 174, 176, *see also* land; personalty; realty; subject matter
proprietary actions 150, 191, 194, 207-19, *see also* equitable tracing
proprietary estoppel 62, 71, 77, 130-3, 140-3, 145-7, *see also* estoppel; family home trusts
public benefit requirements, charitable purpose trusts 104, 105-6, 108, 109, 110, 111, 112
Public Trustees 173-4
public trusts 98-9, 104-8, *see also* charitable trusts
purchase in the name of another scenario, presumed resulting trusts 117, 119-22, 124-5, 130-4, 137-9, 146
purchase price contributions, family home trusts 130, 132-4, 137-9, 146, *see also* land; mortgage instalments/repayments
purchases in good faith (bona fide) 155-6, 166, 207, 208, 211, 219-20, 225-6
purchases of trust property duty, fiduciary relationship 156, 159-60, 162-3, 164-5, 167

purpose trusts 87, 97–113, 122–3; summary 103, 107–8, *see also* charitable; non-charitable private

realty trusts 24–5, 26–8, 37, 39, 40–1, 43, 63–9, 117–19, 135–6, 170–3; definition 24–5, 26–8; evidenced in writing 25, 27–8, 39, 40–1, 63–4, 135–6; formalities for the creation of trusts 24–5, 26–8, 37, 39, 40–1, 43, 135–6, 170–3; presumed resulting trusts 117–19; unenforceable/void issues 27, 37, 135–6

reasonable income wording, objective assessments by courts 11

reasonableness requirements, equitable tracing 207, 210–11; trustees' duty/standard of care/skill 176–80, 184, 187, 189–91, 197, 200–1, 202–6

rebutting the presumption 119–21, 122, 125, 128, 132

recipient (knowing receipt) liability 148–50, 151, 152–3, 155–6, 163, 166, 225–6

recovery remedy 118–19, 150, 155–6, 159, 163, 199, 201, 204, 209; definition 150, 155–6

registrars of companies 46, 77

reimbursed expenses, fiduciary relationship 159, 166

'relatives' term, conceptual uncertainty issues 16, 20

religious purpose trusts 101, 103–5, 106, 110, 111, *see also* charitable trusts

remainder interest 14, 34, 37, 81–3, 89–95, 115, 177, 180–2, 186–8, 193, 198–206; definition 34, 82–3, 94, 95, 177, 180; minors 180, 186, 202,

205–6, *see also* life interest; vested in interest

remedies 45, 54–60, 127, 140–1, 148–67, 189–93, 194–206, 207–26; account of profits 157, 161, 163, 164–6, 167, 205; constructive trusts 150–67, 209–10, 213, 222, 225; definition 54, 55, 60, 189, 207–9, 219–22, 225–6; injunctions 55, 200, 205, 207, 219, 221–2; liability of strangers 148–56, 210, 225–6; personal claims 150–5, 191–3, 194–206, 207–10, 211–12, 218, 225; proprietary estoppel 140–1; recovery remedy 118–19, 150, 155–6, 159, 163, 199, 201, 204, 209; specific performance orders 45, 54–5, 57–60, 200, 207, 219–22, *see also* damages; equitable remedies; equitable tracing

remuneration of trustees 156, 158–9, 161–3, 166

renewals, leasehold land 157

replacement trustees 171–5, 176, 184–5, 187–8

residuary estate, definition 10–11, 19, 21, 39, 41, 115, 126

restitution concepts, equitable remedies 151, 163, 194–5, 201, 225, *see also* constructive trusts

resulting trusts 18, 27–8, 37, 114–29, 130–47; summary 121–2, 124, *see also* automatic; family home trusts; presumed

retirement of trustees 169, 172–3, 175, 176, 184, 192–3

scholarships 98, 105

self-dealing purchases from the trust 159–60, 165, 166–7

Index   239

settlors 1-9, 15-19, 22-42, 43-51, 64-79, 83-6, 107-8, 114-29, 169-88; binding aspects 43-6; covenants to settle 52-6, 58-60, 66-7; definition 3-4, 43-4, 48, 170-4; as trustee 3, 44, 46-50, 55-6, 59, 64, *see also* donors; intention; testators
shares 2, 10-13, 21-3, 31-44, 46, 50, 58-65, 70, 81, 118, 158, 161, 174-80, 191-2, 202; modern portfolio theory 177-8, 179; stock transfer forms 46, 50, 62-5, 174; transfer formalities 46, 50, 62-5, 70, 118, *see also* intangible assets; investments
signatures 27-8, 30, 39, 40-1, 50, 54-6, 75
simple interest awards, damages 195, 201
sitting tenants 130, 133-4, 138, 142, 144, 146, *see also* family home trusts
six-year limitation period trustee defence/protection 189, 190, 196, 198-202, 204, 205-6, 208, 213, 225
sole name 132, 142, 171, *see also* family home trusts
specific performance orders 45, 54-5, 57-60, 200, 207, 219-22
stamp duty 31-2, 34, 40, 41-2
stock transfer forms 46, 50, 62-5, 174
strangers 37, 148-56, 163-7, 176, 210, 225-6, *see also* liability of strangers
sub-equitable interest 35-6
sub-trusts 35-6, 38, 41
subject matter (property) certainty requirement 1-4, 10-13, 18-19, 22-3, 26-8; beneficial interest uncertainties 10-11; definition 10-13, 18-19, 22-3, *see also* property
subsisting equitable interest 29-42

substituted property, equitable tracing requirements 209, 211-12, 217
sui juris beneficiaries 88-91, 94, 158-9, 197-8
suing for damages 54-5, 189-93, 194-6, 198-201, 209, 211, 225, *see also* damages
surplus funds, automatic resulting trusts 122-4
survivorship rights 170-1, 175, 184, 188

tangible assets 11-13, 19, 26-8, 50-1, 69-71, 117-19, 170-1, *see also* chattels; property
taxes, charitable purpose trusts 107; death duty (inheritance tax) 34-5, 37, 63, 182; stamp duty 31-2, 34, 40, 41-2
termination rights 80-1, 88-91, 92-5; discretionary trusts 89-90, 95; fixed trusts 88-9, 90-1; Saunders v Vautier case 80-1, 88-91, 94-6, *see also* beneficial rights
termination/removal of trustees 168-71, 172-3, 174, 175-6, 184; summary 176
testamentary trusts (wills), definition 3, 24, 28; formalities for the creation of trusts 24-6, 28, 39, 41, 65-9; intestate situations 174
testators 2-6, 10-11, 17, 19-23, 65-6, 161, 170-1; definition 3, *see also* settlors
third parties, equitable interest transfers (dispositions) 28-37; Re Rose rule 63-5, 73-4, 77
title deeds 49-50, 63-4, 69-70, 72-4, *see also* land
tombs/monuments, purpose trusts 100-1, 103, 111-13, 122-3

traceable-property requirement 207, 210-12, 218, see also tracing
tracing 87, 150, 151, 155, 191, 194, 207-19; common law remedy option 209; definition 155, 194, 207-19, 221-2; see also equitable tracing
transfers of equitable interest see equitable interest transfers
transfers of legal title to the trustees see vesting the property
trust corporations 173, 184
trust deeds 7, 16, 25, 32, 41, 46-7, 52, 55, 62-4, 170-5, 184, 187, 190, 196-7, see also express private trusts; writing
'trust' word effects, creation of trusts 6-7, 9, 22
trustee de son tort 154-5, 163
trustees 3-4, 44-51, 156-63, 168-88, 195-6, 200-1; additional appointments of trustees 172-3, 174; appointment of trustees 46-51, 168-76, 184-8, 192-3; appointments/removals of trustees by beneficiaries 172-3, 174, 175-6; bare trusts 31-3, 37, 40, 41-2, 80-1, 88, 91, 94; choice of trustees 46-51, 168-74; conflicts of interest 156-67, 176, 195, 205; constitution of trusts 43-60; constructive trusts 37, 148-51, 156-67, 209-10, 213, 222, 225; court appointments/removals of trustees 173-4, 175-6, 184, 187; death of trustees 170-1, 175, 176; declaring oneself a trustee equitable interest transfer method 29, 35-6, 38, 41; definition 3-4, 44-51, 156-63, 168-88, 195-6, 200-1; disclaimer termination of trusteeship 175, 176; eligibility requirements 170-2; equitable interest transfers (dispositions) 28-37, 50-1; ethical investments 178-80, 185-6, 188; impartiality duties of trustees 176-7; incapable appointment factors 171-2; investments 81, 88, 152-3, 168-70, 176-80, 184-8, 190; legal title of the trust assets 3, 29-33, 43-60, 62-79, 80-2, 88-91, 114-29, 170-1, 174, 210-11; number of trustees 170-1, 172-3, 184-5, 187-8; professional/lay trustees 158-9, 166, 173, 177, 184, 187, 197; reimbursed expenses 159, 166; replacement trustees 171-5, 176, 184-5, 187-8; resulting trusts 18, 27-8, 37, 114-29; retirement of trustees 169, 172-3, 175, 176, 184, 192-3; as settlors 3, 44, 46-50, 55-6, 59, 64; summaries 174, 176, 179-80, 183, 195-6, 200-1; survivorship rights 170-1, 175, 184, 188; termination/removal of trustees 168-71, 172-3, 174, 175-6, 184; unfitness appointment factors 170-2, 173, 175; vesting 43-6, 50-2, 55-6, 59-60, 62, 66-7, 69-78, 174, 176, see also fiduciary relationship; separate Tables
trustees' duties 3-4, 35, 81, 88, 148-52, 156-63, 168-70, 176-80, 184-8, 189-206, 207-26; accounts/records duties of trustees 176, 192-3; competition with trust business duty 156, 161-3, 205, 221; definition 168-70, 176-80, 187-8, 192-3, 197, 205-6; directors' fees duty 156, 158, 162-3, 165-6, 167; duty/standard of care/skill 168-70, 176-80, 184, 187, 189-206; purchases

of trust property duty 156, 159-60, 162-3, 164-5, 167; reasonableness requirements 176-80, 184, 187, 189-91, 197, 200-1; remuneration 156, 158-9, 161-3, 166; unauthorised profits 156-8, 161, 162-3, 194-5, 205, see also breaches; conflicts of interest; fiduciary relationship; *individual duties*; investments; trustees' liabilities

trustees' liabilities 189-206, 207-26; acquiescence defence/protection 198, 200-1; beneficiary-involvement defence/protection 189, 197-8, 200-1, 205; consent defence/ protection 189, 196, 197-9, 200-1, 205; court discretionary excuse defence/protection 189, 196, 197, 200-1, 206; defences/protection means 189-90, 196-206, 207-9, 213, 218-19, 224-6; definition 189-93, 195-6, 204-6; doctrine of laches defence/protection 200-1, 205, 207, 213, 219, 225; exemption clause defence/protection 189, 196-7, 200-1, 204-6; six-year limitation period defence/protection 189, 190, 196, 198-202, 204, 205-6, 208, 213, 225; summary 195-6, 200-1, see also breaches; liability of strangers; trustees' duties

trustees' powers 13-15, 27, 80-1, 88, 148-70, 176, 178, 179, 180-4, 186-8, 196-206; advancement power 168, 181-4, 186-8; definition 178, 179, 180-4, 187-8; discretionary aspects 180-1; investments duty of trustees 178, 179, 190-2, 202, 205; maintenance power 168, 180-1, 183-4, 186-7, 188;

statutes 178-84; summary 183, see also breaches; trustees

trusts, against public policy 123, 125; certainty requirements 1-23, 24-8, 37, 43-7, 97-101; creation xiv, 2-23, 24-42, 43-60, 114-29, 130-47, 170-4, 189, 196-7; definitions 1-19, 22-3, 24-37, 40-2, 43-56, 61-3, 80-2, 170; exemption clauses 189, 196-7, 200-1, 204-6; formalities xiv, 2-9, 24-42, 43-7, 50-1, 56, 63-9, 135-6, 170-4; intention 1-3, 4-9, 18-19, 22-3, 26-8, 48-9, 51, 116-17; objects 1-4, 10-11, 13-19, 20, 22-3, 26-8, 82, 97-9, 112-13; subject matter 1-4, 10-13, 18-19, 22-3, 26-8; that carry the intermediate income 181, 184; void trusts 7, 16-17, 27-35, 37, 43-7, 48-9, 85-6, 98, 99-104, 108-13, see also constitution; *individual trust types*; *separate Tables*

unauthorised profits duty, fiduciary relationship 156-8, 161, 162-3, 167, 194-5, 205

undertaking as to damages concept 221, 222

undue influence 138

unenforceable/void issues, realty trusts 27, 37, 135-6

unfitness trustee appointment factors 170-2, 173, 175

unjust enrichment 27, 151, 225-6, see also constructive trusts

unmixed funds tracing rule 207-17, 222

unregistered land 69-70

vested beneficial interest 80, 82-4, 87, 91-2, 181; contingent interest

contrasts 84; definition 80, 82-3, 84, 87, 91, 94, *see also* beneficial interest
vested in interest beneficial interest 80, 82-4, 87, 90-2, 93-5, *see also* remainder interest; vested
vested in possession beneficial interest 80, 82-4, 87, 89-90, 91-2, 93-5, *see also* life interest
vesting the property to the trustees 43-7, 50-2, 55-6, 59-60, 62, 66-7, 69-78, 174, 176; definition 45-7, 50-1, 55-6, 174, 176; stock transfer forms 46, 50, 62-5, 174, *see also* constitution; legal title
vicarious liabilities 189, 193
void trusts 7, 16-17, 27-35, 37, 43-7, 48-9, 85-6, 98, 99-104, 110-13, *see also* incomplete constitution
voluntary transfer of property to another scenario, presumed resulting trusts 117-19, 122, 124-5
volunteer beneficiaries xiv, 44-6, 49, 52-4, 55-60, 61-79, 156; definition 45-6, 59; exceptions to the maxim that equity will not assist a volunteer xiv, 45, 61-79; marriage consideration 52-4, 55-6, 59-60

wilful blindness, liability of strangers 152

wills *see* testamentary trusts (wills)

witnesses 28, 50

words/conduct, common intention constructive trusts 135, 138-40; conceptual uncertainty issues 16, 20, 22-3; creation of trusts 3-9, 16, 19, 22-3, 25, 26-8, 32, 34-5, 38-42, 135-42, 151; informal words and actions 7-9, 19, 22; precatory words 5-7, 9, 19, 22-3; 'trust' word effects 6-7, 9, 22

writing 3, 7, 16, 25-32, 39-47, 50-2, 62-4, 69-78, 135-40, 170-5, 181-4, 187, 190, 196-7; evidenced in writing 3, 25-30, 32, 39-42, 50-1, 63-4, 69-74, 77-8, 135-6; signatures 27-8, 30, 39, 40-1, 50, 54-6, 75; trust deeds 7, 16, 25, 32, 41, 46-7, 52, 62-4, 170-5, 184, 187, 190, 196-7